THE WARD

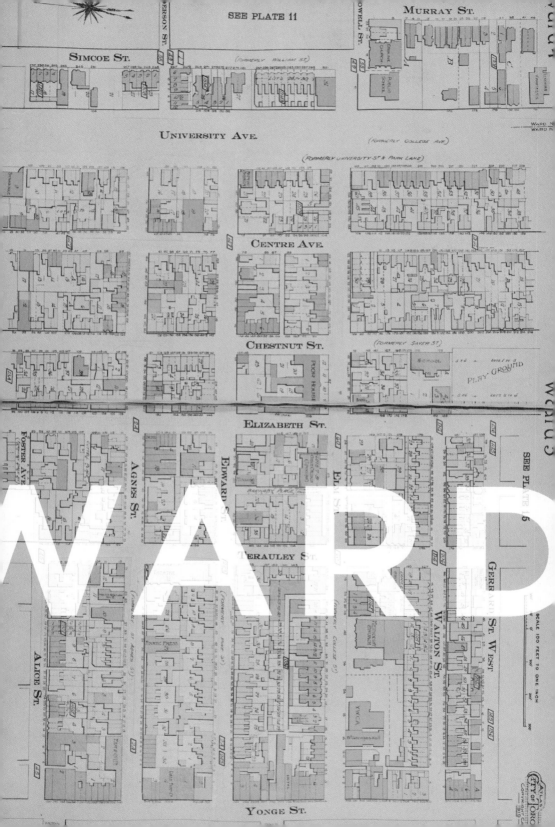

John Lorinc dedicates this book to Jeff Preyra and Matt Blackett.
Michael McClelland dedicates this book to Alex.
Ellen Scheinberg dedicates this book to her husband, Jack, and sons Cory and Mitchell.
Tatum Taylor dedicates this book to Mekhala.

first edition

Published with the generous assistance of the Canada Council for the Arts and the Ontario Arts Council. Coach House Books also acknowledges the support of the Government of Canada through the Canada Book Fund.

The editors and publisher would like to thank the Metcalf Foundation, the Centre for Urban Growth and Renewal, and the Architectural Conservancy of Ontario for their generous support of this project.

The views expressed by the contributors to *The Ward* do not necessarily reflect the opinions of the editors, Coach House Books or the foundations that supported the project.

LIBRARY AND ARCHIVES CANADA CATALOGUING IN PUBLICATION

The Ward : the life and loss of Toronto's first immigrant neighbourhood / edited by John Lorinc, Michael McClelland, Ellen Scheinberg and Tatum Taylor.

Issued in print and electronic formats.
ISBN 978-1-55245-311-7 (pbk.)

1. Ward (Toronto, Ont.)--History. 2. Neighborhoods--Ontario- Toronto--History. 3. Immigrants--Ontario--Toronto--History. I. Lorinc, John, 1963-, author, editor II. McClelland, Michael, 1951-, author, editor III. Scheinberg, Ellen, 1964-, author, editor IV. Taylor, Tatum, author, editor

FC3097.52.W27 2015   971.3'541   C2015-902035-2

CONTENTS

Immigrants arriving in Toronto, ca. 1910.

T**HE MONEY COULD** scarcely have arrived at a more opportune moment.

In late 1845, John Strachan, the first Anglican bishop of Toronto, learned his financially struggling diocese had received an anonymous £5,000 bequest from England. The funds were to be used to build and sustain a new Gothic-style church that would serve the city's poor. In contrast to most churches, which charged congregants for the use of the pews, in this church, the donor's will specified, the seats must be 'free and un-appropriated forever.'

JOHN LORINC

INTRODUCTION

Strachan, a Tory legislator and educator, was a key figure in the Family Compact that controlled Upper Canada. Yet after the 1837 rebellion, he faced criticism over his affluent lifestyle, as well as his political challenges to the Anglican Church's dominance. Strachan was also battling with his superiors in London to ensure he had funds to pay priests and spread the gospel.

With this new tranche of cash, Strachan hired Henry Bowyer Lane to design the church, to be located on the site of the Terauley Cottage – a country estate located west of Yonge Street, a few hundred yards north of Queen. The land had been donated by an old Upper Canadian family, the Macaulays, who owned much of the swampy, forested real estate extending northwest of Queen and Yonge. The English-raised Lane enjoyed a reputation as the city's go-to architect. He'd completed Little Trinity Anglican Church, on King Street East, as well as the new city hall, the city market (later St. Lawrence) and additions to Osgoode Hall.

Almost fifty years later, it was revealed that the mystery donation came from a young British woman named Mary

Previous: Ice Wagon on Elizabeth Street, September 16, 1916.

Left: 1842 Cane Topographical Plan of the City and Liberties of Toronto. Macaulaytown, Toronto's first suburb, is shown, running from Yonge Street to University and from Queen to College.

Lambert Swale. Born to a family of wealthy bankers and lawyers, she married Hogarth Swale, a Yorkshire Anglican priest. Though they never visited Canada, the couple learned about Toronto from Strachan's articles in a journal published by the Society for the Propagation of the Gospel in Foreign Parts, an Anglican missionary network. Swale died after giving birth, in May 1845, at the age of twenty-five. The bequest had been part of her will, as was a similar gift to establish a place of worship for convicts on an Australian island.

None of that back story was known immediately after her death because Reverend Swale wanted the gift to remain a secret. When builders finished the Church of the Holy Trinity in 1847, writes Eric Arthur in *No Mean City*, 'Strachan published a notice inviting "the poor families of the United Church of England and Ireland to make the church their own" and another announcing the opening for service of the "Parochial Church of the Poor of Toronto."'

Long before St. John's Ward came to be branded, in the early twentieth century, as Toronto's most impoverished – and most notorious – 'slum,' the working-class enclave bounded by Queen, College, Yonge and University had a distinctive, diverse character that set it apart from the surrounding city. And, contrary to the Holy Trinity's founding mission, it was anything but uniformly 'poor.'

According to historian Barry Dyster, Macaulaytown was known in the 1850s for its 'boisterous, plebian and clannish qualities.' This gritty, tight-knit community, nestled just past the city's northern fringe, served as a recruiting ground for populist local politicians, as well as a destination for sailors on furlough drawn to its bowling alleys, taverns and brothels, writes Dyster. The inhabitants were predominantly Protestant, with lots of Methodists and Baptists.

The Ward was also home to much of the city's thriving African-Canadian community, whose ranks included successful entrepreneurs, merchants and professionals. Many were escaped slaves or freemen who had fled to Canada via the Underground Railroad and were drawn to Toronto for its reputation as a hotbed of abolitionist sentiment.

As it happens, Toronto's African-Canadian community in 1845 had acquired a piece of land in The Ward, just four blocks from the future Holy Trinity site. The lot was to be the site of a new church for a congregation founded eight years earlier. When it opened, the British Methodist Episcopal Church, located at 94 Chestnut Street, offered not just services, but educational programs and

space for public meetings for members of the black community, many of whom lived nearby.

Then, in 1847, another Victorian-era institution relocated to The Ward. The trustees of the Poor House – at Elizabeth and Elm, and three blocks from the British Methodist church – dispensed welfare to destitute women and children in need of food and shelter. The Poor House wardens forced the men to break stones in order to receive their allotment.

Intriguingly, these three structures – and the communities they aspired to serve – epitomized The Ward, and offered clues about its future evolution. As far back as the 1850s, here was a complex and recognizably urban neighbour- hood already characterized by ethnocultural diversity, crushing poverty and upward mobility, as well as the presence of sturdy institutions that claimed to be acting in the best interests of the area's inhabitants.

Physically, however, The Ward was being squeezed by the surrounding city. During the latter half of the nineteenth century, some of Toronto's most significant institutions – University College, the Ontario Legislature, the Victoria Hospital for Sick Children – sprang up just beyond the borders of The Ward. Members of the city's business elite built mansions along University Avenue, then an elegant boulevard, and north of Queen's Park. Closer to Yonge, the T. Eaton Co., in the 1890s, began constructing a series of massive factories, which eventually surrounded Holy Trinity, forming a wall of brick and glass on The Ward's eastern border. Finally, in 1899, after a decade of construction and scandal, builders completed E. J. Lennox's monumental new city hall/ courthouse at Bay and Queen. The towering sandstone structure – designed in the Romanesque Revival style and overlooking the financial district – sym- bolized Toronto's turn-of-the-century confidence and economic heft.

So what became of the community – or communities – wedged between all this growth? By the early 1880s, eight churches, including Holy Trinity and British Methodist, served a growing neighbourhood of about a thousand people. While The Ward's cottage-lined streets now extended further north, toward College, little had changed socially. It was still a predominantly working-class area with pockets of poverty, whose residents were mainly of British, Scottish, Irish or African origin.

But just over a decade later, as Toronto's economy roared back following the great recession of 1893, the area began to transform rapidly. Immigrants

RUSSIAN BAPTIST MISSION
РУССКАЯ МИССІЯ
ВЕЧЕРНЯ ШКОЛА и ЧИТАЛЬНЯ

The new Registry Office site at 38–42 Elizabeth Street, May 23, 1912. The location corresponds to the present-day playground on the west side of City Hall.

from Italy, Eastern Europe and China – as well as places like Macedonia and Finland – arrived in large numbers. The Ward (and other older working-class districts) offered a supply of cheap, filthy rooms in crumbling stucco-and-wood cottages once occupied by an earlier generation that had relocated to newer neighbourhoods outside the core.

The whole city was in the midst of a period of intense flux, according to historian J. M. S. Careless. Union membership doubled between 1900 and 1906. Women's rights networks were actively pushing for universal suffrage and social reform. Temperance activists and missionaries, meanwhile, railed against vice, alcohol and violations of the Lord's Day Act.

It's not difficult to understand the source of all this upheaval. Between 1871 and 1911, Toronto's population exploded, from 56,000 to over 376,000 – an almost sevenfold increase that drove outward expansion and placed enormous strains on municipal infrastructure. (Toronto, notes historian James Lemon, didn't boom as rapidly in this period as cities like New

York, Chicago and Boston.) Foreign-born residents, moreover, now accounted for almost 10 per cent of the population, and a significant proportion came from non-English-speaking countries. (The Ward's residents were predominantly Jewish and Italian in the early twentieth century. The area became increasingly populated by Chinese bachelors after the First World War and the passage of the Exclusion Act in 1923. The Ward's Jews migrated to Kensington Market while the Italians decamped to College west of Bathurst.)

With speculative commercial and institutional development pushing in from all sides, Ward landlords had little incentive to upgrade aging residential buildings – mostly one- or two-storey wood-frame houses. But they responded to demand for inexpensive living space – a single labourer earning two or three dollars a day could pay as little as seventy-five cents to $1.25 per week for lodging and washing – by erecting rough-hewn shacks in The Ward's litter-strewn rear alleyways. Some of these so-called 'rear houses' had no street frontage and could be accessed only through dirt-floor basements with creaking stairs leading up to backyards piled high with junk.

In 1911, a shocking report by Toronto medical officer of health Dr. Charles Hastings stated that The Ward's now predominantly immigrant population had ballooned to over 11,000 (by 1918, the number reached 17,000). New immigrants were arriving every day, many of them packed into overcrowded rooming houses that lacked the most basic sanitary amenities. Hastings ordered city photographer Arthur Goss to document the conditions, and Goss's images of revolting toilets and derelict flophouses full of labourers graphically illustrated the report.

The streets of this 'slum' teemed with newcomers who were visibly, audibly and culturally different from the majority. Today, one might describe the area using journalist Doug Saunders' resonant phrase, 'arrival city.' In fact, that period marked an historic point of inflection. It was the moment when 'Toronto the good,' a staunchly Anglo outpost preoccupied with defending its Christian values, came face to face with concentrated ethnic diversity and grinding poverty, all in one place.

'Few residents of the Ward had the time or inclination to notice the wretched conditions and pungent smells,' observes journalist/historian Charlotte Gray in *The Massey Murder*. The blocks bustled with commerce – peddlers, butchers and bakeries, small factories, lumberyards and sweatshops. The inhabitants,

Gray continues, 'were too busy scraping together the money to bring to Canada the relatives they had left facing poverty or pogroms in the Old Country. Yet The Ward was not a relentless dark place. Its unpaved streets were lively with entertainers, local preachers, and small stores selling fresh vegetables. Women wearing brightly coloured shawls over their heads haggled in unfamiliar languages over prices.'

Public reaction to all that conspicuous difference was hardly sanguine. A 1905 *Globe* article, entitled 'An Invasion of Foreigners,' fretted about an 'influx of a large population foreign in race, speech and customs.' The writer raised red flags: declining downtown church congregations and a worrisome propensity on the part of newcomers, including many Jews from Russia, to cluster together.

Three years later, a somewhat less anxious *Globe* feature noted the proliferation of synagogues in The Ward, as well as new 'penny banks,' night schools and shops. As the reporter lyrically observed:

> What is familiarly known as 'the Ward' has undergone a radical change in nationality. The little rough-cast houses of Centre Avenue, Terauley, and Elizabeth streets, from which three or four years ago the Irish wash lady wended her way to us on Monday mornings, where the Italian fruit vendor ripened his bananas under his bed at night, and the negro plasterer and barber gave colour to the social scene of a summer evening, have in these later days thrown their shelter over the oppressed Slavonic Jew. Practically the whole Ward is a city ghetto...

Yet this tract of apparently impoverished exoticism drew not only waves of striving immigrants; the area also garnered attention from the city beyond The Ward's well-defined boundaries. Toronto the Good simply could not look away.

Writers, journalists, painters and photographers explored the neighbourhood's busy avenues, filled as they were with peddlers and children. Missionaries and social reformers set up street-front operations to recruit new souls, prevent juvenile delinquency and encourage newcomers to learn Canadian customs. Public health nurses fanned out, visiting the homes of immigrant women to offer stern housekeeping and parenting advice. Psychiatrists trawled for 'feeble-minded' or apparently morally deficient foreigners. Civic officials and policy researchers (among them, an ambitious young graduate student named William Lyon Mackenzie King) went from

sweatshop to sweatshop, and from door to door, dutifully recording everything from the number of flophouse beds and so-called 'dark rooms' to language and behavioural shortcomings within individual families. More institutions, like baths, settlement agencies and even an Italian consulate, opened up to provide various services to residents.

The Ward was also attracting interest, however tentative, from ordinary Torontonians. Audiences flocked to the large vaudeville and burlesque theatres on Terauley (now Bay) and Queen. Onlookers crowded into the Elizabeth Street playground (located on the current site of the new wing of the Hospital for Sick Children) to watch amateur baseball and youth festivals. By the 1920s, a growing number of intrepid diners ventured into The Ward for Italian ice cream or the 'chop suey' served in Chinese eateries. Fortune tellers worked other Ward restaurants, like Mary John's, a popular café at Elizabeth and Gerrard. From the 1930s, artists also began gravitating to The Ward's northern half, where they rented old cottages inexpensively and used them as studios. In the 1950s and 1960s, those blocks, which had the look and feel of contemporary Kensington, became a precursor to Yorkville in its heyday.

Not all this outside interest was benign. Jewish peddlers and Chinese café owners found themselves on the receiving end of attacks by young thugs, including former soldiers back from First World War battlefields. Meanwhile, the police, tasked with upholding Toronto's Protestant values, patrolled The Ward's streets, looking for bootleggers, gambling dens, houses of ill repute and merchants doing business on 'Protestant Sundays.' There was more than a hint of moral panic. The Ward was known to encompass a notorious a red-light district, on Centre Avenue. And at one point, council passed a bylaw preventing white women from working for Chinese businesses.

News coverage, in turn, ranged from alarmist to intrigued, or at least bewildered. 'Negros and Chinese seem to mingle well together,' a *Globe* reporter noted evenly in a 1922 story that makes no reference to the decades-long African-Canadian presence in The Ward. '[T]he native Chinese restaurants are filled with negro customers, several of them women, while here and there an occasional white girl can be seen partaking of a meal with either a brown or yellow skinned partner.'

Was the writer here sending a dog-whistle warning to socially conservative readers, alerting them to the threat of mixed-race relationships or prostitution?

Or was the reporter merely recording something, well, unusual about the way people from different backgrounds encountered one another? The latter question begets another two: did such 'sightings' subtly validate a form of social mixing that may have been taboo until then? And is this how ethnocultural acceptance in Toronto germinated?

It's possible. But louder voices, and more strident calls for civic and social reform, prevailed, especially when it came to determining the area's future uses.

Well before city leaders focused on the most visible symptoms of poverty and overcrowding, the blocks north of Queen had been targeted for redevelopment. Early plans for E. J. Lennox's new city hall, for example, envisioned razing the southern blocks of The Ward to create a square anchored by a giant statue of Queen Victoria. Subsequent civic beautification plans, released in 1911 and 1929, proposed open squares, parade grounds and neo-classical government buildings situated above Queen, at the head of a new north-south boulevard leading to Front Street.

The promulgation of these ideas accompanied increasingly anxious warnings about the dangers of slums. At a conference in 1907, Toronto controllers convened to consider the 'evils' of tenements, with Dr. Charles Sheard, the medical officer of health, alleging that Jewish investors had snapped up derelict Ward dwellings and were charging steep rents. 'He suggested the rookeries in St. John's Ward be expropriated by the city and … turned into playgrounds,' the *Globe* reported.

Even as the most decrepit Ward buildings were gradually torn down and replaced with the sort of two- and three-storey brick structures (store at grade, apartments above) still common in Toronto, civic leaders became ever more preoccupied with the spread of New York– or London-style slums. While he didn't disparage poor immigrants, Dr. Charles Hastings warned Torontonians that they were living in a 'fool's paradise' if they thought the city was immune to the problems of concentrated, visible poverty. Less cautious headline writers slung around shrill words and phrases like 'canker,' 'menace' and 'human derelicts.' Nativist sentiment was palpable, and especially directed at The Ward's Chinese residents. As a 1922 *Globe* article about The Ward all but shouted, 'Moral leprosy spreads.'

The message was clear.

The roots of Toronto's preoccupation with the 'spread' of so-called slum conditions can be traced to England during the early- to mid-nineteenth century. Cities had been home to enclaves of desperately poor people for centuries, of course. But the rise of industrialism triggered the mass urban migrations that transformed the nineteenth century. London's population, for example, jumped from 1 million to 6 million within that period, and other cities experienced similarly explosive growth.

The influx of newcomers placed extreme pressures on urban living conditions, municipal infrastructure, housing and transportation networks. As Peter D. Smith, author of *City: A Guidebook for the Urban Age*, wrote of London during that era, 'Cesspools were overflowing, the cemeteries were bursting with stinking corpses, the streets coated with noxious black mud, rotting rubbish clogged its alleys, and its citizens living in overcrowded decrepit buildings, breathing air that was heavily polluted with soot and sulphurous fumes. This was the filthy reality of London for most of its inhabitants.'

Charles Dickens documented this world in novels like *Our Mutual Friend* and *Oliver Twist*. Beginning in 1842, the young Friedrich Engels spent two years exploring the crowded, dehumanizing slums of Manchester, and the book that emerged from his observations, *The Condition of the Working Class in England*, became a hugely influential manifesto about the plight of the urban underclass.

Governments, of course, responded in various ways to these conditions. The British Parliament, in the 1830s, reformed the country's long-standing 'poor laws,' creating new centralized administrations that operated large workhouses (the Poor House in The Ward opened only a few years after the British reform legislation received royal assent).

Overcrowded, unsanitary conditions also gave rise to lethal epidemics. Victorian physicians believed infectious diseases spread through smell, and fixated on 'miasma' and fetid odours. But during the 1854 cholera outbreak in central London, Dr. John Snow, the father of epidemiology, decided to map fatalities – the so-called Ghost Map – and ultimately concluded that the source of infection was a pump-operated drinking well on Broad Street, in Soho, that had been contaminated by a leaking sanitary sewer nearby. Workers at a neighbouring brewery didn't contract the disease because they mainly drank beer. Snow famously cut off the source of contamination by removing the pump's handle.

To counter slum living conditions, public health and 'sanitary' advocates pressed for the construction of public baths that would allow working-class people to not only clean their bodies but also cleanse their souls – filth, in Victorian England, was considered symptomatic of moral decay.

On a broader urban scale, the obviously putrid state of the Thames, and public alarm over incidents such as 'the great stink' of 1858, prompted London civic authorities in the 1860s and 1870s to embark on a massive sewer-works campaign. Sir Joseph Bazalgette oversaw the construction of 2,100 kilometres of new tunnels, including so-called interceptors, which ran along the banks of the Thames and connected with ancient sewer outflows so runoff could be discharged downriver.

Well before The Ward became a subject of concern here, Toronto, with its large concentration of British immigrants, was paying attention to such developments. In 1885, a *Globe* correspondent travelled to London and sent back a detailed account of Bazalgette's vast sewer-construction campaign, published on November 4 of that year. Noting the sharp drop in cholera cases since Snow's 1854 discovery, the reporter opined that Toronto 'before long will have resolutely to face the great sewage question.' He continued: '[M]any useful lessons may be learnt from London's experience.'

Authorities also turned their attention to housing conditions in notorious slums such as Old Nichol, in London's East End, with the national government establishing a royal commission on housing in 1884. 'The working class housing question was like a great blocked drain,' writes Sarah Wise, author of *The Blackest Streets: The Life and Death of a Victorian Slum*. 'But a number of well informed and articulate individuals were determined to flush it through.' As if foreshadowing Toronto's preoccupation with The Ward in the 1910s and 1920s, British missionaries, child welfare advocates, university settlement workers, social reformers and 'slumming' journalists gravitated to Old Nichol, with its 5,700 residents, exposing municipal corruption and Dickensian conditions.

Meanwhile, social researcher Charles Booth began one of the first and most influential exercises in fine-grain urban poverty mapping – an analytical approach still in use in Toronto, with projects such as University of Toronto sociologist David Hulchanski's 'Three Cities' study in income inequality. Working with a team of investigators, Booth categorized income levels for over 900,000 Londoners, and published colour-coded block-by-block maps showing

areas of high need. His work ultimately led to reforms such as the shortened workweek, rent controls, old age pensions and adoption of a 'poverty line' to assess family need.

As Wise observes, 'The more significant achievement of the outsiders who came to Nichol and to the other pockets of deep deprivation was the steady accumulation of data – both dry figures and startling anecdote – that eventually led to moves towards greater social justice at both the local and national government levels.' Old Nichol, however, was demolished in favour of upmarket apartments.

London wasn't the only city grappling with questions of concentrated poverty, immigration and housing shortages. At the same time Booth was probing the extent and intensity of London's poorest, American journalist and social reformer Jacob Riis was wandering through the congested streets of New York's Lower East Side, an area considered at the time to have the world's highest population density. He not only wrote about what he saw, but he also photographed the residents of a world where large immigrant families packed into cramped tenements and eked out a living in the garment trade.

It was a new and powerful way of documenting social conditions. Riis's book, *How the Other Half Lives* (1890), became an influential bestseller, and drew the attention of progressives like Theodore Roosevelt, who would describe Riis as 'the most useful citizen of New York.' (Roosevelt was also heavily influenced Upton Sinclair's 1906 novel *The Jungle*, a fictionalized account of working-class Chicago and the city's corrupt and unsanitary meat-packing industry.)

As Charles Madison noted in his 1970 preface to *The Other Half*, Riis 'not only substantiated his case against the tenements – with photographs duplicating conditions to the last crack in the wall and the most minute wrinkle – but he was also the first to show the power of photography as a journalistic weapon.' It is not known whether Arthur Goss or William James, the photographers who documented Ward conditions in the 1910s and 1920s, were familiar with Riis's efforts, but the similarities are impossible to ignore; like that of Riis, the work of Goss and James allowed a broader audience to observe life as it was lived in the city's poorest and most crowded enclave.

The historical record clearly shows that Toronto officials were well aware of the concerns about slums and tenements (a word used to describe early

apartment buildings as well) emanating from American and British cities. Some of these places were demolished. In the case of the Lower East Side, according to journalist Taras Grescoe, author of *Straphanger*, the construction of subways to Brooklyn 'decanted' the ghastly, overcrowded conditions on the Lower East Side (gentrification, however, didn't reach Mulberry Street and the Bend until recently).

In Toronto, Charles Hastings vehemently opposed the development of modern apartment buildings as a solution to downtown housing needs, claiming they'd degenerate into tenements. Instead, he advocated for planned 'garden city'–style suburbs and improved rapid transit between outer areas and the core. He even urged council to begin buying land that could be developed with modern housing. In the mid-1930s, Lieutenant Governor-General Herbert Bruce recommended the development of modern public housing projects following his inquiry into slum conditions around the city. His proposal led to the post-war demolition of hundreds of derelict east-end row houses and the subsequent construction of Regent Park, itself the subject of a massive redevelopment effort that has sought to undo some of the damage inflicted by well-meaning housing reform.

As for The Ward, years of anti-slum rhetoric inevitably hit the mark. Council in 1946 authorized the expropriation and clearance of the lower Ward, which at that point encompassed Chinatown. The process of razing, land assembly and redevelopment all the way up to College continued steadily until the 1990s, with office, apartment and institutional buildings (most notably City Hall, the Toronto General and Sick Kids) replacing almost all of the older structures, including stores, homes, synagogues, churches, theatres, cafés, studios, offices and Chinatown's landmark restaurants, as well as a public school and a popular playground. Streetcar tracks were pulled up, and several roads were cut or erased altogether, including the southern portion of Elizabeth, which had served as The Ward's main thoroughfare for over a century and, since the 1930s, Chinatown's high street. In fact, the City combined several blocks of Chinatown into the parcel that would become Nathan Phillips Square.

Besides a handful of row houses on Dundas, Gerrard and Elm streets, as well as Holy Trinity and the Poor House, scant tangible evidence remains. (The British Methodist Episcopal Church was sold and then demolished in the late 1950s after the diminished congregation relocated to Shaw Street; the land

where it stood for over a hundred years remains a parking lot near City Hall.) To find The Ward today, in fact, we must imagine our way back into a complicated world whose physical traces have been systematically expunged. Yet The Ward's deeply compelling stories, and its wider legacy, remain woven into the fabric of a global city now defined by the diversity it first encountered well over a century ago, within a few cramped blocks of the downtown. Now, as then, we still struggle with questions about difference and deprivation, heritage and renewal, equity and political exclusion.

The entries that follow are an attempt to embark on that imaginative journey, and to then contemplate how The Ward's past informs Toronto's present.

Because this community was such a jumbled place – one that churned with vitality and variety as well as conflict and hardship for almost a century – we have opted not to relate its narrative(s) in a conventional way. The book is arranged neither chronologically nor thematically, and some entries offer contradictory or multiple views of what happened, and why. Certain essays provide detailed historical accounts of aspects of The Ward's existence, while others adopt more impressionistic, speculative or polemical perspectives. The collection also includes entries about the many representations of The Ward, because these refracted images, and the impact they made, constitute an important part of the area's story, and its ultimate fate. Throughout, we have sought to make connections across time and space. Indeed, we invite the reader to think about this neighbourhood in four dimensions, because one must always acknowledge time as a powerful actor in the lives of cities.

Lastly, we make no claim of comprehensiveness. We sought to push past the existing literature in compiling these entries. As we came to discover while working on the book, The Ward is still giving up its secrets to those who care to look: there are many more stories out there, at the edge of living memory or tucked away in old photo albums, diaries and archival vaults. The fact that they continue to surface, and to resonate in a city so devoted to the future, is surely interesting in and of itself.

WHEN SEARCHING FOR the old Ward, you can wander east and west along Dundas Street, looking at the ramshackle buildings on the south side – restaurants or print shops mainly – and wonder if they are originals. Some look old enough. But when did The Ward stop being The Ward? Was it when most of the buildings were demolished to make way for City Hall, or do the old bits that survived maintain this area's Wardness?

Perhaps the old gables peeking over retail facades tacked on decades ago are enough to convey the neighbourhood's essence. The clotheslines full of kitchen towels drying in the alley behind the restaurants off Elizabeth Street are also evocative of the old photos of laundry drying between the shacks – Toronto's low-rise version of teeming tenements – once found throughout this neighbourhood. Here is a Lady and the Tramp landscape that doesn't exist much in a prosperous inner city where the poor aren't as visible as they once were, having been relegated in recent decades to the inner suburbs.

These traces may hold some neighbourhood essence, but the people are missing; few live here now, save those renting above stores on Dundas, the condos, the hotels on Chestnut and the gorgeous new YMCA affordable-housing residence on Elm Street that incorporates the 1848 House of Industry.

Yet a few Ward people hang on, for example on the second floor of 121 Dundas, a shoebox building surrounded on three sides by new residential buildings. The Lum Family Association makes its home on the second floor, above a new Denny's. Family associations like the Lums' were once the foundation

SHAWN MICALLEF

SEARCHING FOR THE OLD WARD

Previous: Old houses, Price's Lane, February 23, 1912.

Left: Ken Lum sculpture, Two Children of Toronto.

| **27**

of Chinatown, the place new immigrants went when they arrived in Canada seeking help to find accommodation and work. They still exist, though all but the Lums moved to Spadina, where the new Chinatown was established.

Few of the original Chinese restaurants, where so many of those new immigrants worked and ate, remain. The Sai Woo

restaurant was near the Lums' office, and it was the kind of place people from other parts of the city came to visit. Opened in the mid-1950s, it had a long run until closing in 2000. My aunt briefly lived in

Price's Lane, now known as Barnaby Place, as it looks today, running north from a parking lot opposite the bus station, February 23, 2012.

Toronto in 1974 while working for the provincial government and kept a small condiment dish from those days with 'SAI WOO' written above the image of a sinuous red dragon. She gave it to me a few years ago and it now sits on the table by the door, my very own genuine Ward artifact, collecting loose change and unopened cough drops. The Ward is a disembodied notion now, found more in memory than in physical form.

Maybe The Ward today begins in the two parking lots here, some of the last in downtown Toronto. There's one just north of Dundas and another a few metres south. Both span entire blocks – vast spaces of asphalt in an increasingly dense city, absurdly hot on summer days and tundra-cold in the winter. The story of The Ward is so bound to its destruction – to the city's need to clear space for all this parking that municipal officials once thought we needed – these two lots might be the most Wardish places of all.

The north one runs along the top of the Toronto Coach Terminal site; it's not a mere station, but a terminal. The buses leave every day and every hour, but the emphasis is on termination: this is a place of arrival, either coming home or starting a new life in this city. Travellers are welcomed by a big parking lot that even has a parking lot hut, a bit of Toronto's vernacular heritage. (We should give this hut a heritage listing to

commemorate the post-war period when Toronto, and so many cities like it, devoured itself for parking.) The buses also dominate, and the sound is one continuous diesel-engine idle, from those parked in the terminal bays, to the hop-on/hop-off buses parked along Elm waiting to pick up tourists.

Besides the coming and going of buses, there is lots of work taking place here as The Ward has become an institutional hub, with hospitals and courthouses, government and private-sector offices. Like the financial district before condos, The Ward today can feel a little lifeless at times, especially in the evening when the sidewalk traffic evaporates and there isn't the critical mass of pubs or cafés needed to keep the streets lively after hours. At night, you've got the city to yourself here. The culture that's here – like the gem of a Textile Museum on a stretch of Centre Street long ago dotted by synagogues – is hidden, except during Nuit Blanche, when crowds surge into the area, seeking art and food trucks.

If one searches amid the concrete and pavement, there are also unexpected pockets of green that seem reminiscent of The Ward, with its dirt lots and unrefined urbanism. Directly behind City Hall, along Bay, is Larry Sefton Park, a concrete-and-steel nook that is well-treed, with a memorial to the long-time Steelworkers union leader. Just to the west is a gravel parking lot with two large trees growing in the middle of it. There's a looseness to this place that's at odds with the formality of City Hall and Nathan Phillips Square, a looseness reminiscent of The Ward's haphazard topography. This marginal space morphs into the Downtown Diversity Garden, a lot-sized swath of benches and overt, policy-driven multiculturalism that did not exist in The Ward's day. Adjacent to all this is a 1880s-vintage Toronto Hydro substation, an imposing power pusher with oversized doors that no doubt allowed for the installation of transformers to feed the large institutional buildings that would soon crowd out The Ward's original inhabitants.

Between the power station and a new apartment building on the corner of Bay and Dundas is a narrow east-west passage that leads to the adjacent condo and then over to Elizabeth Street. Here there is a pair of sculptures by the Canadian artist Ken Lum, *Two Children of Toronto*. These Ward kids are hanging out, eternally playing, and from old Chinatown perhaps. Only those curious enough to venture down this walkway will find them. They're there, waiting to be discovered, just as only those with a curious and informed eye will detect the bits of the old Ward all around the new Ward, or whatever we call this not-quite-a-neighbourhood today.

HOWARD AKLER

NO PLACE LIKE HOME

LET'S SAY YOU'RE a little down on your luck. You've got a wife and young daughter to support and your dollar goes only so far. Your first concern, of course, is accommodation. Something decent, affordable. It won't be easy. Everyone knows the rental market is tight. The papers say the private sector stopped all construction of apartment buildings during the Depression, and now, just a few years after the Second World War, the city has over 5,000 families in emergency housing.

So what do you do?

Maybe you go see Mr. L. F. Kirk, of Toronto Trailers Ltd. Put a down payment on one of his company's mobile homes and then park it on a vacant lot just off University Avenue, at Centre and Gerrard, near the old Elizabeth Street Playground. There's over eighty of them there already, an odd little neighbourhood. Sure, some of the residents are a little rough – day labourers and the like – but also plenty of regular folks: veterans, students, small families like yours.

So you move in and it's not half bad. The trailer is snug but clean, cleaner than any of the dingy firetraps for rent out there. And you've got some privacy – no need to cram into some cheap room with another family, no nosy landlord, no one stomping around the apartment above. This is the best you can afford. This, you tell yourself as you settle in over the weeks and months, is home.

Too bad, then, that the city eventually decides to kick you out. Trailer camps are too unseemly, they say – unsuitable for a big city to have hundreds living in such crude conditions. Right out in the open too. This is an official flip-flop: back in 1941, council

eased up the housing standards bylaw to allow the trailer option. *Trailers in front* But now they're starting to crack down. Public Health has been *of Centre Avenue* by to tell you the outhouses and water taps aren't up to code. *and Gerrard Street,* And if that official warning doesn't force you out, then this will: *with the Toronto* the city has deeded this land to the new hospital for sick kids. *General Hospital*

Your eviction notice tells you to be gone by April 30, 1947. *in the background,* Again: what do you do? *May 6, 1940.*

You could pull up stakes, like some folks have done, and set out for Long Branch or Weston. But hell, your job is here. Your daughter's school is here. So maybe you should just stick it out. Bertie Moore and that Mrs. Laws, the war widow, have established the Toronto Trailer Residents Association. They've been writing letters to the Welfare Council, the building commissioner, even Mayor Saunders. And they're getting results: a special committee meeting is scheduled at City Hall later this month. Some say you'll get an extension on your eviction date; there's even some talk that the city will buy up land at the Ontario Stockyards and move everyone there. Better than nothing, you guess, and then you curse yourself for setting the bar so low for you and your family.

You take a stroll through the trailer camp. Discuss the matter with your neighbours. You look around and are amazed. While this city can grow bigger, taller, better and newer, still there are people like you who have to ask the same old question: where will we live?

THE SOUTH PART of St. John's Ward, known as Macaulaytown, was Toronto's first suburb. Two months after the city's incorporation, in March 1834, Alpheus Todd, a thirteen-year-old prodigy who went on to become the librarian of Parliament, published an engraved map of the first formal plan for the City of Toronto. It included a subdivision three blocks wide and one block deep on the north side of Lot (Queen) Street, between Osgoode Hall and Yonge Street.

STEPHEN A. OTTO

BEFORE
THE WARD
MACAULAYTOWN

Todd's lines were based on surveys conducted forty years earlier, when colonial land officials parcelled out the forests on the Town of York's north edge into 100-acre park lots. Nothing much distinguished the properties that became the future St. John's Ward. (As was the case with the whole city, that land had long been occupied by the Mississaugas of the New Credit, and Ojibwa nation that sold its territorial rights to the British in 1787 in a treaty known as the Toronto Purchase.) That particular segment was well-drained ground enclosed by road allowances for University Avenue and Yonge, Queen and Bloor streets. The land sloped slightly toward Lake Ontario from a sandhill near present-day St. Joseph Street. There were no deep ravines, although a small brook, later called Taddle Creek, meandered from north of Queen Street and emptied into the lake near what is now the Distillery.

Park lots numbers 9, 10 and 11 were patented in 1797 and 1798 by James Macaulay, John Elmsley and Thomas Raddish respectively. All three men received their land grants due to their positions in colonial society and the public offices they held. Macaulay was senior military surgeon for Upper Canada,

Top: Bishop Strachan School, at its Wykeham Hall location on the south side of College Street, just west of Yonge, 1915.

Bottom: A detached house and adjoining terrace of four dwellings at 68 Charles Street off of Bay. They were built by Henry Schomberg in 1871. March 1921.

while Elmsley served as the colony's first chief justice and Raddish had become the first missionary for the Church of England in York.

Shortly after receiving their patents, the owners began selling their lands or trading them for others. This sort of speculation was not unusual, since property was one of the few negotiable assets people had. In late 1798, Raddish sold his lot to Elmsley. The following year, Macaulay and Elmsley swapped the northern and southern halves of their respective lots, which were adjacent. That deal made present-day College Street the new boundary between their holdings. There things stood until the 1820s, when Elmsley's widow sold the north half of her lot to King's College (later the University of Toronto). Soon after, the south half of Elmsley's land was acquired by jurist John Beverley Robinson, who designated the corner of Lot Street and University Avenue, then called 'College Avenue to Lot Street,' as the future seat of the provincial courts and Law Society of Upper Canada.

The Macaulays' lands developed more quickly, maybe because they were slightly closer to town. Macaulaytown grew up as an area of workers' houses. In the mid-1840s, the family subdivided other swaths of land between Macaulaytown and present-day Dundas Street, endowing the Church of the Holy Trinity with a site where the Macaulay home, known as Terauley Cottage, once stood. The Macaulays also sold several lots in a desirable area on the west side of Yonge Street, north of Queen. In 1859, after the death of Macaulay's second son, the family sold part of their ten-acre homestead – located south of College Street, just west of Yonge – to Bishop Strachan School, which opened an expanded three-storey facility there in 1870. (The school decamped to Forest Hill in 1915 when the city's industrial and commercial expansion encroached on the property.)

The area north of College evolved quite differently. Until the middle of the nineteenth century, the Elmsleys' hundred acres between College and Bloor remained divided into three large estates: Elmsley Villa, Barnstable and Clover Hill. When the owners did move to subdivide them, their great interest in Roman Catholic institutions left an enduring mark. In 1853, the Elmsleys donated part of the Clover Hill estate to St. Michael's College. Subsequently, they set aside other lots nearby for two convents. Development closer to Bloor occurred toward the end of the nineteenth century.

By then, the pace of urbanization in Toronto had become a subject of public interest. From about 1870, the city's newspapers began to publish annual reports about building activity in each ward. St. John's was usually well down

the list in terms of the dollar value of construction activity, although 10,868 people lived in The Ward as of 1871. In 1879, the *Globe* offered this explanation: 'Little can be expected from this Ward, which is the most densely populated in the city. Any new buildings that have been erected this year are situated in the upper portion of the ward.'

The newspaper continued to bemoan the fact that there was little evidence of any redevelopment of the tiny workers' dwellings that dominated the southern tier of The Ward: 'In the south half of this ward,' the *Globe* reported in 1879, 'there have been but few alterations made, and a few additions to the buildings this year. The central part of this south half especially is composed of little old frame cottages. These seem something more dilapidated and cheerless than a year ago, and that is all.'

In the decades to come, the civic conversation about The Ward's dilapidated housing stock would be sharply amplified by the surge of immigration to Toronto. As the new century dawned, the population of St. John's Ward's had nosed well above 13,000, with many of the residents packed into hundreds of wood cottages located just steps from E. J. Lennox's majestic new city hall and the hulking Eaton's factory next door. By that point, civic officials could no longer ignore the poverty on their doorstep.

William S. Boulton Atlas of the City of Toronto and Vicinity. Detail from Plate 16, St. John's Ward, 1858.

HOWARD MOSCOE

MY GRANDMOTHER THE BOOTLEGGER

MY MATERNAL GRANDMOTHER, Getel (Gertrude) Shumacher, and her husband, Pesach (Percy), came to Canada from Russia in 1908 and settled in The Ward. They lived at 16 Centre Avenue and relocated to 96 Edward Street – near Elizabeth Street – a year or two later. Their first son, Morris, was born in 1910. Their daughters Sarah and Betty were born in 1912 and 1914 respectively. Betty was my mother.

Everyone in the neighbourhood did what they had to do to survive. This was particularly true after the big Eaton's strike in 1912, which resulted in unemployment for many of the local Jews who earned a living as garment workers. My grandfather worked as a peddler and likely did not earn enough to support his family. Like most recent Jewish immigrants, my grandmother spoke very little English, was illiterate and had young children to raise. Confronted with dire economic prospects for her family and few job opportunities, my resourceful grandmother became a bootlegger.

Grandma Gussie opened a so-called 'grocery store' in her home where she dispensed booze by the shot. The grocery business was likely the one she reported to the census takers and the state; it served as a front for her illegal bootlegging operation. Although I knew few details of this family enterprise, my daughter Vicki interviewed my mother for a history essay while she was a student at York University. I asked Vicki if my mother told her that Bubby was a bootlegger, and she said she hadn't. When Vicki specifically asked about it, my mother responded, 'Her brother Shmuel was a bootlegger, but he was very observant, so on the Sabbath, Bubby took over.'

After that time, we did a little digging and discovered a *Toronto Star* article from 1925 that revealed that my grandmother had been charged, along with her sister, for assaulting a woman named Eva Posner on Centre Avenue using a heavy piece of hose and tire from a baby carriage. When questioned by the magistrate, Posner stated, 'She claims I squealed to the police and she wanted me to pay the fine.' My uncle Morris also testified at the hearing, defending his mother by claiming she didn't get along with Mrs. Posner and the two of them got into a fight at a department store over a bargain counter. According to a second *Star* article, in addition to paying the $50 fine for illegal possession of liquor, she was forced to spend a week in jail and was given a suspended sentence of two years if she 'kept the peace with Posner.'

Top: Southeast view of Edward and Bay streets, October 3, 1928. The Shumacher family lived at 96 Edward Street near Elizabeth Street in 1911 and moved to 55 Edward Street, east of Bay, likely after the First World War.

Bottom: Family portrait of Getel and Percy Shumacher with their three children, ca. 1915.

LAUNDRIES ARE THE oldest Chinese businesses in Canada, dating back to the 1858 gold rush in British Columbia. Not surprisingly, the first Chinese immigrant in Toronto, recorded in the city directory of 1878 as Sam Ching, worked as a laundryman at 9 Adelaide Street East. By 1911, Toronto had 301 Chinese laundries, twenty of them in The Ward, the heart of which would soon develop into the city's first Chinatown.

ARLENE CHAN

AGAINST ALL ODDS
THE CHINESE LAUNDRY

Why were laundries so popular among the early Chinese immigrants to Toronto? The Chinese were no more adept at laundering than other immigrants at the time. By tradition, men were not responsible for this household task in China; washing clothes was considered women's work. What the Chinese seized upon was a niche business that could be pursued, in those early years, without persecution and objection. It was not so much a choice, but a practical response to the limited options available to them in that era. The Chinese provided an affordable and valuable service to the burgeoning workforce of single men in the city who needed their clothes laundered.

The Chinese opened their laundries with little start-up capital by pooling their money, saved or borrowed. With inexpensive equipment and simple supplies, they eked out a modest living from the slim profit margins of their small operations. Charging less than their non-Chinese competitors enabled them to attract customers. What's more, they could be their own bosses, hire their relatives and friends, and be free of discrimination from white employers. In 1911, for example, Guan Leying ran a laundry business at 166 Chestnut

Left: The Lung Kong Brotherhood was established in 1911 and served as a mutual benefit society for the Chinese community. It purchased the building at 24 Elizabeth Street in 1922. The photograph was taken in 1957.

Street at Elm, just across from the House of Labour. He relied on his brother and two lodgers to help him out with the rent and laundry work.

Little could be done to make laundry work easier or more pleasant. These laundries typically operated sixteen to eighteen hours a day, six or seven days a week. Chores, confined to a cramped space, started before sunrise with the lighting of the stove fire, which was fed throughout the day with wood or coal. The laundrymen boiled water in a large pot, scrubbed dirty clothes in washtubs and then hung them to dry. They used a heavy iron, heated on the stove, to press out the wrinkles. All the work was completed by hand – hence the phrase 'hand laundry.' Most laundry workers earned an average wage of $8 to $18 a month, including room and board.

The Chinese not only worked at their laundries, they ate and slept in their stores too. Saving on rent and foregoing personal comforts meant that more money could be sent home to support their wives and children. After the introduction of the prohibitive head tax within the Chinese Immigration Act of 1885, most men were forced to leave their families behind in China. In 1921, there were only thirteen Chinese families in Toronto, nine of them living in The Ward. At that time, over half of the 2,134 Chinese recorded in the city census did laundry work. They lived as single men in what came to be known as a bachelor society. In their meagre spare time, they watched performances of beloved Cantonese operas at halls or theatres on Dundas, Queen and Elizabeth streets, gambled or attended free English classes. A network of mutual benefit associations (such as the Lung Kong Brotherhood) – their membership eligibility based on surnames, geographical origin in China and political affiliation – provided welcoming places for these bachelors to socialize and access such essential but scarce services as banking, job placement and legal aid.

As the Chinese population increased, the media stoked the fears of local residents by publishing articles that would be considered racist by today's standards. An 1894 *Toronto Daily Star* item, 'The Evil the Chinese Do,' complained that 'Chinamen were crowding white laundrymen out of business.' An 1896 report in the same paper condemned Chinese laundries as having 'not the first shadow of claim for public patronage.' The biweekly newspaper *Jack Canuck*, in 1911, reported that 'throngs of Chinamen lounging in the streets and doorways' comprised Toronto's 'yellow peril.' The reporter further warned about

'the awful menace lurking behind the partitions or screens of some of these innocent appearing laundries.'

Interior view of Chinese laundry, ca. 1900.

Chinese laundries had also been condemned by labour leaders and trade guilds for many years. The Laundry Association of white owners pressured health authorities to attack 'dirty laundries' to prevent the spread of infection. As early as 1883, the Trades and Labour Congress of Canada advised delegates not to disregard the 'Chinese immigration curse.' While these and other complaints were positioned as threats to public health, the underlying reason had more to do with the competitive edge that Chinese laundries possessed in relation to their competitors, realized through lower operating expenses.

In reality, Chinese hand laundries never posed a threat to the white-owned steam laundries that supplied more profitable bulk washing for hotels and restaurants. Nonetheless, the city and the province reacted with a heavy hand. In 1902, a municipal bylaw imposed a hefty licensing fee of $50, which was

strongly protested by Chinese laundrymen. It was Alderman William P. Hubbard, Toronto's first African-Canadian politician, who successfully advocated on their behalf. Chinese laundries subsequently paid a graduated licensing fee of $5 to $20, depending on the size of the business or the number of employees on staff.

Against all odds, Chinese laundries kept multiplying, at least until the Chinese Exclusion Act was introduced in 1923, effectively shutting the door to Chinese immigrants. For the next twenty-four years, these establishments endured a downward spiral. The modernization of laundry equipment proved too expensive for these businesses to stay competitive. The introduction of synthetic fibres, coin-operated laundromats and home washers and dryers also took a toll. And, ultimately, there was no next generation to take over from the aging laundrymen.

The golden age of the Chinese laundry was over by the 1950s. The legacy of the Chinese laundry, however, endures as one of the most recognizable icons of the Chinese-Canadian experience. While their lives were characterized by adversity, discrimination and hostility, these immigrants confronted the challenges with resilience, determination and a legendary work ethic.

Ghong Yee Laundry at 48 Elizabeth Street, 1912.

ARLENE CHAN

V-J DAY

THE WAR IN the Pacific ended on V-J Day, August 15, 1945. The revellers were joyous because Japan, which had occupied China and Hong Kong and was the common enemy of both Canada and China, surrendered. Thousands of people filled Elizabeth Street for Chinatown's V-J Day parade, resplendent with joyous music, colourful floats and lively lion dances. The war marked a turning point for the Chinese in Toronto and across Canada. They had proven their loyalty, their sons and daughters having put their lives on the line alongside Canadians. Their war-relief efforts to raise funds, more than any other group in Canada on a per capita basis for the Victory Loan Drive alone, did not go unnoticed. All of these wartime contributions paved the way for dramatic reforms in the anti-Chinese government policies that restricted immigration, citizenship, employment and the franchise.

MERLE FOSTER HAD just finished making a papier-mâché head and put it in the shed at the back of the studio she shared with her business-manager sister, at Yonge and Walton streets, just south of Gerrard. But the head was too great a temptation for a neighbourhood boy who, within seconds, hopped the fence and made off with it. The theft didn't escape Foster's notice, and she gave chase, soon rescuing a work destined for a masquerade ball.

TERRY MURRAY

MERLE FOSTER'S STUDIO
'A SPOT OF ENCHANTMENT'

Observing the incident, a police officer shook his head. 'Well,' he told Foster's mother, who was visiting that day, 'your daughters are on a very bad corner.' It was the early 1920s and Foster's studio sat in the northeast quadrant of The Ward, an area notorious for its squalor.

'As if we cared about that,' Foster later told a journalist. 'All we wanted was the head and we got it.'

Foster knew the children of The Ward well enough to have an easygoing attitude toward them. She often used them as models for her sculptures. She paid them, and didn't discourage them from passing the time in her studio.

In fact, a *Toronto Star* reporter dubbed Foster's studio 'a spot of enchantment to the children of the Ward.' As an artist, Foster was becoming a household name, attracting attention for her gargoyles and other architectural decorations, monumental works, portrait busts, public fountains, garden statuary, small works such as sports trophies and bookends, and clay modelling demonstrations at the Canadian National Exhibition.

Her studio – located initially on Walton Street, although she eventually moved to Church Street and then Grosvenor during the 1920s and early 1930s – was known among local children as a 'make-shop.'

'What does she make?' one uninitiated child asked another, who was a regular visitor to Foster's studio.

'Jus' everythin',' the boy answered breathlessly.

Not only was it full of fantastic creations, including figures for the T. Eaton Co.'s annual Santa Claus Parade, there was also clay to play with, and biscuits were always on offer.

And there was also the undeniable appeal of Foster herself. She was just a big kid. Until she was well into her thirties, newspaper stories and magazine profiles invariably called her 'Toronto's girl sculptor.' Her zaftig form, 'jolly' demeanour (as it was inevitably described in articles about her), trilling voice and self-deprecation must have been irresistible to the neighbourhood children. She sometimes denied she was an artist, calling herself instead 'just a mud-slinger' who 'made mud pies for a living.'

Artist Merle Foster working on a bust of novelist W. A. Fraser, ca. 1925.

A writer for *Maclean's* (or *MacLean's*, as it was spelled at the time) was on hand one morning when another boy popped his head in the door. 'Don't you want a model this morning, miss?' he asked, but showed no disappointment when Merle replied, 'I wonder if you would go get your brother.'

The brothers, like so many children in The Ward, might have been guests at one or more of the annual Christmas parties she gave over the course of a decade. Foster's parties – known at the time as 'Christmas Trees' – began in 1922, when she invited nine of her models to the decorated studio for food and gifts. She later expanded the guest list by asking the letter carrier for names of other children in the area whom he thought would have 'little pleasure' during the festive season (meaning they had to forego presents either because of poverty or religion; many Ward children were Jewish). The numbers grew to thirty, fifty and just short of seventy by the time of the last party, in 1931.

'I have no choice in the matter,' Foster said. 'I simply set the date.'

For the first party, the gifts came from her own childhood toy box. By the second year, her toy box was empty and the number of guests increased, so Foster turned to friends for donations. One of her more highly placed friends was Justin Cork, a co-founder of Loblaws, who provided hundreds of dollars' worth of oranges and candy over the years. Toronto newspapers and other local publications also obliged by printing calls for toys and other gifts.

Local newspapers and even national magazines seemed not to tire of covering the parties. With each passing year, the kudos became more lavish and the descriptions more colourful.

'Yesterday found boxes of candy for each child, oranges, sample bottles of sauces, sample packages of powder and toilet accessories for the small girls, 20 pounds of nuts, quantities of animal biscuits, numbers of dolls, all gifts from friends,' the *Daily Star* reported of the 1927 party. 'Games and the distribution of gifts occupied the afternoon, which began at three o'clock and still waxed strong at seven. The children brought their own musical instruments, their banjos and violins, and entertained Miss Foster and her sister and their friends with their quaint music. Many of them danced and gave comic exhibitions of the black bottom [dance].'

In 1928, *Chatelaine* held up Foster's annual party as an example of how an individual could give a Christmas Tree, calling hers a 'success that has evolved into a triumph from a very small beginning.'

The 1930 party was 'a howling success,' according to the *Mail and Empire*. As Foster told the newspaper, 'I'm just so grateful to the people who send me things and help me to keep this party going. I'd hate to give it up.'

But the next year's party was to be the last. Foster's Grosvenor Street studio had been expropriated in the development of Women's College Hospital, and she had moved to York Mills – too far for the children to travel.

On New Year's Eve, 1932, the women's page of the *Toronto Daily Star* carried the news: 'Toys and provisions have been rolling in all week to Merle Foster, the sculptress, the aftermath of her annual holiday party given for the children of the "Ward" who used to model for her when she lived there. This year, living in York Mills, she did not give the party but contributions poured in just the same. She had no difficulty in disposing of them, however, and they went to many deserving and appreciative folk.'

But other events, global and personal, would no doubt have interfered with her ability to continue sponsoring the party. The onset of the Depression led to a sharp decline in commissions. In 1930, moreover, Merle and her sister became guardians of an infant girl; in time, they were also supporting their elderly parents.

In the decades that followed, the children of The Ward did not forget Merle Foster, visiting her until she moved from Toronto to Cornwall shortly before her death in 1986. Among them was Lillian Pearlstein, who grew up in The Ward. She had modelled for Foster as a child and helped her earn at least one commission. Pearlstein later married Sam Shopsowitz, the deli owner who went on to build the Shopsy's restaurant chain and meat processing plant.

'Today,' a magazine noted in 1942, 'atop his [Canadian National] Exhibition stand there's a larger than life size model of Shopsy, executed by Merle Foster who has been remembered all these years by the little model who became Mrs. Shopsy.'

Foster posing with Ward children at one of her annual Christmas parties, which drew donations of gifts from across the city, December 1928.

O N THE EVENING of June 18, 1911, a huge riot erupted at the corner of Agnes (Dundas) and Elizabeth streets. According to the *Toronto Daily Star*'s account, a mob of hundreds of enraged residents hurled stones and debris at a local missionary named Reverend Sabati Rohold, who'd been preaching on the corner. The police intervened, brandishing batons, injuring five participants and arresting eight Jewish residents.

ELLEN SCHEINBERG

MISSIONARY WORK
THE FIGHT FOR JEWISH SOULS

In the aftermath, sympathizers from the Jewish community swarmed a nearby police station. With the support of Holy Blossom's religious leader, Rabbi Solomon Jacobs, they raised the $500 bail required to release the eight men. Until then, the different ethnic and religious groups living in The Ward had coexisted peacefully despite their differences. So what incited the violent brawl between members of the Jewish community and Rev. Rohold?

Presbyterian missions weren't at all unusual in turn-of-the-century Toronto, a city seething with religious reformers. But Rohold's church, located at 156 Terauley (Bay), was something else entirely: it called itself the Christian Synagogue. And the preaching reverend himself was a converted Jew.

The first mission in Toronto emerged in 1894. The movement grew rapidly during the first decade of the twentieth century in response to the arrival of thousands of new Eastern European Jewish immigrants in The Ward. In addition to Rohold's Terauley Street mission, there were two others, one led by Henry Singer, on Centre Avenue, and the other by Paul Berman, on

Left: Henry Singer, in bowler hat, preaching on a corner, 1912.

TO THE JEW FIRS

Service at the
Jewish Church,
ca. 1912.

Edward Street. Like Rohold, both Singer and Berman were Jewish converts who preached on street corners, aiming to proselytize to the Jews and save their souls. In addition to relying on their oratorical skills and familiarity with the scriptures,

these missionaries preyed on the Jewish immigrants' poverty by offering services and products they desperately required, including free breakfasts after morning services. Singer offered to take unemployed immigrants to factories owned by Christians in order to secure jobs for them. The missionaries provided needy Jewish families with coal and rent subsidies.

Presbyterian mission at Elm and Elizabeth, 1913. The site is now a nursing residence. And after the relocation of Rohold's mission in 1913 to a three-storey building at 257 Elizabeth Street, the Christian Synagogue boasted a reading room, nursery, night school and Sabbath school, along with a free dispensary, as well as sewing classes for young people. Some of these services replicated those offered by other entities at the time, such as Central Neighbourhood House and the Jewish community.

The missionaries deliberately situated themselves close to local synagogues or homes of rabbis, shouting provocative and inflammatory statements aimed at taunting these community leaders. The rabbis resisted offers to debate or confront them in public. Many Ward Jews, however, became enraged when the missionaries tried to lure local children into the missions by offering enticements such as lavish Christmas parties, with candy, toys, a special dinner and a visit from Santa Claus. Teachers from Hester How School on Elizabeth Street colluded with these missionaries by releasing the children from classes to attend revival meetings and parties. Indeed, according to

Dr. Stephen Speisman, author of *The Jews of Toronto*, the school and Elizabeth Street Playground became a 'hotbed of attempted proselytizing.'

Jewish parents understood what was taking place and sought to protect their offspring from the clutches of a group Rabbi Jacobs referred to as the 'over-zealous soul-grabbers.' In her autobiography, *The Errand Runner*, Leah Rosenberg, the daughter of a local Polish Orthodox rabbi, revealed that, like many children, she was instructed to avoid the missionaries and not be lured in by their promises of free treats. Another local Jewish girl, Fay Gardner, recalled in an interview preserved by the Ontario Jewish Archives that she attended a Christmas party at one of the missions and received a doll, but had no memory of attempts to convert her.

The three missions run by Rohold, Singer and Berman invested considerable resources into supporting their activities in The Ward. While a sizeable number of Jews took advantage of their offerings, the efforts to convert the recipients appeared to be a dismal failure. According to Shmuel Shapiro, author of *The Rise of the Toronto Jewish Community*, only three people converted.

Years of confronting this incessant assault on their faith created resentment in the community, and the riot represented an opportunity for Jews to release the pent-up hostility they had been harbouring. When the rioters finally had their day in court, an evidently frustrated Rabbi Jacobs told Magistrate Kingsford, 'These missionaries come into the district thickly populated with Jewish citizens, cast aspersions on their religion, wound their feelings, abuse the rabbis, and do the utmost to stir up trouble among peaceful and law-abiding citizens.' Rather than backing down, Rohold replied that the riot only increased his resolve to convert Jews.

As a result, policemen were stationed beside the missionaries during their street-preaching sessions to ensure their safety. While the magistrate sympathized with the Jews during the trial, most local churches, municipal authorities and educators backed the missionaries. In the years to come, as Jews began moving from The Ward to Kensington Market, these missions relocated to that area. They didn't fare much better in their new location. In fact, the missionaries' lack of success prompted the churches to focus on foreign missions instead of local ones. Hence, the Jewish community's staunch efforts to fend off local missionaries and protect their youth ultimately led to the missions' decline in The Ward.

THE WARD WAS Toronto's original 'wrong side of the tracks.' Merely to invoke its name was to conjure up unsavoury images of slums, destitution, disease, crime and the moral deficiency – if not depravity – of its residents. But few Canadians knew The Ward better, or derived more advantage from it, than the man who would become Canada's longest-serving prime minister – Mackenzie King. Indeed, The Ward served as the gateway to his political career.

MYER SIEMIATYCKI
KING OF THE WARD

King never lived in The Ward, but he wrote a series of newspaper articles that drew significant attention to the area, and to himself. In 1897, the twenty-three-year-old aspiring academic spent the summer writing four long articles exploring social problems in Toronto, for the *Mail and Empire*. Not surprisingly, The Ward loomed large in King's reportage.

After an undergraduate degree at the University of Toronto, King spent the 1896–97 academic year pursuing graduate studies in Chicago. There, he worked closely with the inner-city settlement movement, providing support services to the poor and destitute.

King decided to use his stint with the *Mail and Empire* to examine whether Toronto, like Chicago, was beset by slum conditions, problem 'foreigners' and sweatshop labour.

'The greatest curse to any city,' King declared in the opening installment, 'is its slums.' And while he acknowledged that Toronto had no areas as deeply scarred as American slums, he believed there were neighbourhoods in the city with all the same characteristics: crime, overcrowded housing, unsanitary living conditions and elevated risks of disease.

The Ward was the only Toronto district King specifically cited: 'The manner in which the majority [of Ward residents] are housed is a disgrace to the city.' The remedies he proposed are stunningly contemporary: transit, cycling and mixed-social-class housing.

King identified 'cheap and rapid transit' expansion as 'the most promising' solution to housing conditions, arguing that by opening up new suburban housing districts through transit access, the city would end the need for workers to live near their inner-city places of employment. The bicycle, he added, was part of the solution: 'Any improvement intended to provide better paths appears to be a move-ment in the right direction.' Lastly, King called on Toronto 'to take any measures to prevent a separation by areas of the different classes of its citizens.'

Portrait of W. L. Mackenzie King, 1904.

In his two articles on foreigners in Toronto, which echo tropes of both a bygone era and our own, King asked readers to consider whether the increasing number of foreigners in the city constituted an 'evil' or a 'strength' for Toronto.

Those articles are among the first writings on immigrant integration in Canada. Reflecting the outlook of his times on who constituted the city's insiders and outsiders, King identi-fied British immigrants as part of the mainstream, and regarded non-British immigrants as foreigners. He focussed his attention on German, Jewish, Italian, Chinese and Syrian groupings in The Ward.

Generally, King struck an optimistic tone about the impact of foreigners on Toronto. (Syrians he portrayed as an excep-tion: 'The men are lazy and inclined to be dirty and quarrelsome.') Overall, he described the city's non-Anglo immi-grants as hard-working, and less reliant on welfare or engaged in crime than 'Canadians themselves.' Still, he advocated that

measures be taken to prevent foreigners from living together in their own districts, which, he claimed, prevented assimilation. (King's favourable view of foreigners bears little resemblance to his record as prime minister, when the federal government adopted highly discriminatory measures, such as a moratorium on Chinese immigration in 1923, the refusal to admit Jews seeking refuge from Nazi persecution in the 1930s and the internment of Japanese-Canadians during the Second World War.)

The final installment of King's series, however, proved to be the blockbuster, and the revelations propelled the young graduate student into politics. In 'Toronto and the Sweating System,' King documented the oppressive sweatshop working conditions in the city's garment industry, which relied largely on a Jewish workforce and was anchored in The Ward.

'Sweated labour' referred to conditions characterized by long work hours for low wages in unhealthy settings. The phenomenon was rampant in The Ward, especially with subcontracted garment work performed in the area's overcrowded homes. This form of cottage industry thrived in The Ward, with entire families working dawn to dusk producing clothing for local wholesalers and retailers.

Based on his visits, King reported examples of ramshackle housing serving as both family lodging and workspace, with children as young as nine toiling in clothing production. Moreover, he reported, a family's combined wages were 'frequently below a living wage.' Sweatshop conditions also bred disease, work injuries and exploitation of female labour, which King demurely described as 'too hideous to admit of publication.'

Another detail King withheld in his reporting would pave his path into politics. As it turned out, the Canadian government, through the post office, was one of the main indirect employers of sweated labour in The Ward. King, scion of a prominent Liberal family, had a close family friend, William Mulock, who happened to serve as the Liberal government's minister responsible for the post office.

During his investigation, King learned that some of the worst Ward sweatshops were producing postal-carrier uniforms and mailbags. As he recounted two decades later:

> In visiting the homes of workers in the garment trades in company with a Labor
> friend, I came across letter carriers' uniforms being made up under contracts
> awarded by the Post Office Department of Canada. On questioning one of the

workers as to the remuneration she was receiving for sewing machine and hand work, I found that it came to a very few cents an hour. I shall never forget the feeling of pained surprise and indignation I experienced as I learned the extent of that woman's toil from early morning till late at night, and figured out the pittance she received. The circumstance that it was Government work, and that the contracting firm was one of high repute in the city, did not lessen the resentment I felt. As I visited other homes and shops, I found the condition of the woman's employment to be in no sense isolated, but all too common.

However, King did not want to publicly embarrass or condemn the Liberal government – in his reporting, he suppressed any reference to Ottawa's complicity. Instead, he arranged a private meeting with Mulock to apprise him of his findings about sweatshops. The outcome, King would later write, 'was even better than I had anticipated.' According to King biographer R. MacGregor Dawson, the session with Mulock put King on track to become prime minister: 'The day proved... to be one of the most decisive in his [King's] life. The investigation then launched was to take him into the federal civil service and eventually open the door to a political career.'

Mulock commissioned King to investigate and write a fuller report (submitted in 1898) on working conditions associated with government clothing contracts. Based on King's recommendations, Mulock and the Liberal government passed a Fair Wages Resolution in Parliament to improve workers' payment.

In the fall of 1897, King left Toronto to pursue his studies at Harvard. But three years later, Mulock, as the new minister of labour, asked King to become the deputy in the just-created Department of Labour. In 1908, King traded his bureaucratic position for elected office. He joined Wilfrid Laurier's cabinet as minister of labour the next year, and succeeded Laurier as Liberal leader a decade later. In 1921, Mackenzie King was elected prime minister of Canada, a position he would hold for a total of twenty-one years, until stepping down in 1948. That late-nineteenth-century summer he had spent exploring the living conditions in the alleys and hovels of The Ward had taken King a very long way indeed.

'**THEY TOOK A** Carlton streetcar and transferred to Bay and got off at Queen. They walked over to Elizabeth, the street of Chinese merchants, chop-houses and dilapidated roughcast houses used for stores. Some cafés were of new tan brick, with electric signs. Chinese men sat on steps or stood in groups under street lights. No women were to be seen.'

This paragraph, from Morley Callaghan's first novel, *Strange Fugitive* (1928), shows two friends about to enter the dark right ventricle of Toronto's heart for a night of drinking and carousing. Callaghan's readers well knew what happened above Queen and Elizabeth streets in Toronto's Ward (a term never used in the novel). If his readers weren't Torontonians, then they probably knew of the Bowery or the Tenderloin or Little Hell or whatever they called the place in their city where immigrants, indigents and the lost congregated and tried to survive.

No division exists as starkly today in Toronto as the one that separated St. John's Ward to the west of Yonge Street from St. James Ward to the east. The east side of Yonge was Protestant, wealthy and respectable. It was home to the city's lordly bank buildings, some of the vaudeville theatres and the best of the new movie houses. In the middle of it, on Mutual Street, the Toronto Maple Leafs (having just changed their name from the St. Pats) packed the arena, home ice before relocating to the Gardens in 1931. The Ward, by contrast, was where the rich went for vice and the poor huddled together in one-room apartments in falling-down shacks.

MICHAEL REDHILL

WHERE THE RICH WENT FOR VICE

Left: Angelo's Hotel, formerly known at Glionna's, at 144 Chestnut Street, 1955. Hemingway was said to have frequented its bar in the early 1920s. The Faculty of Dentistry now occupies the site.

You can't walk over to Queen and Elizabeth now. That's because there is no Queen and Elizabeth, but if you stand in present-day Toronto on the north side of Queen Street directly underneath the overhead walkway that connects the Sheraton Centre to Nathan Phillips Square, you'll be exactly where Callaghan's antiheroes begin their excursion north, into The Ward.

'They turned another corner, and the neighbourhood was poor, now mainly ramshackle old houses, fifteen blocks west of the centre of the city. Along the street the city hall tower and the big clock stuck up over the roofs of houses and small stores ... ' Harry Trotter, the main character, and his friend Jimmie stop in at Angelina's, a speakeasy where Jimmie's a regular. They drink some whisky, they have some beer, they ogle the girls. Trotter is a hard-drinking cheat and a liar, with a rage kept on a low burn. He's introduced to us in the first sentence of the novel as someone who is 'determined everyone should understand he loved his wife.' But there is scant evidence of his love for his wife in this novel and even less for his fellow man.

From Angelina's, Harry and Jimmy drift up into the fetid centre of The Ward and come upon two men loading a truck with illegal liquor. They have the idea to rob them, thus inaugurating their new careers as bootleggers and sending our heroes along to their inevitable punishment.

Strange Fugitive is almost certainly the first novel of Toronto, and Morley Callaghan its first flâneur. He is not romanticizing or memorializing Toronto; he's living in it. The novel is alive with ghostly place names: Bowles Lunch, Shea's Hippodrome, the Arcadia Dance Hall, Childs Café. The ease with which the author walks through the city's streets and names its places shows him as a man of his time, a writer attuned to his personal now.

The Morley Callaghan of legend is more widely remembered as the winner of a hotly contested boxing match in which he knocked Ernest Hemingway to the mat (after F. Scott Fitzgerald allowed the round to continue beyond three minutes). But the real Callaghan had been a reporter for the *Toronto Star* in the 1920s, where he not only became friends with Hemingway, but found the raw material for his first novel. Some readers of *Strange Fugitive* contend that the story of Harry Trotter is based on a real crime that either or both of the men reported on for the *Star*, but there were a hundred Harry Trotters in every city in North America, going for the main chance and failing.

You can also stand in front of old City Hall and look south across at Bannock, the restaurant there now, and imagine in its place one of the chain of Bowles Lunches in the city. At the end of the novel, and at height of their notoriety, the two bootleggers stop at Bowles for toast and coffee. In a few short pages, they'll both be gunned down in the street. But before that, Callaghan offers us a final view:

> They walked the wet pavement over to the corner. Water was rushing along gutters and over curbs to the sidewalk, swinging past gurgling drains that couldn't take it in. People were coming out on the street after the rain, women walking timorously, doubtfully putting down umbrellas, coming from doorways and from under awnings, hurrying along the street.
>
> In Bowles, men in white jackets stood idly behind the glass counter. The rain had kept out customers and given the boy a chance to clean white armchairs. The tiled floor was clean but there was a line of muddy boot marks to the counter. 'Whole-wheat toast, well-browned, well-buttered,' Harry said. 'Toast the same,' Jimmy yelled.
>
> The baldheaded man with glasses had lots of time to sing, 'Holeee-wheat toast have it well-browned and we-l-l buttered twice.' The man in the kitchen yelled 'Holeee-wheat toast on the fire twice.' They waited, a hand shoved the toast along the slab from the kitchen. The man at the counter held up his forefinger. 'Coffee,' Harry said. 'Coffee,' Jimmie nodded.
>
> They sat down in the armchair. The coffee was very hot.

Morley Callaghan's highest accomplishment in *Strange Fugitive* is preserving a part of Toronto that is truly gone now, its filth and suffering and sins replaced by space-age architecture, a skating rink and a modern plaza. In 2014, there is barely a hint of it left, but you can walk across the square and peer through the gaps in the large concrete tiles to the dark below, where the spirit of The Ward is permanently interred, along with Harry Trotter's (and Toronto's) restless and untrue heart.

Childs at 293 Yonge Street, April 5, 1954.

KAROLYN SMARDZ FROST

A FRESH START

BLACK TORONTO IN THE 19TH CENTURY

ST. JOHN'S WARD has been sadly maligned. Labelled a 'slum' for its overcrowding, poverty and dilapidated housing, it began as a dynamic transitional neighbourhood where thousands of immigrants found their first homes. St. John's Ward was also, from 1830 through the 1880s, the heart and soul of African Canadian Toronto.

Like the rest of Toronto's residential districts, St. John's Ward was never segregated, nor were the city's churches, schools or institutions of higher learning. Unlike most of Upper Canada, the Town of York from the outset was an unusually integrated place.

The earliest Torontonians of African descent were enslaved men, women and children brought from the U.S. by their Loyalist owners. There were free people too. Most lived along Church Street and operated grocery stalls and barbershops at St. Lawrence Market. A few were Black Loyalists who fought for the Crown in the American Revolution. Others moved to York in search of employment and business opportunities.

Although the term 'Underground Railroad' was not used until the 1830s, freedom-seeking African Americans began travelling to Upper Canada after the War of 1812. By the 1820s, both fugitive slaves and free black people occupied modest cottages, mostly wood and some neatly stuccoed, lining Macaulaytown's narrow streets.

Free black families living south of Lot (Queen) who arrived from Richmond, Virginia, in the 1830s purchased properties, started businesses and constructed Toronto's first 'African Chapel' at 40 Hospital (Richmond) Street in 1832–33.

Refugees continued to arrive, seeking full participation in a civil society as naturalized British subjects. About 35,000 African Americans came to British North America before the Civil War – artisans, barbers, seamstresses, hostlers and other skilled workers gravitated to urban centres. Women, alone or with small children, found employment, while elderly newcomers relied on the African Canadian community's support networks.

Wilson Ruffin Abbott and his wife, Ellen Toyer Abbott, arrived via New York in 1835 after jealous white competitors destroyed their shop in Mobile, Alabama. Along with hundreds of African Canadians, Abbott enlisted to help quash the 1837 Rebellion. Loyal to Queen Victoria, they feared that the introduction of American-style 'republicanism' in Upper Canada might mean re-enslavement.

The year of the rebellion, Abbott opened a tobacco shop on Albert Street (which once ran from Chestnut to Yonge), and the Abbotts soon embarked on a real estate career that would make them very wealthy. One son attended Upper Canada College while another, Anderson Ruffin Abbott, would become the first African Canadian doctor. One of eight surgeons who served in the United States Colored Troops in the Civil War (three were graduates of Toronto medical schools), Abbott eventually returned to Toronto and opened a successful practice.

Toronto's African Canadian community grew as tensions mounted between the industrializing northern U.S. and the slaveholding South. Young people from across the province boarded with families on Centre, Agnes and Elm streets to attend the provincial Normal School. Black children like William Peyton Hubbard, who would be Toronto's first – and last – black deputy mayor (1904–1907), enrolled in the Model School, and black youths won scholarships at King's College. By 1850, the city's black population had reached 1,000, out of 47,000 people.

By then, St. John's Ward's population had surged with the arrival of African Americans and immigrants from Ireland, Scotland, England and Germany. Newcomers shared homes, shopped for groceries and worked side by side in local lumberyards, small factories and construction businesses. Together, they made in the area north and east of Osgoode Hall a vibrant neighbourhood redolent with possibility and ambition.

In those blocks, a Maryland woman fleeing slavery, a man from South Carolina seeking a new start in freedom or a free couple and their children arriving from New York or Cincinnati could find a room, rent a flat, purchase

their first small house or set up a modest business. While prejudice and racial discrimination were pernicious facts of African Canadian life, census and tax records show that white homeowners had black tenants, and African Canadians shared homes with European immigrants. Intermarriage was common: young men found wives among the local Irish, German and English girls. Black and white children attended the area's public schools, unlike the rest of the province, where segregated – and inferior – education prevailed.

People of African ancestry were welcome in Toronto's many churches, but separate denominations also thrived. Black churches served as community centres, hubs for benevolent societies and fraternal orders that offered newcomer, self-insurance and burial services, while Ellen Toyer Abbott's Queen Victoria Benevolent Society had branches across the province. Successful businesspeople provided newcomers with low-cost housing. The sixth-largest taxpayer of African descent in St. John's Ward was Thornton Blackburn. Formerly enslaved in Kentucky, he and his wife, Lucie, operated the city's first taxi business. They lived in a small house near the Don River mouth but built six small homes in St. John's Ward, which they rented to families of freedom-seekers at nominal prices.

The African Methodist Episcopal Church on Sayer (Chestnut) Street provided Sunday-school education to children and adults deprived of education and literacy in slavery. In 1856, this became the British Methodist Episcopal Church. This denomination was created after the draconian Fugitive Slave Law, passed by U.S. Congress in 1850, prevented Canadian-based clergymen, many of them former slaves, from attending American church meetings. As the neighbourhood expanded northward, the community built the Agnes Street Baptist Church near the corner of Terauley (Bay) and Dundas.

Those churches served as platforms for political activism. Noted American and British abolitionists, including Frederick Douglass, thundered forth from St. John's Ward pulpits to highly motivated local audiences. Robin Philips, who lived on Centre Street, operated an informal waystation for incoming freedom-seekers. Working with William Still, secretary of the Pennsylvania Anti-Slavery Society, Philips and his family provided temporary accommodation for black immigrants. Some worked for saw maker Thomas Smallwood, a former Underground Railroad operator from Washington who moved to 82 York Street in 1843. John M. Tinsley, in turn, migrated from Richmond and lived

on Agnes (Dundas). His construction company provided many formerly enslaved men with their first Toronto employment. Tinsley would die at the age of 109, lauded for his good works in a long obituary in the *Toronto Globe*.

Choir in the Agnes Street Methodist Church near Terauley Street, 1907.

Alongside sermons and settlement assistance, there were celebrations and picnics, musical events and bazaars, often to raise money to help incoming refugees and advance the work of anti-slavery. Politicians, clergymen and their families, and multi-ethnic neighbours, joined local Blacks in celebrating Emancipation Day on August 1. In the 1830s, Trinidadian-born 'Big Charlie,' a drummer with the 32nd Regiment of Foot, led the annual parade to a picnic at Government House, where Roy Thomson Hall now stands. Toronto's mayor, city councillors, ministers and prominent members of the city's black community addressed the crowds, who enjoyed performances by church choirs, talented soloists and the bands of various fraternal orders.

By mid-century, the ranks of African American expatriates grew sharply. No longer safe in the northern states because of the Fugitive Slave Law, free people sold everything and moved

to Canada. Along with increasing numbers of refugees from slavery, they sought new homes in Canada. The loss of the 1851 census for Toronto makes it impossible to precisely trace this wave of immigration, but it is estimated that about 10,000 people moved to Canada between 1850 and the end of the American Civil War.

Migrants included the family of Ann Maria Jackson, who fled Delaware after two of her sons were sold and her husband died. She arrived in Toronto with seven children, aged five to seventeen, and they settled at 93 Edward Street. Ann Maria took in washing and sent her younger children to school. The youngest son, Albert Calvin Jackson, become Toronto's first black postman. In 1882, white inside workers objected to his hiring in a post of higher rank than their own, but Sir John A. Macdonald himself intervened in Jackson's case: he needed the black vote from St. John's Ward to secure the election in Toronto.

Incoming families of wealth and education arrived with the Victorian penchant for self-help. Dr. Alexander T. Augusta's Provincial Association for the Education and Elevation of Colored People offered lectures on various subjects. A physician at the House of Industry on Elm Street, he operated an apothecary on Yonge Street while his wife, Toronto's most successful business-woman, managed an elegant York Street ladies' accessory shop. The St. John's Benevolent Association offered burial services, while the Provincial Union Association refused donations of used clothing from American and British charities on behalf of fugitive slaves. The practice of 'begging,' they believed, demeaned hard-working African Canadians who could care for their own.

Young black men from St John's Ward fought in the Union Army during the Civil War, and families returned south afterwards. But many remained, contributing to Toronto's development.

In the latter part of the nineteenth century, prosperous black families moved away from St. John's Ward in search of larger homes and less crowded conditions, some settling near Bathurst and College. By then, remaining black families shared the neighbourhood with Italian, Jewish and Chinese immi-grants. The area became 'The Ward,' a pejorative term that betrays a deep disassociation of white Torontonians from new immigrants with different cultural backgrounds, languages and beliefs. Yet for generations, the densely occupied neighbourhood served the hopes of ambitious newcomers who came in search of liberty, opportunity and the right to self-determination.

TORONTONIANS OF A certain age remember the legal fights waged in the 1980s by Edward's Books and Art and fur-coat retailer Paul Magder to have courts strike down the plethora of laws (federal, provincial and municipal) prohibiting Sunday shopping. But few know much about the previous, century-long culture war over 'Sunday observance,' a simmering conflict that reached from Toronto's immigrant neighbourhoods, including The Ward, all the way to the Law Lords in London.

MARIANA VALVERDE

POLICING THE LORD'S DAY

The annual reports of Toronto's chief constable reveal that stamping out non-Protestant cultural practices was a top priority for the police from the 1880s to 1914, a formative period when Toronto's population was exploding. While trade unions saw the Sunday issue as the establishment of a common day of rest, the police sought to ensure that all immigrants adopted the negative Protestant view of Sunday pastimes.

In the 1890s, Toronto police devoted most of their energy to 'houses of ill fame,' 'liquor cases' and 'cruelty to animals.' But they also laid many charges under the provincial Lord's Day Act, which prohibited not only retail sales on Sundays but also public transportation. Workers could only go to the beach or High Park on Sundays, and had to take a streetcar to get there. But the pent-up demand for Sunday streetcars only made Toronto's Protestant elite redouble their efforts to impose on immigrants what the nationwide Lord's Day Alliance, led by Toronto Presbyterian minister John G. Shearer, explicitly called 'the Protestant Sunday.' And the municipal police were only too happy to use their powers to enforce the elite's moral and cultural norms.

In his 1895 annual report, Toronto's chief constable reported that the Lord's Day Act 'is generally well observed, the only infringements being some small shopkeepers ... and a few foreigners working at their trade.' This refrain about an orderly city marred only by 'a few foreigners' was repeated almost every year for the next two decades. Vegetable vendors on Spadina Avenue (at that time more likely to be Jewish than Chinese) caused much concern. Police also targeted ice-cream parlours, a new invention. The chief doesn't explain why his officers scrutinized ice-cream sales, but the likely reason was that Italian immigrants were the pioneering purveyors of ice cream in Toronto. In fact, Italian men, in the popular Anglo imagination, were associated with pleasure, vice and even 'white slavery.' (Incidentally, the Catholic Church, which considered Sunday Mass compulsory, never promoted Puritan Sunday observance, just as it had remained cool to the closely related temperance movement).

In 1901, the chief constable again declared that only 'a few foreigners working at their trade and some ice cream sellers' were charged under the Lord's Day Act. But the 'few' foreigners kept multiplying: by the following year, breaches of the Lord's Day Act had climbed to 10 per cent of all police charges. While offence numbers climbed steadily until the First World War, the police nevertheless continued to reassure city leaders that moral order prevailed, noting, in 1910, that, 'considering the number of foreigners in the city, Sunday observance is well sustained.'

The compulsory Protestant Sunday met a serious challenge in 1902, when the Hamilton Street Railway Company led a legal battle against the Lord's Day Act. At that time, there were no human rights laws, so the argument against the Protestant Sunday had to be the legalistic one that the Province of Ontario had no jurisdiction to pass the act in the first place. The English Law Lords, sitting as the Judicial Committee of the Privy Council (which was until about 1950 the final court of appeal for Canadian constitutional issues), ruled that the law was indeed invalid because the province had no jurisdiction. Why not? Since the act was not really about the provincial domains of commerce and labour, the Law Lords concluded that its purpose related to the basis of criminal law, namely society's need to impose a moral standard. The criminalization of moral offences being exclusively federal, the provincial act was struck down by the Law Lords.

SUNDAY LAWS

In Force in the Province of Ontario

PROHIBIT

1. LABOR. With certain exceptions this includes:

(a) THE WORK OF LABORERS, MECHANICS and MANUFACTURERS.

(b) ALL FARM WORK, such as SEEDING, HARVESTING, FENCING, DITCHING.

(c) WORK ON RAILWAYS, such as BUILDING and CONSTRUCTION, and also REPAIR WORK, except in emergencies, and TRAFFIC, excepting the forwarding of PASSENGER AND CERTAIN FREIGHT TRAINS.

(d) ALL BUILDING, TEAMING, DRIVING FOR BUSINESS PURPOSES, THE WORK OF BAKERS AND BARBERS, Etc.

(e) THE WORK OF MUSICIANS AND PAID PERFORMERS OF ANY KIND. Works of necessity and mercy excepted.

2. BUSINESS. It is unlawful to MAKE CONTRACTS or to BUY, SELL or DELIVER ANYTHING on Sunday, including LIQUORS, CIGARS, NEWSPAPERS, Etc. Generally speaking the only exceptions are DELIVERING PASSENGERS' BAGGAGE, MILK for domestic use, and SUPPLYING MEALS AND MEDICINES.

3. ALL GAMES, RACES OR OTHER SPORTS FOR MONEY OR PRIZES, or which are noisy, or at which a fee is charged, and the business of AMUSEMENT or ENTERTAINMENT.

4. ALL EXCURSIONS for hire and with the object of pleasure, by TRAIN, STEAMER or OTHER CONVEYANCE.

5. ADVERTISING in Canada, unlawful things to take place on Sunday, either in Canada or across the line.

6. IMPORTING, SELLING or DISTRIBUTING FOREIGN NEWSPAPERS on Sunday.

7. ALL GAMBLING, TIPPLING, USING PROFANE LAN-GUAGE, and all other acts which disturb the public quiet.

8. ALL PUBLIC MEETINGS, except in Churches.

9. HUNTING, SHOOTING, FISHING; also BATHING in any public place or in sight of a place of public worship, or private residence.

THE PENALTY IS FROM $1.00 TO $500.00

THE GAME LAW

Of the Province makes Sunday a CLOSE SEASON for all GAME and HUNTING and SHOOTING UNLAWFUL on that day.

THE PENALTY IS FROM $5.00 TO $25.00

The Lords Day Alliance Of Canada

The British judicial decision alarmed Toronto's Protestant social reformers. The chief of police tried to mollify them, saying (incorrectly) that the Privy Council's striking down the act made it 'more difficult' for the police to enforce Sunday observance but that 'the Police will not relax their efforts.' To enable police to continue their cultural profiling, the federal government quickly passed a law that served the same

Ontario's Sunday Laws poster, 1911. Police relied on this legislation to crack down on peddlers, musicians, newsboys and recreational pursuits in The Ward.

purpose – though to keep Catholic Quebec happy, Ottawa also provided an option for provinces to opt out. Ontario and Toronto, however, continued to use their various legal powers to supplement the federal law.

During this period, the city's Protestant leaders also worked hard on the temperance file, with the prohibition movement peaking just before the First World War. At the same time, they also publicized the new and titillating issue of 'white slavery' (the precursor to today's sex trafficking) through unattributed melodramatic tales featuring white Canadian girls being lured by Italian or Jewish procurers into a life of vice. As Rev. T. Hunter Boyd, a Presbyterian minister, typically claimed, 'A young girl of British parentage in service in Montreal was inveigled by another girl... into a room occupied by two Italians... She was held in bondage vile for a period of several weeks.' Anecdotal tales of this type did not always highlight the ethnicity of the procurers and

Policeman and new recruit at the Armouries, ca. 1914.

traffickers, but when they did, Jews and Italians predominated. The Toronto police annual reports reveal that white slavers could not be found – at least not by Toronto police – but it was easy to find Sabbath-breakers.

By and large, the historical record has few traces of any organized resistance to the Protestant cultural hegemony embodied in Sunday observance laws. But a story published in May 1909 in the *Globe* reports that The Ward's Jewish merchants joined together to ask that the police use their discretion sensibly in regard to the deliveries of meat and bread that took place on Saturday evenings, during the brief time after the Jewish Sabbath ended and before the Protestant Sunday began. Under the headline 'Object to Sunday Law: Hebrew Tradesmen Think They Have a Grievance,' the *Globe* reported that the

merchants asked police to stop charging shopkeepers who had to work late into the night on Saturdays (which they did precisely to avoid openly flaunting the law with Sunday-morning deliveries): '[T]he butchers who sell kosher meat complain that the limited time does not allow them to deliver their meat to customers who live outside the Ward.'

The zealous policing of Sunday and even late-Saturday-night commerce crested in the run-up to the First World War. Between 1910 and 1914, when immigrants were flooding into the city, breaches of the Lord's Day Act surged, reaching a high of 921 (or 23.5 per cent of all offences) in 1913. But as senior police officials had done throughout the previous decade, the chief again reassured city leaders that all was well on his watch and that 'breaches of the Lord's Day Act are largely confined to trade on Sundays by foreigners who take a chance when they can.' It is, of course, ironic that Toronto police, who were predominantly Irish Protestants, worked overtime on Sundays, indeed often starting to work at midnight, as the story about the Jewish merchants suggests.

Sunday observance laws began to fall into disrepute after the Second World War, when policing priorities changed. But it took a very long time to reform the law. In 1964, law professor Bora Laskin, who later became the first Jewish justice on the Supreme Court, deplored the continuing legal validity of the Law Lords' view that the federal Lord's Day Act was a legitimate expression of 'federal power in relation to the criminal law, considered to embrace a Christian religious value.' Years before being named the first Jewish Supreme Court judge, Laskin lamented the fact that the then-new Canadian Bill of Rights did nothing to erode the use of criminal-law powers to impose culturally specific moral codes. Indeed, only with the 1982 Charter of Rights did Torontonians and other Canadians gain the necessary tools to ask courts to overturn laws imposing 'Toronto the Good' cultural practices on all. Even then, battles had to be fought one at the time, over many years and at great expense.

Today, Sunday shopping is regarded not as a sin but as an economy-boosting necessity. But the continued prevalence of racial profiling tells us that while the Lord's Day Act may be history, the overpolicing of groups considered to be culturally prone to vice and crime is still with us.

'11-YEAR-OLD GIRL SLAIN AND FOUR MEN INJURED BY A MANIAC CHINAMAN: Oriental Formerly Deported From Asylum Stabs and Slashes in a Mad Rage – WILD SCENE IN STREET – Mounted Constable Makes a Courageous Arrest – Victims Innocent Passers-by' – *Toronto Daily Star*, March 31, 1927

EDWARD KEENAN

'THE MANIAC CHINAMAN'

CAST OF CHARACTERS:

Fong Yong: A 'demented Chinaman' – the villain

Elsie Mokrzycka: An eleven-year-old girl – the innocent victim

Harry Wong, Quan Chee, Peter Lenoskey, Lem Yee: The surviving victims

Mounted Constable Charles Whitford: The hero

Mayflower: His mount

O N MARCH 30, 1927, with the sun still in the sky around 6 p.m., Elsie Mokrzycka was walking up Elizabeth Street carrying her brother's lunch in her hands. She was one of nine children of Polish immigrants Antone and Katarina Mokrzycka, who lived on Nelson Street, which runs between Adelaide and Richmond west of University Avenue.

Usually it was her older sister Frances who ran lunch up to the Olympia Bowling Alley at Yonge and Gerrard streets when her brother worked the late shift there. At the time, it was common for children to play a role – working or helping their working relatives – in supporting their families. On this day, eleven-year-old Elsie, with her blunt bob of dark hair, was allowed for the first time ever to be the errand girl, a fact that would haunt her big sister for the rest of her life. Elsie was less

than halfway through her journey from her home near John and Richmond streets when she encountered Fong Yong. Their meeting would make both of them briefly famous, and trigger an anti-Chinese panic in Toronto.

Fong Yong – or 'Tong Yong,' as a later police report referred to him – was a troubled man, and had been incarcerated at the Queen Street Mental Asylum. A year earlier, he had been ordered deported to China, but had managed to avoid authorities charged with kicking him out of the country. Later immigration and asylum authorities would blame each other for allowing him to slip through the cracks. Immigration agent J. C. Mitchell said it was a matter of 'the common habit of Chinamen changing their names so often' that allowed him to evade expulsion.

In any event, by 1927 he was living at the ominous address of 666 Lansdowne and, it soon became clear, remained mentally unstable.

About a half-hour before meeting young Elsie, Yong began drawing the notice of people on Elizabeth Street. At five minutes to six, he wandered into a butcher shop at 15 Elizabeth, lit a pipe and, according to the *Toronto Daily Star*, 'sulkily aired several grievances.' (The pipe may not have been for tobacco. Yong, like some other Chinese immigrants,

11-YEAR-OLD GIRL SLAIN AND FOUR MEN INJURED BY A MANIAC CHINAMAN

Oriental Formerly Deported From Asylum Stabs and Slashes in a Mad Rage

WILD SCENE IN STREET

Mounted Constable Makes a Courageous Arrest—Victims Innocent Passers-by

Wielding a sixteen inch butcher knife with deadly effect, a demented Chinaman ran amok on Elizabeth street last night, and when his insane orgy was over, little Elsie Mokrzcka of 57 Nelson street lay dead and four others were suffering from knife wounds. A stout band of returning workers witnessed the insane outburst, and fled terror-stricken from the path of the flashing blade.

Those wounded were Harry Wong, 830 Bay street, stabbed in the back; Quan Con, 54 Elizabeth street, stabbed on the left side; Peter Lenosev 214 [illegible] street and Lem Yea, 124 Dupont street.

In less than ten minutes after his wild rush up Elizabeth street, Fong Yong aged 40, of 666 Lansdowne avenue, was taken into custody at Hagerman street by Mounted Constable Charles Whitford after a sharp struggle.

Yong had arrived, had been in an insane way and was deported to China and in some way he managed to evade the immigration officials and got back to Canada recently. He now is to face a charge of murder.

Seizes Butcher's Knife

Like a Scene In Melodrama Of the Movies

A vivid description of the lurid scenes in Toronto's Chinatown last night was given to The Star to-day by F. Howard Annis, one of the passengers in the Toronto-Whitby bus, which was starting from that vicinity.

"As we turned into Elizabeth street," he said, "we found it in an uproar; men, women and children were running in all directions, shouting and screaming. Then they carried that little girl to within a short distance of the bus, and she lay there weltering in her blood a terrible, pitiful sight.

"Up the street we heard the galloping approach of the mounted constable. When the bullets began to fly there was almost a panic among the passengers, for fear of stray shots penetrating.

"The arrest was like a scene from a movie rather than real life. The policeman's struggle, first with his rearing steed, then, after a heavy fall, with the maddened Chinaman, was breathless.

"When the whole thing was over it was a highly-excited bunch of passengers who were transported to Whitby and Oshawa to spread a hectic tale of Toronto's underworld."

constable credit for considerable courage in arresting the man But Whitford himself insisted in giving his more. "Mayflower' as much credit as any other agency.

"She's a wonderful mare," he told The Star "When I jumped off her last night, she just followed me along and as I dealt with the Chinese who came up on the sidewalk and kept walking up and down in front of the [illegible]

Toronto Star, *March 31, 1927. Press accounts of Fong Yong's attacks were sensational and racist in tone.*

may have been suffering from an untreated opium addiction; indeed, the subject of opium had generated much fretful debate in nativist Toronto at the time.) It was there that he grabbed a long narrow butcher knife and made for the door. Before leaving, he slashed, unprovoked, three times at Lem Yee, who was trying to enter the store, tearing his coat and cutting him.

Yong then staggered out into the street and headed north in what the *Star* characterized as a 'dog trot,' muttering about killing everyone. About a block north, he came upon Elsie. As he passed her, he paused and slashed downward into her back, puncturing her lung. As she fell to the sidewalk, he kicked her in the face, before striding on, swinging the knife wildly. He would injure three other adults as he continued, while Elsie was rushed to the hospital by a passerby in his 'motor-car,' where she was declared dead.

One block east, at Bay and Queen, Constable Charles Whitford was astride his horse Mayflower, directing traffic through the off-kilter intersection, when a witness to the crime spree ran up to him, shouting about a 'bad Chinaman' over on Elizabeth trying to kill bystanders. He rode Mayflower at a gallop to the scene, where he encountered Yong holding on to a man, his knife in the air. Whitford pulled his revolver and fired – it went wide, but apparently the sound of the shot created enough fear and surprise that the intended victim was able to wrestle free. A passerby also fainted, causing Mayflower to rear up.

Whitford slid off his horse and ran toward Yong, yelling, 'If you move, I will kill you.'

Yong came toward him with the knife, according to Whitford's account, and the two fought hand-to-hand until the knife dropped to the ground. Whitford then subdued the attacker and placed him in handcuffs.

In relating the story to the press, Whitford was sure to give ample credit to his trusty mount, praising the way she strode back and forth performing crowd control while he 'dealt with the Chinese.'

The news coverage was sensational – the next day's package appeared above the fold on page one of the *Star*, and it featured a diagram of the street, multiple photos of all the characters in the story and even a photo of a knife similar to the one used in the crime. Reading it ninety years later, I am struck by how dated it is in its approach to race and mental health: the frequent references to the 'maniac' or 'demented' 'Chinaman,' as well as the apparently

verbatim Yong quotes, presented in such a way as to caricature his foreigner's English: 'I get 'em,' he's reported to have shouted. 'Me kill everybody.'

There was certainly little risk of negative reader reaction. While media accounts of The Ward's Italian and Jewish residents often emphasized their work ethic and upbeat outlook, the 1920s was a period when Mackenzie King's Liberal government had passed explicitly racist legislation meant to keep out the bulk of Chinese immigrants.

In his 1998 book *Discrimination and Denial,* Washington State University sociologist Clayton James Mosher noted how both the *Star,* and in a report a year later, the Toronto police department, attempted to portray Yong's violent spree as part of a Chinese menace to Toronto, despite the statistically low crime rate among Chinese residents.

While the *Star's* depiction of Yong's crime initially seems antiquated in its presentation, there is also something troublingly familiar and current about this narrative. For in this city of mass immigration, we still contend with regular periods of newcomer panic. The story of the innocent white child murdered by an illegal immigrant or deranged member of a menacing new group could have been written, and often was, at any point in our history. We wrote those stories about the Irish in the 1800s, the Italians in the 1960s, gays in the 1970s, the Vietnamese in the 1980s, Jamaicans in the 1990s and Muslims and Somalis since 9/11. To this day, when tabloids like the *Toronto Sun* publish full-page mug shots of Caribbean-Canadian men, the message is unmistakable.

The precise location of Elsie Mokrzycka's death is gone now – replaced by a city hall where we currently debate new threats mere steps south of the long-celebrated, but quietly eradicated, original Chinatown. Elsie's gravestone, in Prospect Cemetery, once bore the inscription 'Killed by a maniac Chinaman.' Those words have since been erased.

During a visit with her mother to the microfilm section of the Toronto Reference Library many years ago, Toronto writer-actress Patte Rosebank unearthed the details of a terrible episode in her family's past. In 1927, her grandmother Frances's younger sister, Elsie, had been brutally murdered while walking home through The Ward. Over the years, Rosebank gathered news stories, archival records and family accounts about a crime that shook Toronto. 'As I walk through that area, past Hagerman Street and on Elizabeth Street,' she muses, 'I just try to picture what kind of world my grandmother and her siblings grew up in.' Here is the story of Elsie's death, in Rosebank's telling.

PATTE ROSEBANK

ELSIE'S STORY

MY GREAT-GRANDPARENTS WERE very poor [immigrants from Poland], and there was never enough milk for their children. The kids would collect scraps from the garbage bins in the shmatte district and take them home. Great-grandmother sewed everything for those kids, including their underwear.

But there were delights – they lived at 57 Nelson and they would walk down to the Royal Alex. Around intermission, the very rich ladies would have these expensive chocolates. And the kids would look all cute and compliment them: 'Oh, isn't that lady's dress so beautiful? Isn't she lovely like a queen?' The ladies would be so delighted that they'd give their chocolates to these hungry children.

The way the murder happened was that Frances, my grandmother, would run this errand. She was taking a packed dinner to her brother, who worked at the bowling alley on Gerrard

Chinaman Runs Amok on Elizabeth Street—Kills Girl

FRONT LABORITES
GIVE BENEDICTION

Street. But on this particular day, Frances had a music lesson. So for the first time, Elsie was running the errand.

She was going up Elizabeth Street, and ran into a great commotion. Fong Yong, who was an immigrant from China with a long history of extreme mental problems, like hallucinations and paranoid delusions, had found out something terrible. At the time, news from China was printed on the paper that wrapped the tea packages. His brother had seen the news that Fong Yong's family had been captured by bandits in China. The brother realized, 'I've got to keep this from my mentally ill brother.' So they hid the news, and it wasn't until a couple of weeks after the fact that Fong Yong happened to see it. He just went berserk. He was in a butcher shop and grabbed a huge knife.

He just started slashing and screaming. He attacked one man in the doorway of the shop. The guy was wearing a heavy

The Star's front page, the day after the murder. The collage included all the principal characters, the weapon and a schematic of Yong's flight up Elizabeth Street. Elsie is bottom left, and Fong Yong is top row centre.

81

coat so he was fine. He attacked two more people. They were wounded, but survived. But when he got to little Elsie, he came upon her from behind and she was just wearing a thin little sweater. He plunged the knife into her back. It was so long it actually came through her front, and he kicked her twice as she fell. She was still alive, but by the time they got her to the hospital, she was dead.

It was Constable Charles Whitford, on his horse Mayflower, around Hagerman, who caught Fong Yong. The guy was running on so much adrenalin that he even drew the knife across a bystander's throat and tried to kill him. But he was finally apprehended.

When Fong Yong was asked, under questioning, 'Why did you do this?' he replied, 'Her people kill my people.' His reasoning was that white man makes the guns and those are the guns that are used to slaughter his people. His twisted mind equated this with a skinny little girl.

As for how Elsie's family found out: several hours later, as Elsie is lying in the morgue on Lombard Street, which is now a women's shelter, the police started canvassing the neighbourhood. Talking to the children, they said, 'Does anybody here know of any family that's missing a little girl? Anyone didn't come home?' And one kid says, 'Oh yes, little Elsie Mokrzycka didn't come home yet.' So they went to the house and talked to the parents. Then they took Great-grandfather to the morgue to identify the body.

Their troubles were not over. They worshipped at St. Stanislaus Church and wanted to have Elsie's funeral there. The priest at the time was a real bastard. He refused to conduct the funeral service because the children didn't go to Catholic school. Now, the problem was, of course, that you would have to pay for Catholic school. This family could not afford the milk for all the children. This family could not afford to buy underwear.

When word got around the religious community, the minister at [the Church of the Holy Trinity, now behind the Eaton's Centre] was horrified. He went to the family and said, 'This is appalling. I will conduct the service free of charge. It is the Christian thing to do.' In the newspaper accounts, it said the poor little family was so confused in their grief that they had her buried at this other church. That is not true.

I know from research on microfilm that the Chinese community gave something like $310 to the family, which was a huge sum. Subsequently, I

learned that Fong Yong was found to be completely incapable of standing trial and he was remanded to the hospital for the insane. After that, I don't know what happened – if he died there, or if his family sent him home to China.

I do know he had tried to kill himself in the Don River a few years earlier and the police had fished him out. I know he had been committed a couple of times. I know that he reported seeing the Chinese royal family riding on top of the Queen streetcar. Just think of the kind of life someone with mental illness would have had back then. There were no treatments. It was just horrific. So I do feel sorry for him.

Every week after the funeral, the family would ride the streetcar all the way out to Prospect Cemetery [at St. Clair West and Lansdowne]. They'd go to the gravesite and the parents would just wail and weep. It caused serious mental issues for the children in the family.

As for the impact on Frances – there were no more music lessons, because that's what killed Elsie. Her mother kept telling her, 'That should have been you.' You can just imagine the guilt.

The night of Elsie's murder, [Frances] woke up in the middle of the night and she saw her sister Elsie sitting on the big wooden trunk in the corner, swinging her legs and banging her heels against it, as she always did. She started to say, 'Elsie, stop it! Father will come in and kill you.' And she realized and screamed blue murder and Elsie vanished. I kind of like believing it was her sister come back to say goodbye.

I only recently visited the grave, a few months ago [in 2014]. My mother had always insisted it's a big stand-up tomb. Well, no, it's not. Great-grandparents' is a big stand-up stone. Elsie's is flat. I actually had to dig it out, because I think I was the first person to visit it in decades.

Looking at Elsie's gravestone, [I remembered] my mother had told me that originally the inscription had been very, very strongly worded. Many years after the fact, the son of one of Elsie's older brothers saw this inscription and said, 'This is unacceptable. We have to remove it.' I don't know if he did it himself with a hammer and chisel or got someone else to.

But when I visited the grave, I could faintly make out the ghost of the words that were removed. The original inscription was 'Killed by a maniac Chinaman.' Those four really awful words were removed, so now it just says, 'Killed.'

JIM BURANT

LAWREN HARRIS'S WARD PERIOD

O F ALL OF the members of the Group of Seven, Lawren Harris is probably the one most associated with the urban life of Toronto, because of the many paintings he did in The Ward and other parts of Toronto, first downtown and later in the suburbs. During the first twenty years of his career, before the Group of Seven's formation, urban subjects dominated his thinking about art and representation; he was fascinated with the streetscapes of the city, and the patterns of form and colour he saw there.

Harris came to art as an illustrator, studying at first in Toronto, and then in Berlin from 1904 to 1906. There, he was exposed to contemporary European art and trained as a draftsman, with an interest in architectural representation. After returning to Canada, he accompanied a Brantford friend, Norman Duncan, to Palestine, documenting the journey in pencil sketches that were later published in *Harper's Magazine*. By 1910, Harris had returned to Toronto, married and settled down to a career as an artist. He rented a studio over a store in Yorkville and joined the Arts and Letters Club on Elm Street.

There, he befriended J. E. H. MacDonald, another future member of the Group of Seven, and together they began to sketch the city's streets and houses. Initially, Harris made pencil sketches of hitherto neglected subjects: corner stores, backyards and workers' houses in The Ward. Later that year, he switched to paint, and exhibited several Ward paintings during the 1911 exhibition of the Ontario Society of Artists. Characteristic of his works in this early period is an interest in the patterns of urban life: often a painting might be of the

facades or backs of single homes or terraced houses, which are positioned parallel to the picture surface. Harris was interested in architectural details, and his paintings are notable for the absence of any human figures (e.g., *Winter Twilight*, 1911).

Harris said he wanted to capture the strong northern light, especially in his winter pictures, but his palette initially was subdued and conservative, dominated by greys and browns (e.g., *Houses, Gerrard Street, Toronto*).

The first known Ward painting, entitled *In the Ward*, was exhibited in 1912 at the OSA. Typically, works would be described as 'Old Houses,' 'Toronto Street' or 'Corner Store,' without specific addresses. Indeed, the locations can be identified only by comparing the subject matter with contemporary photographs commissioned by city officials. By 1913, in such works as *Hurdy-Gurdy*, Harris had developed a brighter palette and a more impressionistic style. He included more figures, indicative of a developing concern for the human condition within these urban scenes.

Portrait of Lawren Harris by M. O. Hammond, April 25, 1926.

The First World War interrupted Harris's exploration of his urban milieu, and it wasn't until mid-1918 that he returned to these themes. His interest in urban life can be seen in the subjects he presented to the public. Art historian Jeremy Adamson has noted that between March 1919 and August 1921, Harris exhibited sixty-two works in various shows, thirty-seven of which focused on urban themes. Visually vibrant, *Toronto Houses* (c. 1919) is less detailed and more textured than earlier Ward paintings. In another canvas, *In the Ward* (1920), Harris demonstrated his emerging social conscience.

As former National Gallery of Canada curator Charlie Hill notes, 'The anonymous foreground figure seen from the rear ...

and staring at the house, augments the haunting quality of this image of alienation. Lawren Harris was torn by his condemnation of the existence of urban poverty and his ability to see beauty in its midst.'

Harris's ambivalence continues to be present in most of his urban subjects through the 1920s, a period when he was increasingly expressing himself in terms of colour rather than line. His concern about his urban surroundings also found voice in a 1922 book of poems. As he moved farther afield, to locations such as Halifax and the North, Harris's social conscience altered his approach and his philosophy. Poet and editor Gregory Betts comments about Harris's poem 'A Note of Colour,' '[He] marvels at a painted red door that "smiles, and even laughs" in the face of the antipodal "bleary with grime, and bulging, filthy" surroundings.'

As he was drawn further toward abstraction and the Canadian landscape, Harris abandoned the subject of urban life in 1926. He may also have been discouraged that many of his city paintings didn't sell. When the Art Gallery of Toronto mounted a 1948 retrospective, Harris still owned several of the

Ward paintings in the show. In 1960, he donated several of these, including *Return from Church* (1919), *Toronto Street, Winter Morning* (1920) and *Italian Store in the Ward* (1922), to the National Gallery. In the auction market, Harris's Ward paintings now fetched some of the highest prices ever paid for Canadian works. Their charm has worked its magic on current collectors.

Left: Hurdy Gurdy, *1913.*

Above: Italian Store in the Ward, *1922.*

That visual charm, however, belies a deeper meaning. As A. Y. Jackson would later observe, the sweep of Harris's urban work ultimately revealed the emergence of a social conscience: 'The "old house" period in the beginning was gay and picturesque, giving way to gentle satire as he turned to the banalities of the suburban homes around Toronto. Then finally with *Black Court, Halifax* and *Minas Houses, Sydney*, there is a sharp protest that there should be such dismal poverty in a land as bountiful as ours.'

51 NOV. 25 1913

'**E**NOUGH FILTH IN** One Block to Turn a Whole City Sick,' shouted the headline in the July 11, 1911, edition of the *Toronto Daily Star*. With equally breathless prose, the unnamed reporter brought his readers deep into The Ward, a warren of streets so nauseating, he noted early in the article, that he almost had to turn back. The writer observed overcrowded hotels, shops selling bread caked in filth and naked babies crawling in sewage. All of it just blocks from City Hall.

The article introduced the findings of a scathing report on slum conditions released a few days earlier by Dr. Charles Hastings, Toronto's new medical officer of health (MOH). The fifty-three-year-old obstetrician had a thatch of snow-white hair and a bushy moustache, giving him the appearance of a school principal. 'The people of Toronto are living in a fool's paradise,' Hastings told the *Star*. 'They thought they were free from the slum problem, which besets many American cities. The facts, as shown in the "Slum" report, prove that Toronto is not a whit better than other cities of the same class.' In a chapter entitled 'The Slum as a Hotbed for the Germs of Disease,' the report argued that the proliferation of overflowing outdoor 'privies' and filthy, unventilated apartments could be implicated in high levels of infectious diseases, including typhoid, cholera and tuberculosis.

It was strong stuff for a civil servant in Tory Toronto. But Hastings' sharp warnings found a receptive audience among the city's social reformers. In the late nineteenth century, public health had become a hot topic, with British, American and

JOHN LORINC
'FOOL'S PARADISE'
HASTINGS' ANTI-SLUM CRUSADE

Previous: Rear of 96 Elizabeth, February 23, 1912. The Chestnut Hotel/residence now stands on this location.

Left: Image of a privy in The Ward, November 25, 1913. Goss took dozens of photos like this of disgusting toilets in the city's poorest areas.

European public health experts racing to contain epidemics using a combination of vaccines, sanitation and enforceable quarantines. Hastings himself was a pasteurization and breast-feeding activist, having lost a child to contaminated milk.

In the 'Slum Conditions' report, his first move as MOH, Hastings took middle-class Torontonians to task for their wilful blindness. 'The truth is that one half not only does not know,' he said. 'They do not want their peace of mind disturbed by the unpleasant details of the life and sorrows of the lower classes.'

The thirty-two-page, data-filled report focused on four neighbourhoods, including The Ward, with its 11,645 residents crowded into just .57 square kilometres of land (that density level, over 20,000 per square kilometre, is comparable to that of Paris, and four times as much as the present-day City of Toronto). His inspectors entered almost 4,700 homes, spoke to hundreds of tenants and took thousands of photographs.

Many of the poorest immigrants living in those areas, the report found, lived in overcrowded flophouses. The inspectors identified over a hundred dwellings deemed unfit for human habitation. Lane houses and small apartments, or tenements, were crumbling, and a good number had no plumbing or indoor drains. City photographers took hundreds of pictures of filthy toilets and privies.

While the report acknowledged that the conditions didn't match the congestion of New York's Lower East Side, Hastings wrote that the existence of such slums didn't reflect well on the city: 'The people of Toronto, or foreigners coming to Toronto, should not be permitted to be forced into such habitations.'

Unlike many social reformers, Hastings insisted the poor residents of these slums were not necessarily criminals, lunatics or perverts. Still, his writings reflect lingering Victorian obsessions about bad air, and the links between poverty and vice. In one of his monthly MOH reports, Hastings cited a British expert on the subject of 'lodger evil.' (Victorians squirmed about crowded housing because they suspected that close quarters led to sexual depravity and incest.) 'Toronto is a city of homes, and it is in the best interests of the city physically, morally and socially, that it should remain a city of homes,' he wrote.

The publication of the 'Slum Conditions' report in 1911 triggered sweeping changes. Thousands of leaking outhouses were demolished as the city installed new sewer lines and chlorinated Toronto's water supply, and council passed regulations requiring all habitable rooms to have windows. Hastings also recommended that the city ban the practice of allowing housing to be built

behind existing dwellings, to prevent the spread of slum-style density (the report showed pictures of rear houses separated by narrow, muddy alleys). Indeed, he urged council to promote the development of 'garden city' suburbs, connected to the downtown by 'rapid transportation,' to provide new and less congested housing for the working classes.

Hastings' ambitions went beyond The Ward, and his achievements included reforms to the city's corrupt milk industry, the establishment of a municipal abattoir and the deployment of a public health nurse network. He also set up a 'vital statistics' division, which tracked infectious diseases and mortality. Between 1910 and 1915, typhoid mortality plunged from forty-four deaths per 100,000 to two.

Two children in front of rear cottage on Centre Avenue, February 28, 1912. Goss took numerous photos of Ward residents for Hastings' Health Department.

It was a good-news story the press loved: 'Saving Lives on Wholesale Plan/How Toronto Has Been Made the Healthiest of Large Cities,' blared the headline in a lengthy July 1915 feature in *Maclean's*. '[W]ith sufficient organization and proper administration,' Hastings remarked, 'a city can have, within reasonable limits, as much health as it is willing to pay for.'

Hastings retired in 1929, the year when the Rockefeller Foundation selected the University of Toronto, along with Harvard and Johns Hopkins, in Baltimore, as a home for a new public health college. By then, much of the crumbling housing stock in The Ward had been upgraded to conditions we'd recognize today in Kensington Market. His record of reform, however, didn't quiet the calls for slum clearance. Those changes would come later.

DURING THE PROHIBITION era, bootlegging operations, also known as 'blind pigs' and 'doghouses,' served as a hidden and yet pervasive business within St. John's Ward. The Ontario Temperance Act of 1916 led to the closing of all bars and liquor stores in the province. But rather than snuffing out saloons and drinking, the legislation actually produced a boom in home stills and bootlegging operations, as well as glamourized alcohol, speakeasies and gangsters, as depicted in novels such as F. Scott Fitzgerald's *The Great Gatsby* and Morley Callaghan's 1928 crime drama, *Strange Fugitive*.

While it is impossible to determine the number of bootlegging businesses in The Ward, since the proprietors would not have reported their illegal operations to the authorities, we do know they were commonly run by female immigrants – both Italian and Jewish – and there were dozens of them. In his history of drinking, *Booze: A Distilled History*, York University professor Craig Heron indicates that there was a disproportionate number of foreigners, particularly Jews from Poland and Western Russia, involved in bootlegging. Both the Old and New Testaments cast alcohol in a positive light, and beer, wine and spirits were commonly consumed by these immigrants in their countries of origin. There was also a strong distaste among immigrants for the Methodist puritanism of the era, along with a healthy respect for the profits that bootlegging could provide. As a result, immigrants adopted an anti-prohibition stance, rejecting the government's attempts to monitor and control their consumption and sale of alcohol.

ELLEN SCHEINBERG

STRANGE BREW
THE UNDERGROUND ECONOMY OF 'BLIND PIGS'

Left: Man carrying a beer keg in The Ward, 1916. The Eaton's factory is in the background.

The Ward's bootleggers typically ran their operations out of their homes. These ventures were often operated by older women, who relied on bootlegging as a survival strategy – like taking in laundry and borders – to supplement the family income. In his autobiography *Call Me Sammy*, Jewish-Canadian welterweight boxing champion Sammy Luftspring details his family's bootlegging business on Elizabeth Street. Luftspring recalls that their customers would enter via the alley and use the back door that led to their kitchen, where his grandmother and mother would ply them with twenty-five-cent shots of rye until they ran out of money. While the women were running the business, his father would entertain the customers to keep them company and encourage consumption. Sammy's role, starting at age six, was to serve as a lookout for police.

While some of the local bootleggers paid off the police, others, like the Luftsprings, experienced periodic raids that resulted in the confiscation of their liquor as well as forced court appearances. The Toronto Register of Criminals documents many such cases involving Italian and Jewish immigrants who were given the option by the magistrate of either paying a fine of $200 to $300, or serving jail time for their crime. In 1919, Toronto police charged 1,053 offenders with violating the Temperance Act. The vast majority chose to pay the fine, viewing it as part of the cost of doing business. Because of the staggering number of prosecutions, the state reaped a windfall revenue, garnering an astonishing $229,336 in 1919 alone from these fines, equivalent to around $3 million today.

Bootlegging also proved to be an extremely lucrative business for some of these small-scale entrepreneurs. Luftspring notes that selling illegal liquor allowed his father to purchase fourteen houses, with money leftover to buy his wife furs and diamonds. Two of the most notorious Ward bootleggers, Bessie Starkman and Rocco Perri, earned over $1 million in sales during the height of their operation, after they relocated to Hamilton.

Yet the business also brought danger, beyond the risk of fines and incarceration. In 1920, for example, Steven Poppolink, a Romanian immigrant with a wife and two young children living in The Ward, was shot during an argument over the price of liquor at a blind pig at 141½ Centre Avenue, at Edward. And a decade later, one of Al Capone's henchmen assassinated Starkman. Indeed, those who snitched to the police about their bootlegging neighbours were often the victims of retribution.

Municipal officials were responsible for keeping the peace, as well as monitoring and punishing those who violated the Temperance Act. But it was a difficult task due to the scope of the problem, the number of police officers accepting bribes, as well as the secrecy associated with this trade. In 1923, Chief Constable Samuel J. Dickson blamed local foreigners for the proliferation of illegal alcohol. In his annual report for the police force, he declared that the Temperance Act should be 'energetically enforced' and that the Immigration Act be amended to allow for the deportation of aliens who violated the ban.

The police also reached out to the Jewish community, through a local rabbi, to ask for assistance identifying local Jews who were bootlegging. In two editorials published in *Canadian Jewish Review* in 1923 and 1924, Rabbi Barnett Brickner, from Holy Blossom Synagogue, took issue with what he felt was anti-Semitic scapegoating of Toronto's Jews in regards to this crime. He questioned why no other groups were being singled out in the press, noting that the police court column of the *Toronto Evening Telegram* cited only Jews in stories about bootlegging. In the end, the rabbi refused to help enforce the law, advising a seemingly xenophobic police force to do its job. Toronto's Jews, he declared, didn't want to be 'detectives and stool pigeons!'

In 1927, the Conservative government of Ontario premier George Ferguson repealed the Temperance Act, bringing an end to prohibition and establishing the Liquor Control Board of Ontario in its place. The end of prohibition spelled the demise of many of these illegal operations. However, some purveyors continued, like Sammy Luftspring's mother, Bella, who carried on bootlegging until her death in 1940. The family's connection to alcohol ended up trickling down to the next generations: Sammy became the owner of the Mercury Club and the Tropicana, and his son Brian spent part of his career engaged in sports promotion for Molson Ontario Brewery.

A SMALL GIRL IN a clean white dress, her hair in stiff bows, stands on the steps of the Italian consulate at Agnes and Terauley. A woman – likely her mother – looks on.

She puts me in mind of men, this girl. The men of Toronto's first Little Italy clustered in rooming houses on streets to the north and west of the spot where she stands, in the heart of The Ward. I also think of three specific men – my two grandfathers and my maternal great-grandfather. Around the time this photo was taken, in 1910, my great-grandfather was pushing a fruit cart in the streets west of The Ward. I know very little about him, but I've heard he was 'rough.' What manner of personal flaws that term implies, I'm left to guess. The immigrant's journey from southern Italy to Toronto in the late 1800s may well have required some grittiness of character.

ANDREA ADDARIO

THE ITALIAN CONSULATE

The photographer was the consular official at the time. Was he also the girl's father? Judging by the fineness of her clothes, that connection seems plausible. If you look over her shoulder, you'll notice that the consulate shared space in a travel agent's office, representing several steamship lines. Labour agents – or *padroni* – worked with shipping companies and officials to supply labourers to Canadian agriculture and industry, often arranging the joint migration of large groups of men from the same village. It simply made sense to co-locate the consulate, the only such diplomatic outpost in The Ward.

Historian John Zucchi has said that while few members of Italy's political elite would have recognized the names of the Canadian cities and towns to which so many Italians emigrated

Girl in front of Italian consulate at 53 Agnes Street, 1910. The site is now occupied by the Ryerson University business faculty.

in the late 1800s and early 1900s, Toronto was a household word in many small villages and farm fields, thanks to systems of chain migration. *Toronto*: I imagine it as a shouted curse, an excited whisper.

Boarding houses on Centre and Elizabeth streets overflowed in winter with Italian navvies returning from work building the Canadian Pacific Railway. Maybe they took some seasonal labour with the Toronto Street Railway, or in some other segment of Toronto's burgeoning construction industry. Maybe they idled, or gathered at the Glionna Hotel, drinking and cajoling the literate among their ranks to write letters home, seeking news.

It was common at that time for single Italian men to emigrate repeatedly – to come and go, between Toronto and Italy, between Toronto and New York. My paternal grandfather came to Canada in this fashion in the 1910s, an unmarried sojourner or 'bird of passage' seeking work. According to a ship manifest I once found, customs officials noted he was dark-skinned, a labourer who could read and write Italian. He was not, apparently, an anarchist. He returned home, and came once more with my grandmother after they married. They went home to Italy again together, and returned to Canada for good in 1929, now with three young children in tow.

I imagine the conversations they had, deciding whether he would go alone, whether she would join him. Did they fight about such choices? I wonder if their return to Italy, sometime between 1920 and 1929, represented a defeat or a joyous homecoming. What calculus resulted in their final emigration? My grandfather could not have known he'd be dead a decade later, at forty-four, having worked a series of dangerous, dirty jobs in his new country.

A friend of mine, whose family also emigrated from southern Italy, described life in those towns back home as sufficiently hardscrabble that engaging in commerce amounted to walking miles to the next village to trade your potatoes and figs for someone else's potatoes and figs. The intractable old-country poverty must have made the crowded, filthy conditions of The Ward look like hope and possibility – a sensible pooling of risk in order to have a shot at a richer, easier life.

My great-grandfather pushed his fruit cart north and south, east and west. He saved enough to transition from itinerant vendor to shopkeeper, setting up a small store for his son (my maternal grandfather) and his bride as a wedding present. It was given alongside a pronouncement that he and his wife would be coming to live with the newlyweds.

In a 1910 newspaper account of Italian life in The Ward, Emily Weaver wrote, 'The multitude of little fruit stores in Toronto suggests that many an Italian has here attained the summit of his hopes.' Contrary to her patronizing assumption, the inherited, upgraded business was not my maternal grandfather's passion. He didn't want to be the proprietor of a fruit shop located on the edge of a burgeoning new Little Italy, serving the many who had successfully pushed up and out of The Ward into stable neighbourhood life. He had no option. I believe he was happy enough to be here, to have three daughters and a wife born here. But that push-pull, so central to the immigration and settlement experience, is undeniable.

How many families in The Ward lived out variations on that theme, with stakes considerably more fraught than whether or not to open a fruit shop? The act of sending sons and daughters so far away – to break traditions, to locate heart and heft, to do things they did and didn't want to do – it all represented an enormous investment in hope and opportunity for many poor Italians.

Whoever she was, that little girl on the consulate steps would not have been here, in Toronto, without their gamble. And nor would I.

Annunziato Addario and Concetta Albanese Addario, ca. 1920s. Annunziato initially immigrated on his own in the 1910s as a labourer, returned to Italy twice and ultimately settled in Canada with Concetta

EMILY P. WEAVER

THE ITALIANS IN TORONTO
AN EXCERPT

In the early 1900s, Toronto newspapers published numerous stories about slum conditions, overcrowding and immigration, many of which focused on The Ward. Some articles revealed the aggressively nativist sentiment of the age, while others adopted a more benign, albeit patronizing, perspective about 'our new Canadians.' This excerpt comes from a full-page feature with several photos from The Ward, including one showing a pair of children next to a vending cart, with the caption: 'The boy is an Italian, and the girl a Jewess from Roumania.'

WE HAVE MANY Italians in Toronto – something like 7,000, I understand, against two thousand set down in the last census ... As a rule they sail from Naples to New York and come on by rail to Toronto.

Here they have settled, chiefly in the district east of Bathurst Street and south of College, and about Elm and Elizabeth streets, in that picturesquely foreign quarter known as 'The Ward.' Its old houses and tumble-down cottages shelter a population utterly out of proportion to their numbers and accommodations, and every street and lane ... seems to bubble over with eager life. Black-bearded men with sacks of rags on their shoulders and olive-skinned hawkers of ice cream pervade the streets, women with earrings and round brown arms stand in the doorways, and rollicking children, with sun-kissed cheeks, and eyes shaded by long dark lashes, take their pleasure in the dust of the sidewalk or the gutter. A little later in the year, when sleep in crowded rooms seems all but

impossible, the people of 'The Ward' are astir till all hours, and the Italians amuse themselves by singing in their rich, sweet voices the songs of their far-away homeland or dancing their native dances to the music of the mandolin or guitar in the open roadway beneath the stars.

A cheerful folk they are, say those who have lived amongst them; but for the bravest it is no light matter to break with the old life to begin a new one amongst people of other speech and customs, and one has only to wander into the quarters of our city inhabited by our new Canadians late of sunny Italy to gain some hints of their toils and struggles ...

The multitude of little fruit stores in Toronto suggests that many an Italian has here attained the summit of his hopes. Only to look into the cheery faces of some of the vendors of popcorn and peanuts who perambulate our streets with their whistling cooking machines confirms this pleasant sensation ... The peanut sellers come out early in the springtime, like the robins, but, unlike the birds, they keep late hours, and often it must be after midnight when they put out the flaring torches which advertise their stock-in-trade.

Another favourite business of the Italian is that of the street musician. Sometimes a whole family – husband, wife and baby – go round with the organ. Sometimes it is two girls (with short gay skirts and fringed handkerchiefs on their crisp black hair) who appeal to the purses of the passersby with their jingling waltzes and their foreign grace. But their countrymen who know say this is no place for the girls, and with a pride of race that speaks well for the future would have them rather earn their bread, as many Italian maidens do, in the factories and laundries of our city.

At home the Italian women of Toronto work as hard as in their native land, where they used to toil in the fields. They look after the little fruit shops, cook and wash for their large family of little ones, and often for ten or a dozen or even twenty boarders in addition. These are generally single men of their own race of men who have not yet acquired the wherewithal to send for the wives and babies left in Italy. The women, shut within their little homes, are slow to learn either the language or the customs of their adopted country, and do not readily take advantage of organizations intended for their benefit. Their husbands, mixing with workpeople of other nationalities, are less inaccessible to such influences than the women, but of course it is the children with whom the process of assimilation is most rapid and effective.

The Globe, July 16, 1910

BOARD OF EDUCATION TORONTO AUG. 1

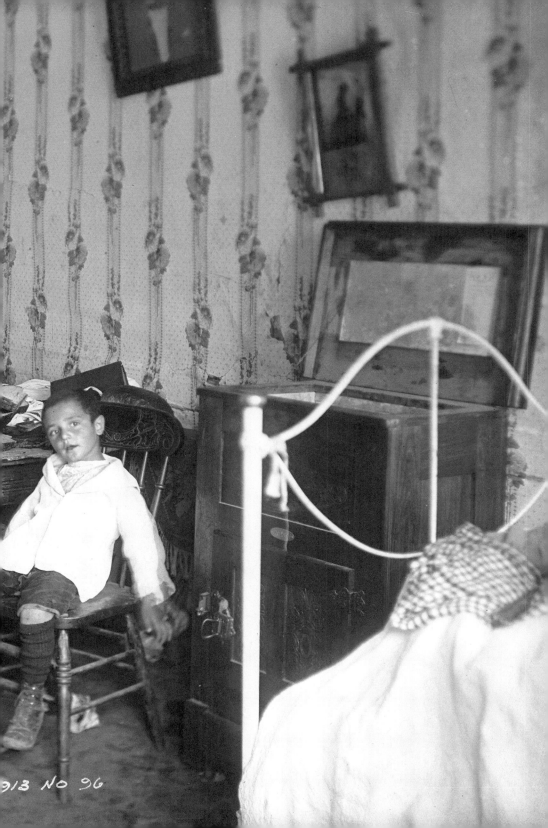

913 NO 96

STEPHEN BULGER

ARTHUR GOSS
DOCUMENTING
HARDSHIP

W**HEN ONE CONJURES** up an image of St. John's Ward, it likely includes dilapidated wooden cottages occupied by poorly dressed, solemn yet stoic immigrants. The individual who helped shape this vision was Arthur Scott Goss. Born in London, Ontario, in 1881, Goss was raised in Cabbagetown, Toronto. The son of a journalist, he was forced to begin his working life at age eleven to support his family after his father's sudden death. At fifteen, he won his first photography contest and further honed his skills throughout the course of his career, developing a reputation as a photographer with great artistic capabilities.

In 1911, Goss was appointed Toronto's first chief photographer, operating under the Photography and Blue Printing Section within the newly formed City Works Department. In addition to tackling civic works projects, this section was also paid by the Department of Public Health and the Board of Education to support and document their initiatives. So Goss was responsible for photographing and documenting all facets of city life.

It is unusual for the output of a city photographer to become popularly known. Working in a salaried position as a civil servant inspires little in the way of creativity and rarely leads to prominence or fame. And the fact that the photographs are owned by the city that commissioned them means *Previous: The* this type of work is seldom seen by the public. Working at a *Don family posing* time of rapid growth and large public works projects, Goss *inside their home,* was afforded the opportunity to document major municipal *August 14, 1913* initiatives such as the Prince Edward Viaduct (Bloor Viaduct),

what would be the R. C. Harris Water Treatment Plant and the laying of the TTC tracks across the city. Exclusive access to these construction projects and the opportunity to document the city's transformation during this period was surely a photographer's dream. Over the course of his career as chief photographer, Goss produced a staggering 35,000 negatives.

In addition to being a prolific photographer, Goss possessed a much more sophisticated and artistic eye than most who carried out this type of photography. His mastery of the complexity of photographing indoors gives us a rare glimpse into the lives and faces of Toronto's working-class immigrants. These residents were typically ostracized by polite society, and despite their numbers, remained segregated and invisible. Goss's compassion for those in need, likely developed at a young age due to his family's difficult financial circumstances, meant that he treated all subjects with the utmost respect. We can assume that Goss was given direction about what to photograph, but it is doubtful he was told *how* to depict his subjects.

Looking at the photograph on pages 104–105, commissioned by the Board of Education, one can assume that Goss was asked to produce an image to illustrate the plight of children or families living in The Ward. Using flash indoors would have created harsh shadows, resulting in a forensic-type photograph. So Goss softened the effect of the flash, and ultimately produced a more flattering portrait that skilfully illuminated the subjects and the details of their surroundings. He also positioned his camera a respectful distance away from the family, to ensure that the camera did not intrude on their personal space.

Although many Torontonians would turn their nose up at such living conditions, this moment frozen in time depicts a family like many others of the day. The mother, Dena Don, is smiling and projects pride, while the children peer curiously into the camera, all seemingly content while posing for Goss. The members of the family are well-groomed and content in their home. The only hints of hardship are the younger boys' tattered short pants, some artwork that hangs askew, a table that seems to be used for both dining and work, as well as cramped living conditions. One might not guess that Dena Don had been abandoned by her husband several years earlier, caring for her four young children alone by taking in laundry.

*Rear of Eaton's
department store on
James Street, south
of Louisa Street,
February 19, 1913.*

Looking at Goss's depictions of the dispossessed, we can see he was a committed social documentary photographer. Whereas a photojournalist strives to capture an objective viewpoint, a social documentarian uses photography to record, interpret and represent social realities in an effort to elicit a certain response from an audience and effect change. In many respects, Goss's photographs of the impoverished residents of The Ward, as well as those taken by William James, shape our vision of how Toronto's lower classes lived in the early part of the twentieth century.

Portrait of Arthur Goss, 1922.

Over the course of his career, Goss had many opportunities to photograph The Ward, which was a multifaceted neighbourhood. Within his body of work, we can find a variety of subjects, scenes and personalities relating to this locale. In addition to capturing the residents within and outside of their homes, Goss also photographed the activities of two of the largest employers and retailers in the area – Eaton's and Simpson's – both located on the south end of The Ward. One interesting project he tackled that was commissioned by the city involved documenting the impact that mail-order businesses had on local traffic. Catalogue shopping offered the utmost convenience at this time, and trucks from both companies remained a common sight within the city until the 1970s. Taking a photograph from approximately the same location each hour, on February 19, 1913,

Goss produced an innovative and fascinating account of this popular service. The image on the previous pages captures the delivery wagons outside of the T. Eaton Company at 8:15 a.m. at the corner of James Street south of Louisa Street.

Each of Goss's photographs has a unique composition that responded to the specific subject, the surroundings, as well as the available light. Whereas many city photographers around the world produced formulaic pictures, Goss upheld a commitment to fine composition as well as documenting his subjects in a realistic yet compassionate manner. He maintained a tremendous work ethic throughout his career and was consequently extremely prolific.

Arthur Goss will be forever memorialized as a character in Michael Ondaatje's 1987 work *In the Skin of a Lion*. Set in 1930s Toronto, the novel fictionalizes Goss's work and recognizes his contribution to the city, honouring the impact his photographs had in inspiring some of the writing in this landmark publication. Goss's legacy and status as a city photographer far surpassed that of most other municipal officers and helped shape our image of early twentieth-century Toronto.

DEPT. OF HEALTH No 150 SEPT 6 1912

CATHY CROWE

FRESH AIR
THE FIGHT
AGAINST TB

BECAUSE THEY CAN vividly expose injustices such as homelessness, poverty or child labour, photographs are powerful tools for advocacy. In the late nineteenth century, photojournalist Jacob Riis documented slum conditions in New York's Lower East Side and helped trigger reforms, such as new schools, sewers and indoor plumbing. During the Great Depression, photographers like Walker Evans and Dorothea Lange – best known for her picture 'Migrant Mother' – documented the impoverished conditions of farmworkers, images that resulted in relief efforts.

In the 1910s, the press responded to Arthur Goss's images with alarmist and sensationalist reporting, using terms like 'vagrant' and 'feeble-minded' to describe The Ward's immigrants, implying that these people bore the blame for their own misfortune.

Despite that response, Goss's searing images played a substantial role in public health history, propelling the poverty conditions in The Ward into the public eye. The exposure created a political case for progressive policies, including better housing, sewage treatment, school health programs and the pasteurization of milk.

As a street nurse, I was always drawn to Goss's photos because they mirrored what I had witnessed in the flophouses, shelters and streets of contemporary Toronto. I was particularly struck by Goss's tuberculosis series. Historically referred to as 'consumption' or 'the white plague,' TB is an infection that most commonly affects the lungs. Although it occurs worldwide, it is more common in regions associated with poverty, crowding, malnutrition and poor medical care.

Previous: Patient in bed in Ward alley, September 6, 1912. The cot and umbrella were supplied to a patient who refused sanatorium care.

114 |

Early in my career, my knowledge of this ancient disease came mainly from popular culture. The development of antibiotics made TB treatable, although we now face the issue of drug resistance. But in the early twentieth century, a TB diagnosis carried a high risk of death. As Canadian activist Dr. Norman Bethune, who experienced tuberculosis himself, once said, 'There is a rich man's tuberculosis and a poor man's tuberculosis. The rich man recovers. The poor man dies.'

It was the poor man's tuberculosis that Goss chronicled so well. In both interior and exterior photos, he revealed how slum conditions – overcrowded housing and malnutrition – left an entire community vulnerable. He also showed how emaciated patients received little formal care. Sanatoriums in Toronto and Muskoka, where patients would be prescribed fresh air, rest and good food, lacked sufficient beds. As Goss's images strongly suggest, immigrants weren't admitted. The notation on this photo – 'refused sanatorium care' – likely meant the person was not given access to free care, or could not afford to leave children behind while seeking treatment.

Instead, the city's health department provided makeshift shacks and tents intended to provide fresh air, isolation and shade – in this case, under the 'Made in Canada' umbrella.

A photograph can answer some questions while posing others. This Goss image has a child in it. Is the patient a parent or older sibling? Did public health nurses come to this bedside? Did the family receive relief from the city or charitable organizations? And what was Goss saying by foregrounding that 'Made in Canada' umbrella? Is this compositional choice a sly social commentary about the way Canada was treating immigrants?

Almost eighty years after Goss took these images, TB returned to Toronto, in the form of a micro-epidemic among the homeless population clustered in a so-called 'hot zone' mere blocks from City Hall. The outbreak, which afflicted both homeless people and shelter workers, was the direct result of the dismantling of social programs in the late 1990s. Seen today, the TB shacks in The Ward evoke the tent-city encampment built by homeless people in 1999 to avoid the poor health conditions, including TB, in the city's shelter system. I can imagine that had he lived today, Goss would have been trying to capture the grim scenes of suffering that street nurses like myself witnessed.

Perhaps we again need an official city photographer with a sense of mission.

THE HOUSE OF Industry, also known as 'the Poor House,' dominated the lives of Toronto's unemployed for more than a century. The city established the original facility in 1837, in the east end, just three years after the British parliament passed the so-called 'new Poor Law,' which forced those without means into workhouses where they had to work in order to obtain 'relief' – food, clothes and shelter. In 1848, this thoroughly Victorian institution relocated to an imposing yellow-brick structure erected on the corner of Elizabeth and Elm streets, in St. John's Ward, then predominantly occupied by Anglo and Irish working-class residents.

GAETAN HEROUX

THE STONE YARD

The House of Industry provided a residence for the elderly, widows and their children, as well as food and coal to destitute families. Through its so-called 'casual ward,' the House also offered relief to single unemployed men, or 'casuals,' who were given food and shelter for the night and then expected to move on. Within a few years, the trustees moved to expand the casual ward as more men entered Toronto looking for work during the winter months. The migration continued as the city grew. A worldwide recession, which began in 1873 and lasted more than two decades, resulted in large numbers of unemployed men flooding into Toronto throughout the 1880s and 1890s.

In November 1890, Rev. Arthur H. Baldwin, a trustee, testified before a provincial commission investigating the problem of vagrancy in Toronto. Reverend Baldwin, like many of his fellow trustees, believed that most of the lodgers were lazy and taking advantage of the House's goodwill. The best way to rid

Left: Exterior of the House of Industry at Elizabeth and Elm, ca. 1890. Modelled on the British poor houses, it served as a shelter and dispensed meals to the unemployed.

Next: Able-bodied men like the ones in this photograph taken ca. 1900, were expected to break stones in the yard behind the poor house in order to qualify for aid.

117

the city of its 'tramps' and 'vagrants,' he argued, was to make the casual ward as uncomfortable and as unwelcoming as possible.

> It seems a great pity that these people should be allowed to go in and dwell there and do nothing but cut a little wood, as we insist upon their doing. I do not see how we can get rid of them if we continue to give them charity. To keep them in comfortable quarters and to allow them to live in idleness is not a way to get rid of them.

Despite Baldwin's claim, a stay at the House of Industry's casual ward was anything but comfortable. 'The residents,' the *Globe* reported in an 1887 article about overcrowding, 'are not provided with beds of any kind. They are kept warm and clean, but the hard boards of the floors are all they have for beds, and a range of boards, a little raised, for pillows. Last Saturday night there were 125, and... they were lying as thickly packed as herring in a barrel. One could scarcely move without stepping on them.

By 1895, the trustees – determined to drive away the apparent malingerers – introduced a new labour requirement for the casuals: breaking 'two yards' of stone in order to qualify for relief. For years to come, The Ward echoed with the noise of men cracking stone in the yard behind the House of Industry (now the site of a new YWCA residence). Haulers brought stone from farms and the lake to the yard, where the casuals had to break it up. Contractors could then haul the rock away to construction sites around the city.

In 1908, a superintendent of the House boasted that the stone yard had, in fact, served as an effective deterrent. 'Our work test is a splendid thing and tends to keep down the number of applicants for help to a minimum,' he said at the time. 'This innovation was pronounced a success, and the applications for relief began to fall off at a rapid rate until we had very few families to take care of.

Those changes, however, didn't go over well with those who needed the aid. In the winter of 1895, more than 1,200 men rebelled against the House's introduction of what they saw as a cruel and degrading labour requirement. Men staying at the casual ward resented being forced to break stone for their relief, and the implication they were responsible for their own destitution. On January 10, 1896, John Curry and Thomas Wilson, two of the casuals, were

charged with vagrancy after refusing to break stone and sentenced to three months in jail. Two years later, sixty men found themselves in court. One told the magistrate that he would rather steal than break stone for his relief.

The protests continued to escalate. On the morning of January 16, 1909, forty-five men ate breakfast at the casual ward but left without doing the required labour. Two days later, another forty men refused to crack stone because of the extreme cold weather. Police were called, and charges laid. In February 1910, seven members of a non-stone-breaking union appeared in court after they refused to crack stone. The House's superintendent testified that one even refused to look at the pile of stones. 'These men,' he complained, 'spend their money in outside towns and then come back to Toronto in droves and expect to be kept.' The seven men received sentences ranging from thirty days to three months.

The jail terms only served to amplify public controversy. 'Though this city claims to be so very religious, you have a savage way of treating poor fellows that have nowhere to go,' noted a letter in the *Daily Star*, simply signed 'Out of Work':

> The statement that some of the men refused to work has appeared in the whole Canadian press from the Atlantic to the Pacific. But nobody ever asked why such a large percentage of men refused to work. No, they are simply put down as lazy. Now, when a man goes to a place like the House of Industry, it is plain that he is half starved already... When he gets up in the morning, after what little sleep he had been able to get, he is required to break a lot of stones. The quantity of stones to be broken will take a man used to it three hours, but a man not used to that kind of work will take from four to six hours... Let the people of Toronto reflect a little on the conditions in this city and cease casting slurs upon those who are for the time being in bad circumstances.

A PHOTOGRAPH THAT IS sometimes known as *Slum Kids,* by William James, one of Toronto's most important yet least known chroniclers, is an ambiguous document. Part of a 1911 series known as *Children of the Ward,* the image is filled with contradictions. Eight girls – immigrants or children of immigrants – dressed in ragged clothes have been immortalized by a roving street photographer in a chance encounter on a sunny day. Yet we know very little about the circumstances of the making of this picture. Where was it taken? Who are these children? Where are they going? What's their story?

While these children lived in poverty, they are far from unkempt, and appear joyous and healthy. The road behind them is wide, the houses are large and possibly one is made of brick, indicating a main street. Two older girls are looking after the younger ones. A baby is in a stroller and two toddlers are being led by the hand.

James (1866–1948) was likely using a cumbersome tripod-mounted camera with long exposure times. He couldn't have made the picture without the explicit consent of the children. It is a candid shot, yet the subjects are complicit with the photographer, who perhaps charmed them with his bizarre-looking equipment.

Indeed, the beauty of the image stems from its seeming spontaneity. The tall girl on the left smiles trustingly, and her gaze indicates she is mesmerized by the photographer.

Because they are slum kids, are they not supposed to be happy? James's image conveys a communion of spirit that

VINCENZO PIETROPAOLO

WILLIAM JAMES
TORONTO'S FIRST PHOTOJOURNALIST

Left: William James Sr. with his sons Bill (left) and Norman (right), 1936.

transcends the social conditions in which these girls live. Their demeanour embodies hopefulness. Their dresses may look rumpled, especially in contrast to a gentleman in a suit and bowler hat walking away from the camera, but they appear cared for and secure. The photograph shows that these slum kids have the inherent qualities of pride and self-respect as much as anyone else.

This image also reveals that William James was, first and foremost, a 'people' photographer, in contrast to his better-known contemporary, Arthur Goss, the city's official photographer. An immigrant from a working-class background, James left England in 1906 with his wife and five children to make a clean break from a class-conscious society. The family sailed to Quebec City and from there took the train to Union Station. James, then forty, had no idea how he was going to make a living.

After three years of doing odd jobs, he decided to become a professional photographer. As a freelancer, he did not have to satisfy the specific demands of an employer, and he used his independence to create diverse bodies of work. Roaming Toronto's streets with only his camera and his curiosity, he shot thousands of pictures and sold them to newspapers and magazines.

Whereas Goss's stark images were formal and mandated by the city, James didn't have to please municipal officials. Instead, he relied on his wits to find subjects on the street or in public places, documenting moments of urban life that would otherwise have remained

Slum Kids: *Girls minding their younger siblings, ca. 1911.*

unrecorded. In so doing, he provided newspaper readers in tony neighbourhoods with glimpses of how the other half was living, to paraphrase the nineteenth-century Danish-American journalist and social activist Jacob Riis.

In both content and emotional power, James's work evokes the street photographs of Lewis Hine, who documented

poverty on New York's Lower East Side and came to be known as one of the founding fathers of social documentary photography. It's unlikely James knew Hine, which further attests to his originality.

As he increasingly earned a living by selling his work to local broadsheets and other publications, James established himself as a photojournalist. In fact, he is considered Canada's first press photographer – at the time, newspapers

Chicken warehouse (left) and a kosher restaurant (right) on Agnes Street (now Dundas), ca. 1910.

did not employ staff photographers. As a contractor, James developed a close relationship with editors, who relied on him for images to illustrate their human-interest stories.

And there were many such stories. During the first four decades of the twentieth century, Toronto's population tripled. James, who worked until the late 1930s, documented upper-class society and working-class communities with equal aplomb, eventually becoming one of the most prolific photographers in the pre–Second World War era.

Of course, he didn't just create pictures of The Ward. He left a legacy of historically important images of Toronto's skyline, lakeside venues, panoramic street views, construction sites and shops, and the bustle of its downtown traffic. For aerial photographs, he even strapped himself into biplanes. The city was his canvas.

Much of this work is preserved in the City of Toronto Archives, which has a collection of some 12,000 images in the James family fonds, including 5,800 glass-lantern slides of landmarks, events and ordinary people going about their lives.

It didn't matter that some of those subjects – such as the girls in the *Children of the Ward* series – lived in a poor, immigrant enclave shunned by more prosperous Torontonians. For James, they too were part of the city he saw in the viewfinder.

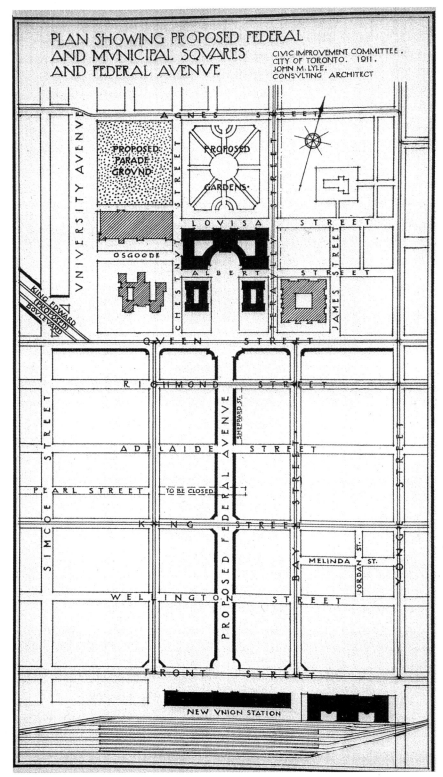

PLAN SHOWING PROPOSED FEDERAL AND MVNICIPAL SQVARES AND FEDERAL AVENVE

CIVIC IMPROVEMENT COMMITTEE.
CITY OF TORONTO. 1911.
JOHN M. LYLE.
CONSVLTING ARCHITECT

PROPOSED PARADE GROVND

PROPOSED GARDENS.

OSGOODE

VNIVERSITY AVENVE

KING EDWARD (PROPOSED) BOVLEVARD

AGNES STREET

LOVISA STREET

ALBERT STREET

CHESTNVT STREET

TERAVLEY STREET

JAMES STREET

STREET

QVEEN STREET

RICHMOND STREET

ADELAIDE STREET

PEARL STREET

TO BE CLOSED

SHEPPARD ST.

SIMCOE STREET

KING STREET

MELINDA STREET

JORDAN ST.

BAY STREET

WELLINGTON STREET

PROPOSED FEDERAL AVENVE

YONGE STREET

FRONT STREET

NEW VNION STATION

Plate 130

I N 1909, THE Civic Guild, a group of well-heeled local citizens, petitioned the city council to carry out a comprehensive plan for beautifying Toronto. In response, council formed the Civic Improvement Committee, which submitted a final document in 1911. The thoroughly illustrated thirty-one-page report – which contained many forward-looking ideas, including more park space, a civic square and a modernized road network – became the first comprehensive plan for Toronto.

MICHAEL McCLELLAND

THE AVENUE NOT TAKEN

The committee's plan was competitive: the members noted that other comparable cities already had such plans, with specific proposals. For example, the West Chicago Park Commission in 1908 had determined that cities should have one acre of parkland for every 100 inhabitants. Toronto's parkland, the authors concluded, would need to be quadrupled so the city could compete effectively: 'The need for breathing spaces and recreation grounds is being forced upon the attention of practical men, who are learning to appreciate that a city, in order to be a good labour market, must provide for the health and pleasure of the great body of workers.'

Transportation was also a key priority. The committee acknowledged that the impact of the private automobile on Toronto's narrow streets was the city's most pressing concern. They created a number of our now familiar streets, like Bay Street, by connecting previously unconnected smaller avenues. Amazingly, the report proposed a viaduct over the Don Valley, and recommended that it make allowances for a subway. Their advice was taken, and the subway, which wasn't constructed

Left: Plan showing proposed Federal and Municipal squares linked by Federal Avenue. John M. Lyle, Architect, 1911.

until some sixty years later, was able to fit snugly on a level beneath the vehicular roadway.

But the committee's most impressive move was the proposed design for Federal Avenue, a broad new boulevard that would cut through the downtown core to create a masterpiece of Beaux-Arts planning. It would run from Front Street to Queen Street, where it would terminate at a new complex of civic buildings, parks and parade grounds. The southern end of Federal Avenue would eventually become the site of the new Union Station, while the northern terminus, in the 1960s, became the new City Hall and Nathan Philips Square. The committee's forward-looking plan also regularized the size of the very large blocks that existed in the downtown, creating more street frontage for prominent buildings and more north-south sidewalks for increasingly jostled pedestrians.

The author of the Federal Avenue scheme was John Lyle, acknowledged then and now as one of Canada's preeminent architects. Appropriately, he had studied at l'École des Beaux-Arts in Paris, where this type of formal planning had developed. Some aspects of the Federal Avenue plan did get built, but the cost of expropriation in the business district eventually killed it. Lyle's design for Union Station was built as cited in the plan and opened in 1927. The initial portion of the Royal York Hotel was built two years later. The structure, then the highest building in the British Empire, was purposely placed off-centre from the station to allow room for the proposed avenue. A few other remaining buildings – including the Federal and the Graphic Arts buildings on Richmond – were developed in anticipation of this grand boulevard.

As an architecture student who admired the work of Lyle, I became enamoured with the genius of his Federal Avenue plan. This is what architects should do, I thought; they should work with engaged citizens and employ creative urban design strategies to build a better city that could hold its own against the best cities in the world.

But it did not dawn on me until much later that the plan contained much that was left unacknowledged. The dense warren of increasingly derelict housing in The Ward would have to disappear to make way for this vision of Toronto's future. When designing what became the Prince Edward Viaduct, the committee commented that the city should exercise the utmost care with this project so the natural beauty of the Rosedale ravine would not be marred.

City officials, however, raised no such concerns about The Ward or its predominantly immigrant population of over 10,000 people. Without specific reference to any location, the committee noted that density of population 'beyond a certain point results in disorder, vice and disease.' Presumably, The Ward, with its crowded and cluttered streets, fell into this category.

While the city never built Federal Avenue, successive generations of municipal planners never relinquished the goal of developing a north-south route through the core. In the 1960s, long after those turn-of-the-century ambitions had been forgotten, the city began promoting an underground pedestrian connection roughly in the same area. It was to run between the proposed TD Centre and New City Hall. What would have driven John Lyle crazy, I like to think, was that his classic straightedge boulevard had morphed into the first stages of Toronto's spiderlike, subterranean PATH system.

Architectural historians have argued that Lyle's unbuilt Federal Avenue is a prime example of Toronto's inability to make the grand gesture. I now see a much more nuanced story, however. The lessons from Federal Avenue may be that big planning gestures are not what makes Toronto tick. We should recognize that most master plans are never fully executed. In fact, large planning gestures may have dangerous blind spots and unintentional impacts for the people who stand in the way. When we approach city-building with the same confidence that John Lyle possessed, we must ask ourselves, where are our blind spots? We need to question whether these grand civic plans are more important than the people who actually inhabit the city.

THE TWELFTH-STOREY ROOFTOP of the T. Eaton Co.'s tallest factory presented a panoramic view of the slum that the once-mighty retailer both helped to create and did much to sustain as Toronto's nineteenth century progressed into the twentieth.

It was a vista dyed grey in the central city's coal-fire industrial smog, a scene bearing the Eatons' feudal imprimatur – The Ward's tumble-down, tottering cottages shoulder-to-shoulder along laneways and alleys, yards filled with garbage, outdoor toilets and the disordered debris of failed habitation, all of it beneath the department store's stern fortifications.

Aggravating The Ward's already over-crowded conditions, more than 175 dwellings had been bought up by Eaton's and demolished at the turn of the century to allow the company to build manufacturing plants for its own goods – primarily clothing and the iconic Eaton's catalogues – within the precinct of its flagship store at Queen and Yonge streets.

Many of The Ward's remaining dwellings were crammed with Eaton's workers (on average eight to ten per building), employed in factories that towered over Bay Street – formerly Terauley Street – near the intersection with what was once Louisa Street, about where the Marriott Hotel now stands.

Four Eaton's factories erected between 1890 and 1913 ringed tiny Church of the Holy Trinity. At its peak, the complex spread over nineteen acres and employed between 6,500 and 9,000 men, young women and girls, working at 5,000 electric garment-making machines.

MICHAEL VALPY

TIMOTHY EATON'S STERN FORTIFICATIONS

Previous: The Ward from the Eaton's factory rooftop, 1912. The two large buildings in the lower right are a synagogue and the Agnes Street Methodist Church.

Left: Eaton's factory buildings overlooking Terauley (now Bay), 1912.

Most of the thousands of Jews who lived in The Ward until they migrated west to Spadina had at least one family member attached to the Eaton's manufacturing force. Among them was Joseph Shlisky, one of the world's most famous cantors between the two world wars. Kidnapped from his family in Poland as a child by an unscrupulous cantor, Shlisky was brought to Toronto to sing in a cantors' choir and sent off to work at a sewing machine in one of the Eatons' factories. Lady Florence Eaton, Timothy's daughter-in-law, overheard him singing while he worked and offered to pay for his education at the Toronto Conservatory of Music.

Shlisky was just a cog in a much larger labour machine. The factories were Toronto's third-largest employer, after the railways and government. Their story is a testament to founder Timothy Eaton's business acumen.

The retailer's foray into manufacturing began in 1889, with the installation of twelve sewing machines on the top floor of the company's original store. Eaton wanted to reduce the cost of goods to his customers first by elbowing aside wholesalers by buying directly from manufacturers, and then by eliminating the manufacturers themselves.

In 1897, Eaton built a paint, oil and chemical factory. By the turn of the century, Eaton's employed more than 700 workers operating more than 500 sewing machines and producing over 4,500 complete garments every day. 'All middle profits have been eliminated,' boasted the company.

In 1907, Eaton's created its own drug-manufacturing operation. It also introduced its own clothing brands – Acme in 1905 and TECO (for T. Eaton Co.) in 1907. By 1915, the factories –including the largest thread-making operation in Canada – were producing 2,000 completed garments an hour and 350 items of fur clothing daily. The factories turned out footwear, while the tailoring shop employed 400 and its machines sewed on 11,500 buttons daily. The print shop and bindery produced Eaton's catalogues, business forms and school textbooks at prices the store claimed were less than half the cost of what students previously paid. In 1916, the company established its Product Research Bureau to oversee quality control of its merchandise. The model worked so well that, by 1922, Eaton's established clothing factories in Montreal and Hamilton.

While the company appeared to be a model of twentieth-century private enterprise, those factories also produced a hotly contested narrative of Toronto's

labour history: What really went on inside those buildings? Were they misogynous, anti-Semitic sweatshops with offensive working conditions for their underpaid employees, as labour organizers alleged? Or were the factories model places of employment paying industry-standard wages and overseen by a benevolent Eaton family patriarchy, as the company insisted?

It depends on who provides the account. According to a 1919 Eaton's pamphlet, the factories were the very embodiment of enlightened manufacturing and working conditions:

Condemned house, rear of 11 Alice Street, with Eaton's in the background. November 9, 1917. Alice Street no longer exists; the site is now the north end of the Eaton Centre.

> Great stretches of floor space bounded by fire-proof walls and
> connected by smoke-proof stairways. Windows on four sides

letting in floods of daylight. Drinking fountains supplying cooled and filtered water. Machinery rendered as noiseless, dustless and dangerless as modern invention can render it. A hospital on the premises with qualified nurses in attendance – in a case of accident or sudden illness. And at the designing boards, the cutting tables, the sewing machines, the printing presses, the binderies, up and down the aisles, here, there and everywhere, men, women, girls and boys who look healthy and happy.

Inquiring as to things not seen – hours, pay, etc., what do we find?

A Saturday afternoon holiday all the year round, and a whole-day holiday on the Saturdays of July and August with full pay for both week and piece-workers. Daily hours for the rest of the week 8 a.m. to 5 p.m. Full pay for all Public Holidays for both week and piece workers. Yearly holiday of two weeks with full pay for all workers who have been in the Eaton employ for two years and over, and of one week with full pay for all who have been one year and over...

For women and girls, privileges of membership in the Eaton Women's Clubs, affording use of library, rest rooms, a reception room where women residing in boarding houses may – under suitable chaperonage – receive their young men friends; and offering opportunity to join classes, at small expense, for instruction in dancing, swimming, gymnasium work and choral music.'

No dark satanic mills here.

But others offered far darker accounts. In 1902, the *Typographical Journal*, the official publication of the International Typographical Union, declared that 'poor old Tim [Eaton] had better put his philanthropic endowments to that of paying living wages to those who create his wealth.' A decade later, the rabble-rousing journal *Jack Canuck* commented, during the 1912 Eaton's strike, that 'President John Eaton [Timothy's son and successor] gives immense amounts of money to hospitals and other institutions to take care of the sick and indigent, and apparently tries very hard to keep these institutions supplied with patients by overworking and underpaying his employees.'

'The conditions in the factories were deplorable,' added a 2012 documentary about the Eaton's factory produced by the Textile Museum of Canada. 'There were gas irons, treadle machines and inadequate toilets. Workers stood for long hours at a time, sixty hours a week. Women and children replaced male workers for less wages.'

Regardless of which narrative provided a more accurate version of the working conditions in the company's looming factories, commercial imperatives would soon overtake the Eatons' vision of vertical integration.

Interior of Eaton's factory, November 9, 1917.

Before the outbreak of the Second World War – the precise dates are not certain – the company decided to shut its Ward operations and lay off its thousands of workers. Smaller garment manufacturers could supply Eaton's with products at prices cheaper than the cost of producing them in-house. Moreover, demand for prime downtown land, for office buildings and institutional development, outstripped the value of those plants.

The view of The Ward from the rooftop changed. The factories disappeared. Time had moved on.

304 JAN. 24 1916 ITALIAN MOTHERCRA

ON MAY 10, 1911, the popular social reformer J. J. Kelso – a former journalist who had founded the Toronto Humane Society, the Children's Aid Society and the Fresh Air Fund – hosted an informal meeting at his house. The agenda: improving the living conditions for newcomers in Toronto's downtown. A few University of Toronto students from Victoria College and local activists joined him.

As the Friday evening lengthened, those gathered at Kelso's Prince Arthur Avenue home formed a committee to help create a democratic meeting place and a social centre where neighbours of all ages, races and religious affiliations could contribute equally. They believed it was about time that Canadians embraced the social (university) settlement movement pioneered by Toynbee Hall in London, England, in 1884.

That movement required voluntary staff, usually college-educated, middle- and upper-class young men and women, to take up residence in poor communities. The idea was to experience poverty by 'settling' in and then using the insights gained to improve life in that very neighbourhood. This paternalistic tactic found favour with religious groups concerned with the lives of the poor but was seen as normative or moralistic by radical social movements.

The Toynbee Hall experiment soon captured the imagination of American social reformers. In 1889, Chicago reformers founded Hull House, which became a model for others in North America. By the end of the nineteenth century, more than a hundred settlement houses had been established in the U.S.

**RATNA OMIDVAR &
RANJIT BHASKAR**

SETTLING IN
CENTRAL NEIGHBOURHOOD HOUSE

Left: Italian mothercraft course held at Central Neighbourhood House, 82–84 Gerrard Street W., January 24, 1916.

| 141

Four months after that initial organizing session, Kelso's group founded Central Neighbourhood House (CNH), which became the second settlement house in Toronto. Kelso, according to one news report about the official opening, noted that 'the visitors would be afforded every facility for learning the English language, and would be taught how to become good and useful citizens.' CNH was part of the effort to 'clean up' The Ward.

To effectively deliver its programs to the new immigrants, CNH did its best to speak to them in their own languages: Italian, Russian, Serbian and German, among others.

When CNH first opened in The Ward, on September 18, 1911, it was at 84 Gerrard Street West. One of its concerns there was occupants not getting a good night's sleep – as the house had once been a brothel, well-dressed young men in search of that earlier service would come knocking in the middle of night.

For the next seventeen years, CNH offered a variety of new services and programs to the area's residents. A weekly schedule listed sixty-four different activities – everything from 'mothercraft' to sports – and monthly attendance reached 2,000. CNH staff delivered their programs at the house or in local schools. The activities were geared toward all ages, and both men and women.

English-language classes and programs aimed at increasing job opportunities and promoting citizenship were on offer for men, along with lectures on topics like 'The Naturalization of the Foreigner.' The women had their social clubs as well as lessons in English, arithmetic and dressmaking. While the programs for boys and girls and men and women reflected the stereotypical gender roles of that era, most would not be out of place today.

Elizabeth Neufeld, an American from Baltimore who served as the first CNH head worker, became involved in almost every social issue of the day. She sat on the executive of the Canadian Conference of Charities and Corrections and the Canadian Welfare League. Neufeld also advocated for universal suffrage and a minimum wage, and her opinions routinely turned up in news stories about issues confronting immigrants and their families.

What's more, she had a knack for influencing politicians. In late February 1914, Neufeld helped organize a march of about 200 children – 'a happy little army,' as the *Toronto Telegram* described the group – down to City Hall to press council for $20,000 for recreation equipment. They took their protest directly to the board of control committee room, on the second floor. 'We, the

Children of The Ward, are asking for a playhouse on the Elizabeth street playground,' said ten-year-old John Senson. 'We need a place where we can have baths, gymnasiums and entertainments.'

Neufeld's efforts drew a positive response from people in the neighbourhood. 'There seems to be a feeling that the Settlement is vitally interested in the lives of working people,' read a Head Worker's Report of February 1912, a sentiment that resonates to this day.

Central Neighbourhood House eventually moved out of The Ward, and currently makes its home in a restored Victorian row house in the east end, where it serves residents of Regent Park, St. James Town and Moss Park. Despite waves of gentrification in areas like Cabbagetown, those east-side neighbourhoods still have the highest concentration of homeless shelters and drop-in centres in Canada, as well as a large number of rooming houses and other low-income housing. 'Much of the needs of our neighbours haven't changed over the years,' says Elizabeth Forestell, the current executive director of CNH. 'What has changed is that I am no longer required to live in the office, not called the Head Worker or Girl and not paid $25 a month.' What hasn't shifted, she adds, is the agency's dedication to community-building.

The New Canadians,' Central Neighbourhood House Bulletin, *August 1913.*

CHN's tradition of social reform advocacy, initiated by Kelso and Neufeld, has also persisted through the years, even during periods when the agency's staff and its board came under attack for being too removed from the communities they served. Three former mayors – John Sewell, Barbara Hall and June Rowlands – all worked there before entering politics. Hall, who began at CNH in 1967, says, 'I came to Toronto from Nova Scotia intent on becoming a youth worker.'

From its inception, CNH focused on building community and providing a means for neighbours to help one another, Hall adds. 'They did that in 1911, we did it in the sixties when I worked there and it continues today. There's so much to be proud of from the past. So many people still need support, and we must also prepare to meet the needs of the next 100 years.' Hall recalls a 1926 comment made by a woman who was a CNH member: 'Settlement House means a place where your troubles are settled.'

WHILE SHE WAS often referred to as 'America's Sweetheart,' Mary Pickford, the glamorous Hollywood film star, was a Torontonian from St. John's Ward. Born Gladys Louise Smith in April 1892, she was the eldest daughter of a British Methodist father and an Irish Catholic mother. The family lived in a brick home at 211 University Street north of present-day Gerrard Street, where the Hospital for Sick Children is located today. Her father, John, a purser for the Niagara Steamship Company, was an alcoholic who abandoned the family in 1895. He died three years later in a work-related accident, leaving his wife, Charlotte, destitute, with Gladys and her two younger siblings – Lottie and Jack – to support.

ELLEN SCHEINBERG

TORONTO'S GIRL WITH THE CURLS

After experiencing a bout of depression following this tragic incident, Charlotte briefly pursued a career as a seamstress, producing and selling dresses to women from the area. She also took in lodgers to bring in a little extra money. One of the tenants ran the Valentine Theatre Company and prodded Charlotte to let Gladys and Lottie take part in one of his productions. This led to other performances with this company and, in 1900, a role in her first major production, *The Silver King*, which played at the Princess Theatre on King Street.

During a radio interview with the CBC in 1959, Pickford reminisced about her early childhood experiences in Toronto. She recalled riding her bike down University Avenue to Queen Street, as well as playing at Queen's Park. Because of her theatrical commitments at a young age, she was mainly home-schooled by her mother, and didn't get the opportunity

to attend public school. A number of her contemporaries who lived in the area claimed to have been friends with her as a child. One interesting anecdote, recounted by Sara Easser (née Foster) during an interview conducted by the Multicultural History Society of Ontario, involved sharing an outhouse with Pickford and her family after their arrival in Toronto around 1900. Due to severe overcrowding and sharing of external water spouts and privies in the neighbourhood, the neighbours would have gotten to know one another well, simply by running into each other during their day-to-day chores and routines.

Mary Pickford
ca. 1898

According to the 1901 census, Gladys and her family were still living on University Avenue; however, she spent much of the year in the United States, acting in theatrical productions. The family formally moved to the U.S. in 1902 so the kids could pursue careers in the theatre, with Charlotte as their manager. At fourteen, Gladys began appearing in Broadway productions, and three years later she commenced her fabled film career.

Gladys changed her name to Mary Pickford around that time, and enjoyed immediate success in the business, turning out fifty-one films that first year and earning a sizeable salary of $10 a day. Mary was not only one of the most famous and recognizable actors of her era, she was also an impressive businesswoman – she was a skilful salary negotiator and a co-founder of United Artists.

Despite her success and glamorous Hollywood lifestyle with Douglas Fairbanks after their 1920 marriage, Pickford maintained a strong Canadian identity and visited her homeland several times throughout her life. In 1924, she posed for a

photograph in front of her childhood home on University Avenue. She returned again in 1943 to contribute to the war effort. Pickford sold her beloved home for $15,000, using the proceeds to build a bungalow in East York. She then auctioned off the new home and raised $250,000, which was donated to Canadian war charities. Although she became an American citizen when she married Fairbanks, she successfully reclaimed her Canadian citizenship before her death in 1979.

A plaque sponsored by the Ontario Film Institute honouring Pickford's illustrious career and contribution to film was unveiled in 1973. It is located in the area where her childhood house would have stood at University and Elm Street, by the Hospital for Sick Children. Her third husband, actor and bandleader Buddy Rogers, attended the ceremony. A decade later, a bronze bust of the star created by artist Eino Gira was placed next to the plaque. These commemorative markers help connect Pickford to her birthplace in The Ward. From the perspective of her contemporaries, she represented a poor Irish girl from the 'slum' who achieved remarkable success as an international film star in the nascent film industry.

Mary Pickford, on the steps of her birthplace, 211 University Ave., March 23, 1924.

IN THE LATE nineteenth century, Chinese immigrants began to settle in cities throughout Canada (except in B.C. and Alberta). Unable to get waged jobs because of the colour of their skin, they mostly went into two lines of work: laundries and cafés. The cafés required more start-up capital, and involved long hours, remaining open from early in the morning until late at night, seven days a week. The owners often lived on the premises to keep costs down.

ELLEN SCHEINBERG & PAUL YEE

CHINESE CAFÉS
SURVIVAL
AND DANGER

Sing Tom opened Toronto's first Chinese café in 1901, at 37½ Queen Street West, opposite E. J. Lennox's towering new City Hall. According to the City of Toronto Directory, there were nineteen Chinese restaurants by 1912, about half in The Ward. Only ten years later (see directory, page 150), the figure had risen dramatically to around 100 cafés.

The Ward had restaurants serving Chinese food, as well as Chinese-run cafés serving western fare. According to author Mariana Valverde, moral reformers circulated warnings about the 'lure of the Chinaman,' particularly the connection reformers felt they had to opium and white slavery. Some xenophobic Canadians therefore viewed these spaces as dens of iniquity that posed a danger to the public, particularly to innocent young white women.

Still, white customers did frequent these restaurants, drawn by the exotic cuisine and affordable prices. In 1917, *Globe* food critic Peter McArthur, in his column 'Food Values,' expressed his appreciation for the more unusual dishes. 'Even when I go to a Chinese restaurant the mystery of chop suey no longer holds me,' he wrote. 'I seek the darker mysteries of Yet Goy

Left: Joe's Café and Chop Suey, 56–58 Elizabeth Street, December 2, 1937.

Main or Egg Foo Young.' Journalist Bruce West, who also dined at these cafés during the 1920s, reminisced about his experience as a teen eating at a Chinese restaurant on the second floor of a building on Elizabeth Street. West described it as painted a 'violent shade of green,' with a coal stove in the middle of the room. He further reflected that he enjoyed watching the cook prepare the meal on an assortment of chopping blocks and huge skillets from his vantage point at the table. He said diners could get a 'sumptuous' Chinese meal for 75 cents and enjoy 'exotic odors wafting out of the kitchen,' evoking memories of Hong Kong or Shanghai.

(Chinese)

Bathurst 76
Bay 130, 132 and 170
Bloor w, 512, 1285, 1286, 1288
Church 103, 106, 131, 134
College 287, 436, 457, 630, 847
Danforth 107, 523, 1335
Dupont 639, 639A
Dundas w 2217, 2219, 2826, 2904, 2961
Elizabeth 12½, 14, 31
King e 75, 152, 245
King w, 72, 128, 350
Lansdowne av, 859
Pape av, 844
Parliament, 408
Queen e 31, 34, 66, 126, 146, 187½, 212, 242, 350, 721, 747, 749, 885
Queen w, 69, 71, 83, 93, 97, 199, 206, 255, 273, 308, 422, 445, 469, 495, 512, 517, 621, 651, 710, 750, 874, 1190, 1194, 1278, 1294, 1336, and 1360
Simcoe, 127
Spadina av, 448
Temperance, 16
Yonge, 143, 245, 305, 331, 365½, 376, 403-403A, 433, 434, 556, 662, 1196
York, 51-53, 99, 122, 144, 156½

List of Chinese restaurants from the Toronto City Directory, 1922.

In addition to food critics, Chinatown's restaurants were also a draw for some celebrities. Arlene Chan notes that Edward G. Robinson and other Jewish vaudeville actors often dined at Chinese restaurants after performing at Shea's Hippodrome during the 1920s. Robinson revealed that his favourite spot was located at 12½ Elizabeth, which was owned by Hung Fah Low and Jung Wah. While this restaurant had mostly Chinese clients, Anglo-Torontonians represented the bulk of the clientele for most of the Chinatown cafés.

Although most proprietors were law-abiding businessmen, they confronted considerable harassment from government and police. For example, in 1908, the city threatened to deny licences to Chinese restaurants that hired white women. Then, in 1914, the province introduced similar legislation. Neither the municipal nor the provincial legislation was well enforced.

By 1923, 126 white women were working in 121 Chinese restaurants in Toronto. In 1928, a protest was held to challenge this seemingly racist Ontario statute. The owners, in fact, had the backing of eighty white women employed in Chinese restaurants as waitresses.

Besides the regulatory controls, police frequently raided Chinese restaurants that served alcohol or allowed gambling, especially after the 1916 passage of the Temperance Act. For instance, in 1918, Youk You, the owner of a restaurant at 12 Elizabeth Street, was arrested for selling Chinese whisky in teapots for twenty-five cents. The police seized two suitcases of whisky and charged him with breaching the law; You was released on bail for $500. Chinese restaurateurs continued to face harassment for alcohol offences even after the legislation was repealed. Chong Wan, the owner of a café at 11 Elizabeth Street, had his business padlocked in May 1929 for allegedly selling liquor on the premises, presumably without a licence.

Gambling was also common in Chinese establishments, since many bachelors enjoyed playing popular games of chance such as 'fan-tan' and 'pai gow.' As a result, the police made numerous raids, particularly on Sundays, for violation of the Lord's Day Act. One took place at a Chinese restaurant at Elizabeth and Albert during the summer of 1919, with twenty-seven men playing fan-tan. They quickly posted $15,000 bail, a staggering amount for that period.

As well as the police harassment, Chinese restaurateurs were also often victims of pranks and abuse by white locals. Some customers would order a meal, eat and then leave without paying. When one young man tried to dodge the bill at a Queen Street West café, the owner and a waiter chased him. The culprit sprinted by a policeman, who jumped onto the running board of a passing car and cornered him on Pearl Street. On hearing the café owner demand payment, passersby took up a collection to pay for the meal. Police released the young man because the café owner did not press charges. Were these bystanders protecting one of their own against 'losing' to the despised Chinese?

Other troublemakers shouted obscenities, sang loudly and pounded the tables to drive away customers. One deliberately slammed a café door hard to shatter the glass. The reason? The owner hadn't made change fast enough. In still another incident, café owner Harry Quon ducked a punch by William Lund, who then broke furniture, poured coffee and soup onto customers, and hurled lids, stools and dishes. John Shore refused to pay twenty cents for a

bowl of soup. He offered fifteen cents instead and told the owner, Yok Lee, to fight for the balance. When Lee appeared in court, he had several stitches in his head and a blood-soaked collar.

Such abuse demonstrated the contempt that some white Torontonians directed toward Chinese residents, who were called 'chinks' and 'Chinamen.' The harassment became especially visible in October 1919, when a crowd of young ex-soldiers raided a Chinese restaurant at 199 Queen Street West, where they broke the windows and threw the cash register into the street. A month later, veterans triggered another major riot on Elizabeth Street. They paraded around Chinatown, throwing stones at Chinese shops and restaurants. They later explained to the police that they wanted to take revenge on a restaurant owner at 33 Elizabeth Street, who they felt had insulted them when they were eating at his restaurant by calling them 'white dogs.' Police used batons on the crowd but made no arrests. The soldiers immediately headed to City Hall to talk to Mayor Tommy Church, who told them to disperse. Following this violence, the Chinese consul general from Ottawa asked Chief of Police H. J. Grassett for special protection for the community.

During the 1940s, some Chinese restaurants fell into disrepair and disrepute. The WK Café, at 56 Elizabeth Street, owned by Mah Keung and Henry Mah, lost its licence after the Police Commission described it as a 'dive and cesspool,' as well as a suspected meeting place for criminals and prostitutes. The owners' lawyer cheekily argued that 'police did not have to chase all over Toronto after criminals because they knew where to find them in the restaurant.' Other owners said they couldn't oust undesirable visitors because they couldn't afford to lose the business.

Curiously, Elizabeth Street experienced a restaurant boom during the late 1940s and 1950s. The first large facility to open was the Nanking in 1947, with the Lichee Gardens Restaurant and Club opening soon after, in 1948. Lichee Gardens boasted an enormous elegant dining room, with capacity to serve as many as 1,500 customers a day. It had a band and offered dining and dancing until closing at 5 a.m. Both establishments mainly catered to a western clientele. Ads for these businesses were published in the mainstream as well as select ethnic newspapers, like the *Canadian Jewish Review*.

Other large competitors who moved into the area in the 1950s included Kwong Chow, the Golden Dragon and Sai Woo. These modern restaurants were not only larger and more sophisticated than their predecessors, but also renowned for their cleanliness, and their authentic and abundant menus. Ironically, by the end of the 1950s, Chinese investors had spent more than a million dollars in improvements to Chinatown on Elizabeth Street, despite the city's moves to demolish the area. Many of these restaurants survived and even thrived, but were forced to relocate to nearby Kensington Market by the 1970s and 1980s.

Chinese festival on Elizabeth Street west of Dundas, 1967

RUTH A. FRAGER

DEFIANCE AND DIVISIONS

THE GREAT EATON'S STRIKE

I N LATE MARCH 1912, the Toronto Trades and Labour Council led a largely female strike parade through the downtown streets while some bystanders scoffed and others cheered at the 2,000 marchers. That same month, some 4,000 people joined a protest meeting at Massey Hall that spilled out onto Shuter and Victoria streets, just a few blocks east of the T. Eaton Co.'s looming clothing factory. At this massive protest, labour leaders stressed how crucial it was to back the striking clothing workers who were locked in combat with Eaton's, one of the country's most powerful employers. Many of the strikers were female immigrants who lived in The Ward. Their customary trip to work was short – the Eaton's clothing factory was located on several city blocks north of Queen Street, not far from their homes.

The strike itself had begun in mid-February, when over a thousand Eaton's garment workers, many of them Jewish women, walked off the job over a dispute in one of the women's clothing departments. At the time, about 60 per cent of the city's garment workers were female, and a large percentage of this group was Jewish. The International Ladies' Garment Workers' Union (ILGWU), which served both female and male clothing workers, directed the strike, which expanded to include many individuals who worked in the men's clothing departments of the same factory.

'Discrimination, intimidation and subjection to the worst prison-like system has been and is the predominant rule of this firm,' declared the defiant workers as they struggled to mobilize support. The strike stemmed not only from deep-seated

discontent with low wages and long hours; it was also a response to the exploitation of child labour. The union charged that 'in this very Kingdom of the Eaton Company, frail children of fourteen years, in busy seasons, work from 8 a.m. to 9 p.m.' But, the union added, 'in slack season, skilled working women, connected with the firm for six, eight or more years, can earn only Five, Four or even less Dollars per week.'

In Toronto at this time, the employment of women and children took place in a context in which the typical male blue-collar worker could not earn enough to keep a family of five above the poverty line. As a result, the working-class family economy was often dependent on secondary wage earners. Labour activists struggled to increase the wages of the male head of the family and limit child labour, but they harboured an ambivalent attitude toward women's paid labour. Even though there were laws on the books prohibiting child labour in Ontario, it was easy for child workers to collude with management to keep their jobs,

Female operators at work within Eaton's tailor shop, ca. 1910.

especially because there were very few official factory inspectors. Meanwhile, the typical blue-collar female worker could not even earn enough to support herself. Some of the women were widows or abandoned wives supporting families. The majority, however, were single young women who undertook paid labour to support their struggling families. In addition to protesting low wages and the exploitation of children, the strikers also objected to 'Graft for Foremen,' protesting that 'foremen and forewomen have power to discriminate most flagrantly in favor of their friends, or vice versa, and may cut wages, ruinously, by intention, or from careless distribution of piece work.' 'Insults to Girls' (i.e., sexual harassment) was another complaint against the T. Eaton Co.

Management had triggered the strike when it ordered sixty-five male sewing-machine operators to sew in the linings of women's coats on their machines. The men refused: they had been making sixty-five cents per garment without sewing in the linings, and management was now insisting they do the extra work without any pay increase. Previously, female workers known as finishers had sewn in the linings by hand. The employer's new directive amounted to more than a pay cut for the men: the women adding the linings were going to lose their jobs.

This solidarity between women and men became one of the main themes of the strike. Joe Salsberg, a Jewish immigrant who became a prominent labour activist and politician, later recalled that one of the strike slogans 'became the folksy expression of simple, honest working men … in Yiddish particularly: "*Mir vellen nisht aroycenemen dem bissle fun broyt fun di mayler fun undzere shvester.*" "We will not take the morsel of bread from the mouths of our sisters."'

Female and male Jews from the Eaton's garment factory remained united against the company, but their solidarity was not matched by the firm's non-Jewish clothing workers. The Jewish nature of the strike was, in fact, a central issue. As the ILGWU newspaper explained: 'Those affected [by the dispute at the T. Eaton Co.] are almost entirely Jewish: and the chief slogan by which it was hoped to cut off public sympathy was the report… that this is "only a strike of Jews." The appeal to race and creed prejudice has succeeded, too, insofar as it has prevented the Gentile Cloak Makers from joining in the sympathetic strike.'

Although this 'strike of Jews' did manage to obtain some significant support from the broader labour movement, the support was limited because of anti-Semitism. For example, the *Lance*, a Toronto labour paper, promoted the strikers'

call for a boycott of Eaton's retail business, while at the same time warning that 'the foreign agitator has few friends in Canadian labour circles.'

Jack Canuck, a populist Toronto newspaper, missed no opportunity to criticize Eaton's and praised the strikers for tackling this villainous enterprise. While declaring, in another context, that 'a dirty Jew is about the dirtiest specimen of humanity in the world,' the editors promoted the cause of the Jewish strikers in article after article.

One letter to the editor opined that Eaton's was 'one of the public's worst enemies' because this 'trust store' was 'in a position to dictate to the manufacturers the price they are to receive for their goods, and [to dictate to] the sales clerks how much they are to

Philanthropist : " Yes, and put bells on it."

receive for selling them.' Hostility to the 'Eaton Octopus' (a term coined by a journalist highlighting the grasping nature and extensive reach of this big business) also stemmed from the fact that its large department stores, together with its mail-order catalogues, were squeezing out small, family-run, retail businesses. These concerns were much like the present-day opposition to Walmart.

Meanwhile, strike supporters also appealed for help from women's groups. Given that about a third of the strikers were

Top: Supporting the strike at the T. Eaton Company's clothing factory, 1912.

Bottom: Cover of Jack Canuck, *May 4, 1912.*

female, the ILGWU and the Toronto Trades and Labour Council asked 'associations of leisure class women' and suffrage organizations 'to defend the rights of the [Eaton's] workers.' However, little support came from these entities, partly because the women's movement reflected the anti-Semitism of Canadian society more broadly. And, as explained by suffrage advocate Alice Chown, women suffragists were especially unwilling to support the female strikers because they feared that 'their pet cause would be hurt through being linked with an unpopular one.'

Given the difficulties building alliances across class, ethnic and gender lines, the opposition proved no match for a powerful, intransigent employer. The adamantly anti-union president of the company, John C. Eaton, had the resources to recruit strikebreakers all the way from Britain and to weather any temporary drop in sales that might be brought about by the boycott. Despite the formidable solidarity between female and male Jewish workers, and the vigorous support of the immigrant Jewish community, Eaton, scathingly referred to by the union's newsletter as the 'King of Canada,' prevailed.

The workers were forced to admit defeat after holding out for four months. The ILGWU was seriously weakened, and 'for a long time' after this strike, a union official recalled, 'the T. Eaton Company would not hire any Jews.' The Ward's immigrant Jewish community was devastated. Although Jewish clothing workers could seek jobs at other firms, Eaton's had been their largest employer. As a result, members of the Jewish community were forced to explore other occupational options outside of the shmatte trade. As many scrambled to find other kinds of work, anti-Semitic hiring restrictions in many sectors sharply limited their prospects. In the end, class, ethnic and gender biases undermined the Jewish labour movement and its chance for success.

'VE ALWAYS CONSIDERED the designation 'Chinatown' for the stretch of Spadina between College and Dundas to be kind of annoying. Reason one: there are a lot of Vietnamese businesses along there. Reason two: it's silly to lionize just one of the GTA's many hubs of East Asian groceries, bubble tea lounges and grab-bag novelty stores blaring extremely loud Cantopop. I grew up in Agincourt (a.k.a. 'Asiancourt,' a term I think should be reclaimed with pride), just southeast of Markham's Pacific Mall, and I now live within walking distance of the Chinatown at Gerrard and Broadview. Each of these areas has its particular charms, and its own roaming packs of Marlboro-puffing, tai-chi-arm-flinging seniors.

DENISE BALKISSOON
ELIZABETH STREET
WHAT THE CITY DIRECTORIES REVEAL

Checking out the pages of the city directories from a long-gone Toronto, it's evident that The Ward went through a Chinatown phase as well. There might never again be such a quick, easy way to take a snapshot of the city's multi-ethnic makeup (never mind what we've lost with the elimination of the long-form census). Elizabeth Street was The Ward's main north-south arterial. When I examined how the names of its residents changed at ten-year intervals, from 1889 to the post–Second World War razing of the neighbourhood, I could see in those stark lists how international migration left its mark on the face of this once-Anglo city.

When Queen Victoria still ruled, Elizabeth Street was predominantly white, but that doesn't mean there wasn't diversity, or division. In the late nineteenth century, I imagine that the

street's Wrights didn't mix too much with its Cullens. Tempers likely flared between the neighbourhood's Protestants and Catholics during the annual Orange Order parade, once a frightening and inescapable show of class and race hierarchies.

But everything changes. By 1900, an intrepid family named Rosen had made its way onto Elizabeth – the Smiths and Rooneys still dominated the directory, but there was now a Hebrew teacher named S. Yaffee at number 44, as well. The next two decades saw a deluge of Bornsteins, Yarmolinskys and Silvermans, as well as the first proprietors of the Chinese laundries. Nine years later, the WASPs and the Irish had almost disappeared, and Elizabeth Street was almost entirely Jewish and Chinese. Many of the latter were saddled with sometimes unfortunate phonetic spellings of their given names. Yep Ship Thoy, Hing Dong and, sigh, Poo Wong were definitely in the majority by 1916, offering neighbours and passersby a chance to eat chop suey, get their hair cut and have their laundry done. One could also buy presumably kosher chickens from the lingering Jacob Wasserman.

In the era of social media, we can trawl through the minutiae of just about anyone's life. But pulling back to see the macro picture is tough. The history lessons contained in the pages of these aging city directories provide the opposite experience. They document how broad waves of immigration washed up onto Elizabeth, but without highlighting the details of individual lives. House number 96 witnessed it all: home to John Frank in 1889, it was Hing Goon's drugstore by 1945, and occupied by Philip Zwior and Ephraim Ziwinski in between. Two men named David Rugenhoff and James Rogers shared the space in 1916. I imagine them as bachelors whom everyone thought would just bunk in together until at least one of them found a wife. But perhaps they were happy on their own, thank you very much. Like the homes of those who populated Elizabeth Street's Chinatown, the remnants of their love may have disappeared. But that doesn't mean it didn't exist, those faint strands woven eternally into the fabric of Toronto.

20 Stollery Wm, bldr
24 Fox Mrs Sarah
26 Nexon Wm C
28 Cameron Mrs Marion K
30 Dobbin David H
32 Sloane Beresford J
34 Cheer John A
34 Cayley Francis O
38 Lawson Mrs Edith
40 Runciman Thomas
42 Jarvis Stephen M
Montgomery John T
44 Williams Fredk C
46 Mather N L C
48 Wily Walter
5. Powis Edmund
52 Sydere A H

.... South Side ....

13 Aikens Isaac R
15 Pardoe Avern
17 Randall Robert E
19 Veck George H
21 Pelham Edgar
25 Suckling I E
27 Muldoon Mrs Lois
29 Geddes Mrs Matilda J
31 Edgar Miss Beatrice
33 Pangman Mrs O F
35 Boyd John W G
37 McCormack John
39 Ballantyne Robt
41 Vacant
45 Macnamara Michael J
47 Dyas Wm J

ELIZABETH
(Mimico)

ELIZABETH
(Swansea)

ELIZABETH
(Weston)

ELIZABETH
North from 102 Queen w
to Grenville, ward 1.

.... East Side ....

7 Allen Charles, blksmith
9 Stevens & Buckley, vet surgs
11 Frazee Storage and Cartage Co, warehouse
15 Mispolet Rene, dairy
17 Smith Samuel
19 Sarkis Geo
21 Licht Hyman
Steinberg Moses, rear
23 Underwood James
25 Robinson Thos
31-33 McLaughlin - Gourley, Ltd, wd wkrs
♦ Albert st intersects
35 Chinese Laundry
37 Most Nathan
39 Shabatta Shapsil
43 Rotterman Solomon
45 Finer Saml
47 Pearl Mrs Ida
47 Shneiderman Israel
51 Altman Samuel
51 Shapiro Solomon
53 Stuart James
55 Tamchinsky Mendel
57 Fawcett Mrs Prudentia
57 Small Daniel, liquors
♦ Louisa st intersects
59 Cohen Benjamin, gro
63-65 Herman David, junk
67 Rabinowitz Abraham, printer
69 Berman Jacob, mlnr
71 Sherman Benj, tinsmith
71½ Miller Mrs Rosa, confy
73 Goldenberg L, dry gds
75 Hagerman st commences
75 Spiegal Louis
77 Halper Samuel
79 Shapiro Mrs Julia, fruits
81 Sigel & Griesman, junk
Freindlich & Mandelsohn, butchers
81½ Weinberg Jockel, wtch-mkr
85 Lebsky Solomon
85 Malinsky Morris
87 Rubintchik Philip, bicycles

89 Greenberg Morris, exp
Karlinsky Simon, shoe maker
91 Smith Mrs Sarah, gro
91½ Tobvis Moses, lock-smith
♦ Foster pl commences
93 Vacant
95 Weserman Saml, tlr
97 Dacks David
99 Plant H, china decorator
101 Cyrkan Hyman
1... Peter Benjamin
105 Manton Bros, printers' supplies
Mitchell W & J, leather goods
107 Haberman Marco
♦ Cuttell pl commences
109 Aber Seth
111 Mitz Harris, rest
113 Swartzman Wilfred, plmbr
113½ Loxdam Hyman
115 Salger Hyman, barber
♦ Agnes st intersects
117 Lepofsky Saml
117½ Liebleman Lazarus
119 Lipshitz & Herman
119½ Tachenblach Louis
121 Midanik L & Sons, dry goods
123 Melnazarian Sorel, rest
125 Glassman Benj, fish
127 Volmar Mrs Gussta, confectionery
127½ Gibbs Julius, clothes repairer
131 Bernstein Louis, btchr
♦ Edward st intersects
145 Rottenberg L & Son, junk
Sabluski Joseph, rear
147 Tator Louis
149 Sherman Joseph
Brown Abraham, rear
Sabluski Joseph, rear
151 Pike Levy
153 Cooper Max
155 Vacant
♦ Elm st intersects
165 Vacant
167 Anderson Miss Divnia
169 Soskin Max
171 Cohen David
173 Cotta Max
179 Mordosky Mrs Rosa, gro
♦ Walton st ends
181 Steiner Joseph, stone ctr
187 Robinson Mrs Eliza
189 Vacant
♦ Gerrard st w ends
191 McConnell John
195-197 Eckl.. ?½, baker
199 Dennis Lewis, gro
201 Gross Hyman
203 Lakes Louie
205 Silverburg Louis
207 Krangle Mrs Mary
209 Chinese lndry
♦ Hayter st intersects
211 Scastaffio R, gro
213 Davis Maurice
221-221 Nurses Home
223 Berman Morris
225 Watson Wm
227 Dulzon Wm
229 Fry Charles P
241 Brown Wm
243 Clarke Frederick
245-255 Children's Hospital
♦ College st intersects
247 Vacant
249 Rensmara Philip
252 Holland Miss Jennie

.... West Side ....

6 Britl Leon, rest
8 Britl Leon, tobacco
10 Ion David
12 Tank W C & Co, Chinese gds
14 Caplan Harry L, shirt waists
16 Ying Tong Co, Chinese goods
18 Foster Joseph
20 Aber Jacob
22 Black Harris
24 Winer Wm
26 Lewis John

30 Kaufman Israel
34 Vacant
34½ Vacant
♦ Albert st intersects
36 Sloboat Harry, shoemkr
38 Vacant
40 Vacant
42 Vacant
42½ Albani Raffaelle
44 Kendler Israel
46 Vacant
48 Chinese lndry
♦ Lenatsky Jacob
50 Levine Jesse, gro
52 Brasher Wm J
54 Lahn Saml, btchr
♦ Louisa st intersects
56 Rosenfeld & Koldofsky, news dlrs
58 Altman Herman, barber
60 Sprechman Jacob, rest
62 Wolfe George, grocer
64 Dworkin Bros, adv agts
Dworkin Saml, staty
C P R Co's Tel (br)
66 Herman Morris, dyer
68 Davis Moses, confy
70 Plaim Maurice, confy
72 Simon Fredk, bkseller
74 Kazashah Joseph, gro
76 Clouth Filippo, fruit
78 Robinoff Moses, plmbr
80 Sturman Samuel, rest
82 Weinberg Samuel, pntr
84 Gold Bros, barbers
86 Shur Max, confy
88 Siebleman Lazarus, fish
90 Kars Hyman, dry gds
92 Goldsmith Reuben, dry goods
94 Grinberg Abraham, clo repairer
Schwartz Jacob
96 Litvik Abram, gro
Vacant, rear
98 Litvik Abram
100 Sleterman Morris
102 Goodbelm Max, hdware
104 Salinsky Saml, gro
106 Rosenfeldt Harold, gro
108 Tucker Mrs Minnie, rest
110-112 Sterling Joseph, bkr
114 Bloom Louis, paints
116 Teplita Rabbi David
118 Dinkin Louis, gro
120 James David, produce
122 Davis Hyman, gro
124 Tovbis Moses, plmbr
124½ Fox Samuel, crockery
126 Chininofsky Gidard, poultry
128 Sakker Samuel, barber
♦ Agnes st intersects
130 Vacant
134 Kindler Leopold
136 Mannheim John
138 Pesachowitz Gimpel, confectionery
140 Powis John
142 Wolfisch Samuel
144 Fioderwasner Samuel
♦ Edward st intersects
♦ Elm st intersects
168 Keeler John
170 Keeler James
176 Harnick Moses
178 Winkler Asher
184 Elizabeth St Sch
Unfinished building
♦ Hayter st intersects
♦ College st intersects

ELIZABETH
(West Toronto), name changed to Runnymede rd.

ELLERBECK
(Chester), north from Danforth av, first east of Don Mills rd, ward 1.

.... East Side ....

7 Maddaford Saml C
♦ Hurndale av commences
♦ Plaster cres commences
♦ Butternut av commences
193 Rooke Wm J

.... West Side ....

♦ Pretoria av ends
22 Brown Saml
24 Vickery Wm R

CYNTHIA MacDOUGALL
GROWING UP ON WALTON STREET

MY GRANDPARENTS, MATTEO and Antonia Principe, were an Italian immigrant couple with eight children, seven of whom were born in Canada. They lost their house when my grandfather died from diabetes, around the time insulin was discovered in 1920, and Antonia and seven of the children moved to a house on Walton Street. Maria (now Mary), my mother, was two years old at the time. Antonia received family assistance, and the children attended St. Michael's College.

My mother recalled that her neighbourhood was full of Italians and Jews who lived together in harmony but minded their own business. She disliked the Christmas boxes the *Toronto Star* distributed because everyone recognized the mitts and hats, and it made her feel poor. When her brothers were old enough to work, they contributed to the family budget. My uncle Leonard gave my mother some of the money he earned from his job so she could take the bus to Northern Secondary School at Mount Pleasant and Eglinton to attend Grade 9, saving her the long walk. But she had to drop out when she turned sixteen.

When she was growing up on Walton Street, my mother played a variety of games with the other neighbourhood children: Red Rover, hopscotch, skipping and Ring-Around-the-Rosie ('A pocket full posies/Husha husha/we all fall down!'). She also played with marbles if and when anyone had them.

My uncles and aunts said Walton Street was a neighbourhood all of its own, and everything was there. You could walk to anything you needed – the shop, the restaurant, the barber. The children played on the street, and sometimes at Queen's Park.

Besides my mother and aunt, two of my uncles are still alive: Peter and Leonard. Leonard became a mechanic, while Peter was a stretcher carrier in the Second World War and lost a leg from a land mine. He returned to Toronto and worked for more than fifty years as a cab driver. He is now over ninety.

In recent years, the brothers have enjoyed sitting down for a coffee at the Chelsea Hotel (formerly the Delta Chelsea) on Gerrard Street – they have determined the coffee shop is where their original family kitchen used to be.

Aunt Lucy Principe, who worked in the kitchen at the Park Plaza, in the 1920s on Walton Street. The Yonge Street Mission is at the end of the block.

**ALINA CHATTERJEE &
DEREK BALLANTYNE**

REVITALIZING GEORGE STREET

THE WARD'S LESSONS

WHEN THE CITY of Toronto razed much of the lower Ward in the late 1950s to make way for a new civic square, slum clearance was the preferred solution for dealing with derelict and inconveniently situated neighbourhoods. By the 1960s, however, residents and planners began to recognize that the vast public housing projects that often followed slum eradi- cation created new, and arguably more severe, social crises. In the 1970s, reformers used those hard-fought lessons to promote mixed-income/ mixed-tenure communities, such as St. Lawrence.

Today, Toronto – which in recent years has directed investment in social infrastructure to priority neighbourhoods – is in the midst of a third wave of housing reform. The city, Toronto Community Housing and private builders are redeveloping TCH properties like Regent Park, Alexandra Park and Lawrence Heights, using a mix of market and subsidized housing, as well as urban design that reflects Jane Jacobs' ideals of small blocks and eyes on the street. The revitalization of Regent Park, now well underway, is an effort to reintegrate a spatially and socially segregated community with the fabric of the central city.

Since 2010, council has also started to consider how to improve the so-called Downtown East area, a.k.a. Moss Park, long known for a high concentration of social service agen- cies catering to homeless people and individuals with addiction issues. At its core is George Street, a long-neglected enclave that's home to the city's largest emergency shelter, Seaton House.

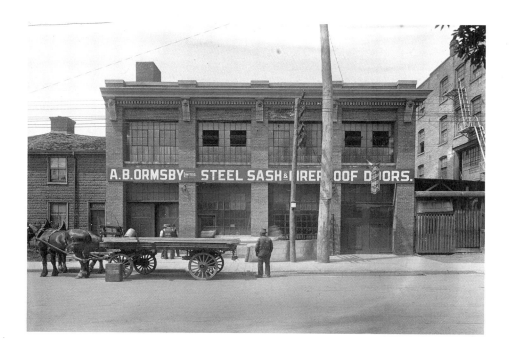

Tucked a block east of Jarvis, the stretch of George Street between Dundas and College streets is a mishmash of crumbling Victorian row houses, aging apartments and some contemporary buildings. This area has been home to social agencies since the nineteenth century, and was officially regarded as a slum by the early twentieth century. Toronto's original YWCA was located a block east of George. The Fegan Boys' Home for orphans, both local and English-born, was situated on George – between 1884 and 1938, 3,166 boys passed through.

154 George Street (west side of George Street, south of Queen). June 4, 1913.

Aside from a few homeowners who bought in anticipation of gentrification, George Street's residents include new immigrants, people living in poverty and those with severe mental illnesses and/or addictions. It's a community largely invisible to most Torontonians. George, in short, is home to those with nowhere else to go.

The Ward's fate continues to offer Toronto lessons on what should occur in areas like George Street. The Ward's post-war

redevelopment, to make way for institutional and office uses, occurred without any social planning – the city simply expropriated the properties and demolished them. The redevelopment proceeded without deep concern for the displacement of the area's residents.

In the 1960s, the transformation of George Street was similarly ill-conceived. As it constructed shelters and social housing on that block, the city gave little thought to the impact on the existing community. At the time, municipal officials felt they could simply concentrate social services in economically marginalized neighbourhoods. The long legacy of a poorly constructed past is what propels a new sort of reform for the George Street/Downtown East area.

There is another parallel between the city's efforts to revitalize Downtown East/George and the razing of The Ward in the 1950s/1960s: rising real estate values in areas where private interests own most of the land. The blocks all around George have experienced intense speculative development activity in recent years. Indeed, this sliver of the Downtown East may have dodged the condo boom because of the social, health and economic challenges its residents experienced, as well as the concentration of publicly owned social service agencies on George. Yet it's only a matter of time before this stretch also begins to experience development pressure, especially as the city looks to break ground in 2015 on a replacement for Seaton House that will include emergency shelter housing, a long-term care facility, affordable housing units and a service hub.

The redevelopment of Regent Park, just to the east, was a pilot for planning processes that put people ahead of development interests. While it will take time to distill all the lessons of Regent Park, we've learned which approaches can have impact. For example, the Regent experience of tenant relocation taught us that public/private co-planning is essential to creating the conditions for successful neighbourhood renewal. We also learned to find ways to protect the local networks and popular community organizations that existed in Regent Park and were threatened by the dislocation of tenants. Indeed, we now understand that planning social and community infrastructure is a necessary condition for creating livable neighbourhoods – these amenities do not just spring to life by accident or through market forces.

Strategies for social development continue to be refined as the revitalizations of Lawrence Heights, Alexandra Park and other priority neighbourhoods proceed. But a planning approach based on the full participation of current

residents, including those who rely on social housing and the area's shelters, holds much promise for the future.

What happens on George will fundamentally change the Downtown East neighbourhood, as well as the heart of the city. This effort offers a unique opportunity for the city to create a healthier community that weaves the area's architectural heritage with new uses while providing affordable housing and services to the residents of a mixed-income/mixed-tenure community. The eventual renewal of George Street should be a far cry from the terse expropriations that led to the dispersal, in the 1950s, of The Ward's mainly Chinese-Canadian residents and business owners. If done mindfully and appropriately, the story of the old George Street will not end abruptly.

Rear of Thomas Meredith House at 305 George Street, 2006.

ELLEN SCHEINBERG

TAKING CARE OF BUSINESS IN THE WARD

WHILE MANY WARD residents toiled as labourers in factories and on construction sites, others worked in or ran a wide array of shops and businesses that operated within the neighbourhood.

Chaim Teichman and his partners Morris Silverberg and Sam Shumaker ran the Toronto Soda Company at 183 Elizabeth Street. Their firm produced seltzer water along with flavoured sodas at their facility and made deliveries to their clients. Mr. S. Himel owned Peerless Bicycle Works, which offered inexpensive bikes at its location on Dundas near Centre Avenue. A few storefronts east, Fanny Fankell ran the Human Hair Company, at 150 Dundas West. Fankell was a young, single hairdresser who split her time coiffing hair and producing high-quality wigs. Her clients for the latter

product were likely local married Orthodox women, who were required to cover their hair with a wig to comply with Jewish law.

Some of the more common and prolific businesses in The Ward included restaurants, butchers, bakers, grocers, cigar and clothing manufacturers, pawn-brokers, steamship agents, machine and printing shops, clothing and shoe shops, confectioners, billiard rooms, ice cream and soda parlours, taxi compan-ies and junk dealers.

This photograph, from the City of Toronto Archives, was taken around 1926. It captures the south side of Queen Street West between York Street and University Avenue – presently the site of the Four Seasons Centre. One can see Simonsky's pawnshop to the far right, the Broadway Café, Queen Printing Company and the Globe Theatre, which was run by S. Sternberg and featured vaudeville shows. The barbershop on the opposite side of the street offered twenty-five-cent haircuts.

South side of Queen Street West between York and University, 1926. The block is now occupied by the Four Seasons Centre.

O N A SNOWY Sunday in February 1907, a large crowd gathered on University Avenue north of Queen Street for the 2 p.m. dedication service of Congregation Goel Tzedec's new synagogue. The *Globe* highlighted the participation of non-Jews in the ceremony, noting, '[M]any Gentiles join their Hebrew brethren in scene of rejoicing.' With Mayor Emerson Coatsworth, local MPs and other dignitaries in attendance, the four-and-a-half-hour ceremony was full of the era's pomp and circumstance, beginning with a solemn procession of the congregation's fourteen Scrolls of the Law from the previous synagogue on Elm Street. Cantor Wollman sang and directed the choir while rabbis Jacob Gordon and Joseph Weinreb recited prayers. The press deemed the Romanesque-style building 'striking,' and praised the 'magnificent dome… Illuminated by electric lights which add greatly to the stained glass panels of the dome.' In fact, the audience gasped when the synagogue's 500 electric lights were turned on as a speaker intoned, 'And the Lord said, "Let there be light."'

JACK LIPINSKY

A 'MAGNIFICENT DOME'
THE GREAT UNIVERSITY AVENUE SYNAGOGUE

The building was designed to be noticed. Planning began in 1896 and picked up speed in 1900, with the hiring of William Limberry Symons. The prominent architect had already completed Upper Canada College's gate lodge and Bellevue Hospital, and would go on to a highly successful career designing many Rosedale and Forest Hill homes and other significant buildings. While the congregation raised funds, synagogue officials gave Symons three years to study

Left: Wedding at Goel Tzedec, 1947.

Jewish Synagogue,
University Ave., Toronto.

*Postcard of Goel
Tzedec, ca. 1910.* Jewish ritual and symbolism. Their decision to choose an establishment architect revealed their desire to create a formidable edifice that would draw praise for its exterior design while including the important interior elements an Orthodox congregation required to practice its religion properly.

The history of Goel Tzedec, from its 1883 inception to the opening of its purpose-built sanctuary in 1907, mirrors both upward mobility and other key trends in the history of Jews in The Ward. The congregation began modestly in 1883 as a place of prayer for immigrants who mostly resided in The Ward. At first the congregation rented space on Richmond Street, as well as Temperance Hall for the High Holidays. The original

members arrived in Canada from different parts of Eastern Europe during the 1880s, but over time, as more synagogues and *shtiblech* (typically single-room synagogues located within homes) emerged within The Ward, the congregation became increasingly dominated by Russian Jews. Jews who came from Poland, Austria, Romania and other countries established their own synagogues with their countrymen. The first president was Jacob Draiman, who immigrated from Poland to Toronto in 1882, and lived at 309 Queen Street West with his large family above his dry-goods store.

Although the early members lived in The Ward, they were socially ambitious individuals like Samuel Weber. He worked as a peddler in 1901, but by 1911 had relocated to a more upscale home at 226 Simcoe with his family and a domestic. Weber ran a second-hand store and later ventured into real estate. This type of occupational trajectory was fairly typical of the Goel Tzedec founders and members. The membership also became quite large, with the huge influx of Jewish immigrants to The Ward. The burgeoning numbers enlarged and enriched the congregation, to the extent that it was able to finance the purchase of a Methodist church at University and Elm streets for conversion into a synagogue in 1886. This building accommodated the members' needs until the turn of the century.

Despite its success, the congregation was viewed as Toronto's second synagogue, after the more religiously moderate and affluent Holy Blossom, which greatly benefited from the desertion of many Goel Tzedec members intent on joining an elite institution. In 1897, Holy Blossom moved into a magnificent new building on Bond Street. The development, a decade later, of Goel Tzedec's synagogue on University Avenue was an attempt by its congregation to be part of a prominent, prestigious Orthodox synagogue. In *The Jews of Toronto*, historian Stephen Speisman observed, '[T]he residents of the Ward gloated over the structure as a symbol of their own self-respect and proof that Holy Blossom was not the only synagogue worthy of public attention.' Some Toronto Jews were so attracted to the appeal of the new building that they took out memberships at two synagogues, some venturing from the Beach, in the east end, in order to be part of Goel Tzedec.

The new building was now Toronto's largest synagogue, with seating for 1,200. Hebrew classes were held in the basement, which was also used for banquets, dances, weddings and bar mitzvahs. Prominent member Ida Siegal set up welfare, Zionist and educational institutions within the community. In fact, she

Samuel Weber and his family in a car in front of his home at 226 Simcoe Street, 1906.

convinced a number of synagogues, besides Goel Tzedec, to open congregational schools to ensure the Jewish education of members' children – including girls, who were overlooked at that time. She later served as a key facilitator of organized community-wide fundraising. A vigorous organizer, Siegal was 'one of the most indefatigable and effective volunteer leaders in the history of the Toronto Jewish community,' according to *The Jewish Women's Archives Encyclopedia.*

Louis Gurofsky, another member, became an influential immigrant agent who often represented the community's interests to Toronto police, especially when Jews were accused of breaking the Sunday laws. The activities of individuals like these underscored Goel Tzedec's belief that it was the pre-eminent 'immigrant synagogue' in Toronto.

The diversity of Goel Tzedec's membership also accounts for some congregational strife. The European-bred older generation wanted religious services to remain close to the European tradition, while younger members pushed for a weekly English sermon every Sabbath. In 1904, the congregation chose Jacob Gordon to be their rabbi. Gordon, who served three smaller congregations to defray costs, mirrored the dissonant influences sweeping through European Jewry. He had trained at leading European rabbinical schools, but he was also a Zionist who quickly learned to speak English. However, despite his

praiseworthy public reputation and his efforts to set up a local Hebrew school for boys, Gordon disappointed younger congregants by refusing to speak in English from the pulpit or deliver weekly services. Rabbi Julius Price, hired in 1914, adopted both practices.

Given the congregation's awareness of its status in the community, it is not surprising that the ceremonial laying of the new synagogue's cornerstone in May 1906 was carefully scripted to ensure that the congregation's importance would now be recognized both within and without the Jewish community. And so it was. During the ceremony, which included prayers for the health of the king, the royal family and the governor-general, Mayor Coatsworth observed that Jews made good citizens for the city. Just to make sure the message was clear, Montreal's Rabbi Abramovitz capped the rhetoric of Empire loyalty by stating, '[W]e are indeed grateful that under the folds of the British flag we are able to erect our places of worship without fear of having to turn them into fortresses.'

Ultimately, the congregation's westward move from the heart of The Ward to University Avenue proved both prophetic and prescient. Overcrowding in The Ward, propelled by an almost sixfold increase in its Jewish population in the early twentieth century, catalyzed a significant population shift toward Bathurst Street. This migration commenced after the turn of the century and peaked during and after the First World War. Despite that migration, the congregation's new home on University Avenue remained accessible both to those Jews who had moved west and those who remained within The Ward. The prestigious site – near the Armouries and Osgoode Hall, on an elegant boulevard leading to Ontario's parliament – also underscored the perception that Goel Tzedec's members had arrived, socially and economically. They had constructed the synagogue of their dreams without abandoning long-cherished traditions and beliefs.

The University Avenue synagogue housed the congregation for close to fifty years. In 1925, it joined the Conservative Synagogue Movement and eventually introduced mixed seating, bat mitzvahs and other egalitarian practices. By the 1950s, in response to the movement of the Jewish community northward to the Bathurst corridor, Goel Tzedec amalgamated with another Conservative institution, the McCaul Street Synagogue (Beth Hamidrash Hagadol), forming Beth Tzedec Congregation. The University Avenue building was demolished in May 1955 and on December 9 of that year, the congregation moved into its newly designed building at 1700 Bathurst Street, just north of Eglinton, where it stands today.

KIM STOREY AND JAMES BROWN

READING THE WARD

THE INEVITABILITY OF LOSS

OUR FASCINATION WITH maps is rooted in their ability to abstract a messy reality, distilling information on landforms, buildings, public spaces and streets. The Goad's fire insurance plans – produced by the Charles E. Goad Company as a record of buildings, materials, fire appliances and waterworks systems for the fire insurance industry – provide a remarkable record of Toronto's evolution, with highly detailed versions for the years 1880, 1884, 1890, 1899, 1903, 1910 and 1913, and continued by others for 1924.

The Goad's maps of 1884 and 1890 for St. John's Ward provide a dispassionate and accurate view of what, at first glance, seems like an ordered and measured settlement. Building materials and their additions are colour-coded, with light yellow for wood structures and red for masonry and brick. The buildings seem tidily placed in tight-knit blocks, with a few scattered 'red' churches and upgraded sites. But if we read more closely into The Ward's maps, reaching further back in time to Lieutenant-Governor John Graves Simcoe's initial Park Lot division in 1793, the signs of inevitable future loss become clear – a lack of public space, the high number of small urban blocks populated by lots of minimal size and the absence of a larger vision for a growing city.

The distance between Toronto's original post-colonial landscape and the regard of the mapmakers is clearly shown in the detail of the Patent Plans of York Township, circa 1796. These reveal Simcoe's vision for the City of Toronto, with all

the charm of an accountant's ledger. Here, the expansion of the original ten blocks of the Town of York has been measured out into Park Lots – long, narrow, hundred-acre parcels that ran between Bloor Street and Lot (Queen) Street.

As interesting as it is to chart the Park Lots' evolution into the imperfect grid of today's Toronto, the 660-by-6,600-foot plots granted by Graves to a new landed gentry erased any possibility for a common goal of a planned city. The creation of Park Lots trumped any collective vision for the expanded Town of York. These holdings did not allow for grand open spaces and places for future institutions, except through circumstantial amalgamation and negotiated trades and sales between privileged landowners. Instead, this arrangement guaranteed development for optimal profit.

The St. John's Ward shown in the Goad's 1884 and 1890 maps is remarkable for its lack of public space. In the later development of more western Park Lots, the traces of former geography, like the Garrison Creek ravine, could often be relied upon to provide an informal set of open spaces, if only because the undulating topography didn't yield easily to development. Although Taddle Creek travelled diagonally across The Ward (as seen in the James Cane map of 1842), it almost immediately vanishes without a trace (as seen in the 1854 Boulton map) in the lot division that was rapidly settled. With similar efficiency, this portion of Taddle Creek seems to have been simply filled in, tamped down and forgotten.

Without the informal adoption of the Taddle Creek ravine as open space, and without the formal designation of common space by a governing hand, the future of The Ward was always at risk. Ironically, the creation of a new playground at the corners of Elizabeth and Gerrard streets in 1912, which was universally welcomed, was later eclipsed by the extension of Gerrard Street west to University Avenue, and the construction of a new wing for the Hospital for Sick Children. The fate of that playground notwithstanding, public spaces are not easily eradicated, and can ensure an anchor that future development will respect. With the Ward, there were no such anchors to give a reliable structure to future land acquisition and assembly.

The public spaces of The Ward were to be found in its streets. But those proved easy enough to appropriate, with the original pattern of forty-three blocks reduced to twenty-six after the late 1950s, with the final expropriation for Toronto City Hall and Nathan Philips Square (and not counting the loss of the laneways

within the original blocks). The Goad's maps reveal a block structure and lot division that in some areas emulated the earliest block development in the Town of York – a dense pattern of square blocks, although the fixed widths of the Park Lots resulted in some 'square blocks' that were more generous, with others as narrow and dense remainders. These smaller, square blocks gave The Ward a high proportion of 25 per cent street area to 75 per cent private land area – a defin-

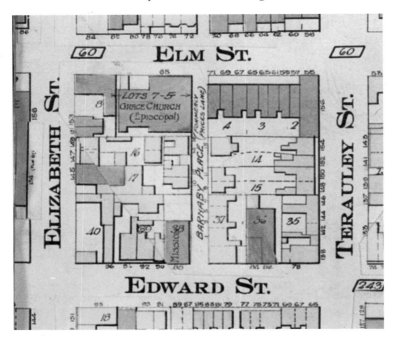

Detail from 1910 Goad's Map, Panel 12. The entire collection can be accessed at goadstoronto.blogspot.ca.

ite plus for a community without any public spaces, but a liability because of the streets' apparent ease for consolidation. While the Goad atlases show only the rights-of-way without the finer definitions of sidewalks and road surfaces, many of the archival photographs depict people in poses within the only public realm that existed – the street.

Another casualty of the haphazard grid of The Ward is the absence of laneways in about three-quarters of the blocks. Laneway infrastructure can provide areas for access, coach houses and manufacturing supports – without them, an incremental development of the cottages of The Ward into, for example, a typical Victorian neighbourhood of brick row-houses was more difficult. The absence of laneways in The

Ward, either through planning indifference or lack of space, initiated an almost organic pattern of sheds, stables and miniature courts in the rear spaces of each lot.

While archival photographs often show these back spaces as clear evidence of 'slum' conditions, one could just as easily imagine these internal courtyards and alleys possessing the qualities of a medieval village, albeit one contained within a late-eighteenth-century grid. Nevertheless, the unstructured blocks made the homes of The Ward an easier target for future amalgamation of blocks at a major scale. The neighbourhood's stability was further eroded by the incremental carving away of The Ward's streets and blocks at its edges – the Eaton's factories off Terauley (Bay), the hospitals on College, City Hall on Queen Street, University Avenue and Yonge Street.

Irrespective of the absence of laneways, public spaces and carefully ordered grids, the Goad's maps still show a compact intensity of modest dwellings that does not automatically suggest 'slums' and the 'underprivileged.' Read with archival photographs, the frame Ward buildings depicted on the Goad's maps reveal a thriving community, with pride of place intact. The Ward filled a vital need for available 'small spaces,' where those not afforded the luxury of one-hundred-acre land grants could begin new lives in Toronto, a requirement still present today.

Today, we generally accept the principle that neighbourhoods that contain mixed incomes and a diversity of uses are good for a city's stability and health. This realization came too late for St. John's Ward, settled almost exclusively by low-income residents well in advance of other neighbourhoods. The early establishment of a population of low-income working-class residents of little influence, perpetuated through private development in lieu of a considered vision of this part of the city, set the stage for the community's eventual, inevitable extinction.

ITALY

Geographical Miles

English Miles 69 to a Degree

Railways shown thus

1 Monteleone di Puglia
2 Modugnese di Bari
3 Pisticci

FROM THE 1880S to the 1930s, the 'commercial centre' of this first Little Italy was Centre Avenue and Elm Street, and fixtures like Glionna's Hotel, just a block north, which historian John Zucchi describes as 'the first saloon for Italian sojourners in Toronto.'

But unlike the waves of Jewish and Chinese settlement in The Ward, the area's Italian population, primarily labourers, ebbed and flowed. 'One travelling emigration inspector from Rome estimated the city's Italian population in 1902 at 4,000, only one-quarter of whom were permanent,' Zucchi observed in *Gathering Places*, a collection of essays about immigration in Toronto. As he noted, census figures showed that in a downtown electoral district that encompassed The Ward, Italian males outnumbered women by almost three to one. The women managed the area's small shops and looked after lodgers. 'Almost every [Italian] household in The Ward ... put up at least one boarder at some point before the First World War.

JOHN LORINC

TORONTO'S FIRST LITTLE ITALY

Left: Labourers from certain villages in Italy often lived together in rooming houses in The Ward.

ELISABETH ST. PLAYGROUND   AUG. 21 1913   NO 70

BRUCE KIDD

THE ELIZABETH STREET PLAYGROUND, REVISITED

ONCE AT A Canada Day dinner party, three distinguished immigrant women spoke about what they most admired about Canada. 'You can go to school free,' said the first. 'You can go to a library and they let you take the books home with you,' said the second. But the answer that elicited the most applause was the third: 'When you go to a beach or swimming pool, they hire someone to see that you don't drown!'

That third defining characteristic of public opportunity in Canada – free, state-funded recreation, with skilled leaders to ensure safety and to provide counselling, instruction and play in sports, dance, arts and crafts – was won in The Ward in Toronto a century ago.

There are uncanny parallels between the circumstances in which playgrounds were established in The Ward in the 1910s and those of today. Then, as now, it was a gilded age, with huge fortunes ostentatiously displayed alongside conditions of abysmal poverty and environmental desecration. Then, as now, the waves of immigration that enabled economic and urban growth elicited a mixture of reactions, from a welcoming, visionary form of humanitarianism to moral panic fuelled by nativism and deep resentment from some quarters that the marginalized and the poor should benefit from tax-supported programs.

As just one expression of progressive reform, the proponents of the early-twentieth-century 'playground movement' were imaginatively committed to child welfare, but also preoccupied by delinquency and disease among slum children, as well as

the children's poor school records. They saw their programs primarily as a way to reduce crime and delinquency.

In an oft-quoted poem, the U.S. public health champion Dennis McCarty advocated:

> Give them a chance for innocent sport, give them a chance for fun;
> Better a playground plot than a court and jail when hard is done;
> Give them a chance – if you stint, tomorrow you will pay
> A larger bill for a darker ill, so give them a chance to play.

Those words could also have served as the manifesto of Toronto's early playground activists. Led by the Toronto Council of Women, the city's playground movement gathered together the efforts of a broad cross-class coalition of reformers concerned about slum and immigrant children. In 1905, after the City of Toronto initiated the public use of schools, including

Previous: Girls playing basketball at Elizabeth Street Playground, August 21, 1913.

Above: Boys playing baseball, August 21, 1913. Hester How Public School is in the background.

schoolyards, the TCW began a 'vacation' school in The Ward, at Hester How School, and hired teachers to serve as supervisors.

Two years later, the Board of Education took over the program, but the reformers – among them journalist-turned-social-activist J. J. Kelso – were soon dissatisfied with the quality of the activities and equipment. So in 1909, they formed a non-governmental organization, the Toronto Playground Association, to show everyone how it could be done. The group first established and operated a purpose-built playground at Adelaide and Brant, just south of The Ward. Then the Trades and Labour Council insisted that playgrounds be publicly operated, and joined ranks with the TPA to persuade the city to assume full financial responsibility.

Between 1910 and the outbreak of the First World War, Toronto invested $1.4 million in playgrounds – a huge sum for a city that watched taxpayer dollars closely. The showcase was the Elizabeth Street Playground in The Ward, on the site of what is now the eastern end of the Hospital for Sick Children. The large asphalt yard, which sat just to the north of Hester How on the west side of Elizabeth Street, contained all sorts of equipment not before seen in a Toronto park – swings, teeter-totters, climbing apparatus, basketball hoops and a baseball diamond.

Yet the project had its detractors, including parochial aldermen who wanted playgrounds in wards inhabited by those 'who have lived here all their lives,' as historian Erica Simmons wrote in *Spacing* (summer 2013): 'Politicians complained loudly about the "outrageous" $164,000 cost of purchasing expropriated properties... Supporters countered by pointing to the social costs of not providing public recreation, asking, "Which are cheaper? Prisons or playgrounds?"'

While the controversies never entirely subsided, Toronto playgrounds for decades provided outstanding opportunities for children to learn sports and play them at increasingly higher levels of ability. The 'Lizzies,' as the teams from Elizabeth Street Playground were known – even after they relocated to Christie Pits – were always a threat. Lizzies captured more than 150 city, provincial and national championships in baseball, basketball, football and hockey. Many of those athletes, including Lionel Conacher, Goody Rosen and Alex Levinsky, made it to the pros.

There's hardly a family in Toronto that hasn't benefited from Toronto's playgrounds in the intervening years, as participants, spectators, lifeguards,

instructors or supervisors. My mother earned her university tuition as a playground leader during the Depression. I made it to the Olympics in the 1960s in part on the basis of the lessons and experiences I gained playing for playground teams. Many Torontonians have similar stories. Municipal parks and recreation is one of the great public goods.

Today's welfare state provides much more protection for the disadvantaged, including poor children, than Canadian society did a century ago. But the idea of public recreation has suffered enormously, with decaying facilities, reduced programs and escalating user fees. None of the NGOs in the vanguard of the 'sport for all' movement call for the expansion of public programs; on the contrary, they fund-raise on the basis of the state's inadequacies. Public programs themselves have shrunk in ambition, especially with respect to competitive sports. The route to the national championships, the Olympics and the pros is now through private clubs, paid coaches and exorbitant user fees – it's a pursuit for rich families.

Clowns at the Elizabeth Street Playground, 1917.

The story of the establishment of the Elizabeth Street Playground in The Ward should remind us of what we have lost in recent decades, and inspire us to put public recreation back on the urban agenda.

ALL TORONTO NEIGHBOURHOODS – rich, middle-class and poor – endured the traumas inflicted by the Great War; the violence in the fields of France and Belgium didn't discriminate. But the poverty of The Ward brought pressures that weren't felt as keenly elsewhere in the city. Young men living in The Ward wanted to show they were patriotic and enlisted, like many other young men across the country, at least in part to leave dead-end jobs. Yet some families simply couldn't do without even those meagre incomes.

SANDRA SHAUL

DIVIDED LOYALTIES

There were, however, other issues that complicated The Ward's war experience.

For example, Central Neighbourhood House (CNH), which provided settlement services to immigrants living in the area, published a magazine called *Ward Graphic*. When the fighting broke out, its editors realized they needed to confront a difficult question dangling over The Ward's Italian and Jewish residents: given the situations of their families and former countrymen, to whom would they be most loyal – King George V, or the Emperor or the Czar?

In the 1916–1917 edition, the opening editorial – 'What Does the Foreigner Mean to You?' – sought to defuse suspicions about divided allegiances and demonstrate that even residents of the poorest part of the city were prepared to make a valuable contribution to Canada's war effort:

Before the war you and I may have had little or no interest in Belgium, in Serbia or Poland, or in any part of Continental Europe for that matter. Now it is different – we know – (you

Left: Italian Canadian reservists preparing for the First World War, ca. 1915.

and I) that the Belgians, the Serbs, the Italians, the Russians and their comrades are closely allied with us in the common struggle for freedom and are even now fighting and dying side by side with our own relatives and friends – for humanity – for us.

The issue included a photo of the wall panel inscribed with the honour roll of those serving in the war, alongside an article stating that sixty-five men from The Ward were serving. (The actual figure for The Ward by the end of the war would have been much higher.) Under the photo there is this appeal: 'The patriotic service of the boys from "The Ward" should find a response in our willingness to sympathetically assist the community they represent.'

CNH officials didn't shy away from reminding Torontonians that some of The Ward's residents suffered greatly because of the war. In 1915, for example, CNH executive director Elizabeth Neufeld wrote about an Italian widow, with eight children, reduced to begging at two missions and a Roman Catholic church.

Yet many Ward residents also took it upon themselves to help out, for example, by assembling boxes of goods to send to the troops. One was the Good Friendship Club, founded by Annie Goldberg, in September 1913, at CNH. In the 1917 edition of *Ward Graphic*, she describes packing boxes of goods for a dozen of the 'house boys' serving overseas.

Meanwhile, suspicion about divided loyalties affected immigrants across the city. At the start of the war, Italy had been allied with the Central Powers. The Italians of The Ward and Little Italy were highly criticized, and many workers were fired from their jobs. With the enforcement of the War Measures Act, passed in 1914, any immigrants who had entered Canada in the fifteen years before the war under the nationality of an enemy nation, such as Austria, Italy or Germany, could be obligated to report monthly to the Registrar for Alien Enemies. Many Ukrainians were classified as 'enemy aliens' and interned in camps across the country, including Exhibition Place in Toronto.

But in 1915, Italy switched sides, joining forces with the Allied nations. Enthusiastically embracing the new allegiance, Canadians raised $60,000 in one day for the Italian Red Cross. Britain agreed to send Italians in the Empire back to Italy to fight if they had been reservists before leaving Italy. In May of that year, the Canadian and Italian governments organized a special train – 'il treno degli italiani' – to travel from Vancouver to Montreal to pick up reservists and

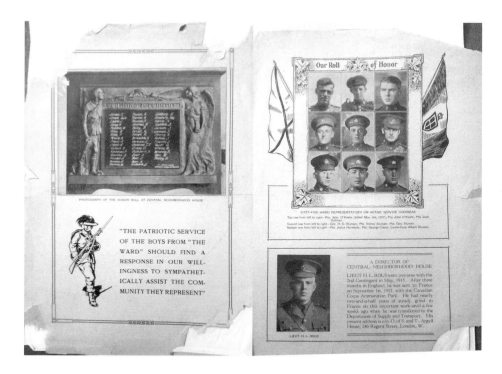

Our Roll of Honor

SIXTY-FIVE WARD REPRESENTATIVES ON ACTIVE SERVICE OVERSEAS
Top row from left to right—Pte. Wm. O'Keefe (killed May 3rd, 1917); Pte. John O'Keefe; Pte. Jack Sullivan.
Second row from left to right—Gnr. H. G. Sluman; Pte. Sidney Sluman; Pte. Geo. Sluman.
Bottom row from left to right—Pte. Julius Havelock; Pte. George Crane; Lance-Corp. Albert Sluman.

PHOTOGRAPH OF THE HONOR ROLL AT CENTRAL NEIGHBORHOOD HOUSE

"THE PATRIOTIC SERVICE OF THE BOYS FROM "THE WARD" SHOULD FIND A RESPONSE IN OUR WILLINGNESS TO SYMPATHETICALLY ASSIST THE COMMUNITY THEY REPRESENT"

A DIRECTOR OF CENTRAL NEIGHBORHOOD HOUSE
LIEUT H. L. ROUS went overseas with the 2nd Contingent in May, 1915. After three months in England, he was sent to France on September 1st, 1915, with the Canadian Corps Ammunition Park. He had nearly two-and-a-half years of steady grind in France on this important work until a few weeks ago when he was transferred to the Department of Supply and Transport. His present address is c/o D. of S. and T., Argyll House, 246 Regent Street, London, W.

LIEUT. H. L. ROUS

volunteers for the Italian army. Central Neighbourhood House posted an honour roll of Italians who served.

Unlike Great Britain and Canada, Italy lacked the funds to pay soldiers. As a result, many large Italian families living in The Ward were left destitute, without breadwinners. Women trying to support their families were so malnourished that they had difficulty performing what little manual labour they could find while still having to care for their children.

Michael Angelo Sansone was among those who served for Canada. In an article in *Ward Graphic*, Sansone explained that he'd been born in Lorenzana, Italy, in 1895 and came to Canada around 1902. At the time he was drafted in June 1918 at the age of twenty-two, he was working as a railway clerk and living with his mother, Carmela, and the rest of his family, at 74 Gerrard Street, just down the block from CNH. He was a breadwinner for the family and at least in the Canadian Expeditionary Force he would be paid.

Spread from 1916–1917 edition of The Ward Graphic, *a magazine published by Central Neighbourhood House. These pages show Ward men who fought in Europe.*

Like the Italian volunteers, many Jews also wished to show their patriotism by enlisting in the British and Canadian armed forces. They were motivated by conflict in two areas: Palestine, where Britain and her Middle Eastern allies were at war with the Ottoman Empire, and in the Pale of Settlement of Eastern Europe.

THE JEWS THE WORLD OVER LOVE LIBERTY
HAVE FOUGHT FOR IT & WILL FIGHT FOR IT.

BRITAIN EXPECTS
EVERY SON OF ISRAEL
TO DO HIS DUTY

ENLIST WITH THE INFANTRY REINFORCEMENTS
FOR OVERSEAS
Under the Command of
Capt. FREEDMAN
Headquarters·
786 ST. LAWRENCE BOULEVARD.
MONTREAL.

Recruitment poster for the Jewish Legion, 1917.

Zionist sympathies lay mainly within the more established upper- and middle-class Jewish communities, but some residents of The Ward also belonged to Zionist organizations. It was through Zionism that support was offered specifically to the British war efforts in Palestine. Men who wished to fight for Palestine joined a special battalion of the British Army called the Jewish Legion. Made up of five British battalions that had originally served on the Gallipoli front as the Mule Corps beginning in 1915–16, the Jewish Legion was officially formed in 1917. Of the 5,000 volunteers who enlisted, 300 came from Canada. After 1919, their cap badges were distinguished by the image of a menorah.

Among those who enlisted in the British Army was Louis Gurofsky. Unlike many of those who lived in The Ward and signed up to fight, he belonged to a family of wealthy leaders in the area, having participated in the establishment of the Shaarei Tzedec synagogue on Centre Avenue at the turn of the century. Joseph, the patriarch, was postmaster for The Ward's local post office and later a manager of an immigrant bank on Terauley (now Bay) Street. Operating out of a store on Queen Street West, Louis was a shipping agent and realtor who also helped immigrants send money back to their families in Russia (though his business was in The Ward, he lived on Markham Street, near College).

Gurofsky's decision to join the war effort in 1918 drew the attention of the *Globe*: 'As the result of his leaving his business,'

the newspaper noted, 'he supported the application of P. J. Cowan, his manager and accountant, for exemption from service before Mr. Justice Riddell's appeal tribunal on Saturday. Cowan is the only remaining man of military age in the Gurofsky offices, and the desire was to leave him to look after the business. Gurofsky stated that his family would not cost the Government anything, and pointed out that the shilling and six pence per day would be his pay.'

When Lord and Lady Allenby visited the city on March 22, 1926, Gurofsky, as sergeant-major, commanded local members of the Jewish Legion in an honour guard at a reception held in front of City Hall. Ironically, only seven years later, Toronto experienced a wave of anti-Semitism that led to violent confrontations in The Beach and Christie Pits.

Despite the attention directed at volunteers such as Sansone and Gurofsky, it would appear that they accounted for only a minority of The Ward's population; most men who went to fight were of British-Celtic origin, many of them tradespeople and typically very young.

One Ward family, the Slumans, sent four brothers off to fight in France. The eldest was George, a tile layer born in 1891. Married and living on Cumberland Street, in Yorkville, he was the first of the four to enlist, on April 12, 1915, at the age of twenty-three. William, born in October 1895 and also a tile layer, signed up five months later, just before his twentieth birthday. Like his two younger siblings, Albert and Sidney, he was still single. All three lived in The Ward, with their parents, Mary and William, at 193 Terauley Street, near Hayter. George, a private, William, a gunner, and Albert, a lance-corporal, would have received a special medal issued to those who volunteered in 1914 and 1915. Sidney, also a private, was wounded in the thigh by shrapnel in May 1917, according to the *Toronto Star*. 'He is 19 years of age, and was rejected three times before he succeeded in enlisting.'

When the fighting ended, in November 1918, a few Ward veterans, like Gurofsky, were able to return to stable businesses or professions. Others found ways to work their way up the economic ladder, securing better-paying jobs and moving out of the neighbourhood. But many of those who did see action between 1914 and 1918 came back to the same grinding poverty and substandard housing that existed in the neighbourhood before the Great War. Like more established Canadians, they had made their sacrifice. But they were still struggling to get by.

JOHN LORINC

CROWDED BY ANY MEASURE

ACCORDING TO DR. Charles Hastings' 1911 report on slum conditions in four impoverished Toronto neighbourhoods, overcrowding in The Ward had begun to reach crisis proportions. He estimated the population density in the area bounded by University, College, Queen and Yonge to be 82 persons per acre, with over 11,000 people living in a 142-acre area. This 1915 info-graphic reveals that the blocks of The Ward, just right of Queen's Park, had the highest densities in the city.

How do The Ward's population densities compare? Some examples from the past and present:

- Mumbai, Central Area (2005) – 182 persons/acre
- Manhattan, 1890s – 143 persons/acre, with some neighbourhoods, such as the Lower East Side, reaching 800
- Paris, late 19th century – 125 persons/acre
- Hong Kong, Central Area (2009) – 89 persons/acre
- Downtown Toronto (2011) – 57 persons/acre
- London, Central Area (2007) – 33 persons/acre
- Suburban Toronto (2011) – 6 persons/acre

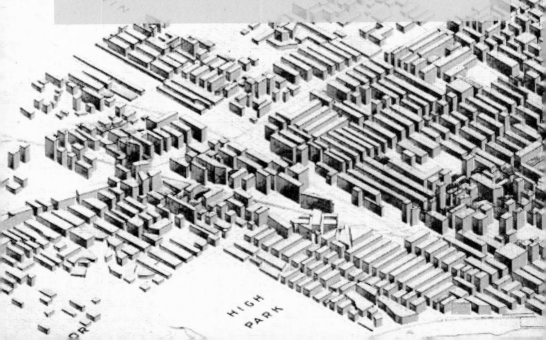

LESLIE

QUEENS PARK

YONGE

QUEEN

*Isometric projection
showing population
density in Toronto.
Civic Transportation
Committee, 1915.*

THE

WARD

LIKE THOUSANDS OF Jews fleeing the threat of pogroms in Eastern Europe, Moses Brody left Galician Poland in the early 1890s and made his way to Toronto. When he arrived, Moses boarded in the home of a family member, Sigmund Brody, at 73 Chestnut Street. It was Sigmund who introduced Moses to junk peddling. By 1896, Moses was lodging at the home of Samuel Greenbaum, another peddler from Galicia, at the rear of 11 Centre Avenue. That same year, he was able to send for his wife, Sara, and their five children, and they lived together at 16 Edward Street. Two years later they had another daughter.

DEENA NATHANSON

A PEDDLER AND HIS CART

THE WARD'S RAG TRADE

Moses continued peddling until 1901, when he had saved enough capital to set up a small grocery store at 109 Elizabeth Street. His eldest son, Harry, however, continued to work as a travelling salesman during the early twentieth century. After losing his spouse in 1902 to heart disease, Moses married his second wife, Hannah, and they had four children together. By 1911, the family resided in a modern, multi-storeyed house on Draper Street, and Moses's occupation was listed as real estate.

Jewish peddlers like Moses Brody arrived in the city virtually penniless, spoke little or no English and needed immediate employment. Between 1890 and 1899, there were over 200 Jewish peddlers in Toronto. Many resided on Centre Avenue and Chestnut and Elizabeth streets. By 1916, the Jewish community had grown, and at least 600 peddlers now lived in the area. The Ward offered peddlers an environment close to important amenities such as synagogues, other communal

Left: Immigrant peddler in The Ward, ca. 1910.

organizations and kosher food, and put them in close proximity to their suppliers.

Peddling was an important occupation in the North American economy around the turn of the twentieth century. The traders played a role later filled by department stores in urban centres and catalogue shopping in rural areas. Patronizing peddlers was more convenient and less expensive than shopping at an established store. In Toronto, peddlers sold produce and dry goods or traded in rags and junk. Some plied their trade in the towns and villages surrounding Toronto, while others worked on the city's streets.

Peddling demanded minimal investment and a strong constitution; it was an ideal entry-level job for a new immigrant. It was also a first step in the business world – many Jewish immigrants used street trading as a threshold occupation from which to launch their careers. It was also one to which they could return when they were between jobs. Toronto peddlers had to pay licensing fees, which, during the 1890s, ranged from $20 to $30 for those using carts and draft animals. Milkmen and meat peddlers were assessed an additional dollar a year. It cost approximately $10 a week to outfit a peddler with dry goods and luxury items. In Toronto, between 1890 and 1899, the total cost of peddling with a horse and cart was roughly $550 per year, about the equivalent of a working man's salary at the time.

Even a small investment could be difficult for a new immigrant to make, so it was common for prospective peddlers to turn to their landsmen, or countrymen, for a loan so they could purchase the first week's supply of goods. Another option was to apply to a merchant or wholesaler who outfitted peddlers. These traders usually advanced their clients merchandise on credit and acted as their bankers. A third funding source for prospective peddlers during the early years was local charities and, later on, charitable organizations established by Toronto's Jewish community, such as the Jewish Free Loan Society, which emerged in 1911.

Jewish Scrap Collector Questioned by a Toronto Police Officer, *William Kurelek, 1975.*

The most important source of investment capital available to new immigrant peddlers was relatives who had preceded them to Toronto. Family members provided immigrants with contacts among wholesalers and often acted as outfitters themselves. It was fairly common for new immigrants to become the assistant peddlers to their relatives who had already established themselves in the trade. Few peddlers began their careers without the help of other members of the immigrant Jewish community in Toronto.

The trajectory of a peddler's career depended on the connections he made. Along with his family ties, the strength of the networks he built were key to achieving socio-economic success. Membership in voluntary organizations played a significant role in the social and business lives of immigrants. Mutual benefit societies – *landsmanschaften* – and synagogues, organized by and comprised of members from the same European town or region, provided immigrants with a sense of security and familiarity. It was also common for landsmen to help one another in their careers. For instance, in

Toronto, Polish Jews, who comprised the largest portion of the Jewish community, established *landsmanschaften* based on their members' hometowns in Poland. Other voluntary organizations were also established on the basis of regional or national groupings.

It was common for peddlers to have memberships in several organizations. This was especially true of the Galician peddlers who joined the congregation at Goel Tzedec, the elegant synagogue on University Avenue. Though it was originally established as a Lithuanian organization, Goel Tzedec became the synagogue of the new elite among Toronto's Eastern European Jewish community. Some of the peddlers joined this synagogue specifically for networking purposes, as well as to benefit from the status associated with being a member.

In turn-of-the-twentieth-century Toronto, peddling was hard and sometimes dangerous work. Established storekeepers were often opposed to peddlers selling similar goods to their customers at lower prices. Police blotters are filled with complaints by storekeepers about peddlers setting up shop outside their stores. The police usually responded by telling peddlers to move along, though they were sometimes arrested and fined. Other types of charges lodged against peddlers included peddling without a licence, obstructing the street, having an insecurely hitched horse and, for those who worked on Sunday, breaking the Lord's Day Act. The offenders were typically given a choice of paying fines ranging from $1 to $5 or spending ten to thirty days in jail. Peddlers usually paid the fine and viewed it as part of the price of conducting this type of business in Toronto.

Jewish peddlers also suffered the consequences of anti-Semitism. They were harassed and occasionally beaten for being both Jewish and nuisances. An article published in the *Daily Star* on July 26, 1907, addressed this concern, stating that many peddlers were confronted with profanity and ill treatment from the public while working. During this period, a group of Jewish peddlers opted to band together to form the Hebrew Peddlers' Protective Association. They appealed to the citizens of Toronto and asked that they provide their names to the authorities as well as those of the victims when they witnessed assaults. Their intent was to gather as much evidence as possible in order to prosecute these cases. Although the HPPA was established in response to immediate needs, its members were concerned with their own social mobility.

As small businessmen, the original members left the group as soon as they had amassed enough capital to abandon peddling.

The ambivalence of its members toward the HPPA speaks to the entrepreneurial spirit of the Jewish peddlers who began their careers in St. John's Ward. They preferred not to support associations based on trade and ideology, but were willing to join other groupings based on family, region and socio-economic mobility. In this way, the peddlers established a wide variety of networks and connections that bolstered their success in Toronto.

Most of the immigrants who began their careers in Toronto as peddlers achieved some degree of upward mobility. Some, of course, were more successful than others. Many were natural entrepreneurs, who abandoned peddling and went on to establish companies in fields like salvage or manufacturing. Among their ranks were Harry Winberg and Henry Greisman. Winberg relied on peddling to make a living after he came to Toronto, and ended up becoming a significant property owner and even mayoral candidate in 1915. Greisman, in turn, was a Russian Jew who immigrated to Toronto in 1888. He lived in The Ward and toiled as a peddler during the late nineteenth century. He quickly achieved success, and by 1897, Greisman owned all of the properties between 45 and 57 Chestnut Street, and later expanded his empire to include two significant structures in the new garment district, along with several apartment buildings. He also ran the King Suspender Company. By the time of his death in 1938, he was living in a stately Victorian Annex home and was one of the most prominent and successful businessmen in the city.

Yet many peddlers didn't attain that kind of economic success. They ran shops or tiny businesses, even as they continued to peddle to the end of their working lives. Still others spent the bulk of their careers as travelling salesmen, working for specific firms and assured of a product and a market in which to sell it. But when their businesses failed or unemployment loomed, they returned to peddling as an occupation they could fall back on during hard times.

View from the Toronto
General Hospital
(1931), Doris McCarthy.

RICHARD DENNIS

TORONTO'S ORIGINAL TENEMENT

WINEBERG APARTMENTS

HARRY WINEBERG (LATER Winberg) came to Toronto as a ten-year-old in the late nineteenth century, having migrated 'friendless and without a penny' from his home in Kovno (now Kaunas, Lithuania, but then in the Russian Empire), via Hamburg and New York. Upon arrival, he moved in with a married sister living on Queen Street and took to peddling goods on the street. By age twenty-four, he'd gained enough experience and capital to rent a jeweller's counter inside Morris Bachrack's department store at Yonge and Albert. From 1904 to 1913, he lived in homes on Cameron, Baldwin and Beverley, and eventually married Bachrack's daughter Frances.

Wineberg also established a reputation beyond his business activities. He lobbied for protections for the members of an association of Jewish peddlers, published a Jewish newspaper and even mounted a long-shot bid for mayor in 1915. Historian Stephen Speisman has carefully described him as 'a man of varied ambitions' and a 'multiplicity of interests.'

Yet Wineberg's most enduring legacy still stands at the northeast corner of Elizabeth Street and Dundas – the elegant three-storey apartment he developed and built in 1907.

It was a speculative and controversial venture. According to a lengthy editorial in *Canadian Architect and Builder*, the development industry's mouthpiece, apartments undermined family life. But in November 1907, *Construction*, a new architectural magazine, published a major feature about the 'sociological and economic advantages of the apartment house.'

FRONT ELEVATION, WINEBERG APARTMENTS, IN THE "WARD," TORONTO. A NOTEWORTHY DESIGN OF MODERATE PRICED APARTMENTS. A STYLE OF BUILDING MOST NEEDED IN THE CONGESTED DISTRICTS OF OUR LARGER CITIES. A GOOD EXAMPLE OF A PLAIN, SIMPLE, ECONOMICAL STRUCTURE IN WHICH THE DESIGNER HAS ACCOMPLISHED HIS PURPOSE WITHOUT THE USELESS EXPENDITURE OF MONEY ON UNNECESSARY ORNAMENTATION. FRED HERBERT, ARCHITECT.

Construction's editors were eager to distance themselves from the architectural establishment. They championed such housing, citing examples of luxury and middle-class buildings such as the Traders Bank Apartments at Yonge and Bloor (rents ran from $40 to $100 per month), the understated modernist Wardlow Apartments in Winnipeg ($85 monthly) and the Madison in the Annex, which offered six-room apartments, including a servant's bedroom, for $75 a month. *Construction* also highlighted 'a large three-storey apartment building, which has been erected on unique lines and an entirely original plan from anything hitherto conceived,' situated in The Ward.

Sketch of exterior of Wineberg Apartment Building, by Architect Fred Herbert, 1907.

The Wineberg Apartments, which Harry had promoted, shared the same E-shape as the Madison, with rooms opening off long corridors running the depth of the building and light shafts extending between the parallel ranges of rooms for more than half the building's depth. But the Wineberg's light shafts were much narrower – little more than slits – and there were two apartments on each corridor, compared to only one in the Madison. Moreover, some rooms near the front of the building depended on 'borrowed light' (with windows onto adjacent rooms), little better than can still be seen today in New York's Tenement House Museum. In total there were twenty-eight four-room apartments, twelve on each of the upper floors and four situated in the rear of eleven shops that fronted the two streets.

The novelty really lay in the management strategy, which claimed to subsidize and minimize the rents paid by residential tenants by charging commercial rents to shopkeepers. The latter were to pay $25 to $30 a month, with rents of $18 to $25 for each apartment. This was slightly higher than the average rents in The Ward, which ranged from $10 to $20 a month.

The building permit estimated construction outlay at $75,000 (more than double the cost of the Madison). The 1910 assessment valued the land on which the apartments were situated at $13,067 and the building at $48,000, not out of line with the permit value. The roll listed the owners as not only Harry Wineberg but also his wife, Frances, and Morris Bachrack.

Wineberg's architect, F. H. Herbert, was a prolific designer of middle-class homes in Toronto. Four appeared in illustrations in the *Canadian Architect and Builder*, and *Construction* carried an illustrated article featuring several of his dwellings in 1910. *Construction* praised the Wineberg as 'a good example of a plain, simple, economical structure ... without the useless expenditure of money on unnecessary ornamentation.' As the editors speculated, 'a few buildings of this character would soon effect a solution of "the Ward" problem in Toronto' – a reference to the area's infamously degraded and overcrowded housing stock.

The Wineberg had no trouble attracting tenants. According to a 1914 assessment roll, the building had eight street-level stores, including a billiard hall, dry-goods store, confectioner, barber, fishmonger, milliner, delicatessen and a jeweller – a village in the heart of the city. Two of the shopkeepers lived in flats in the building, and all but one of the eighteen residential tenants were Jewish.

In 1911, most of the Wineberg's residents lived in family groups. More than 90 per cent were Jewish, with two-thirds born in Russia or Eastern Europe. Many of the immigrant tenants had arrived in Canada since 1906. But unlike many Ward residences, the Wineberg wasn't a lodging house. More than a third of occupants were children fourteen and under. While there were more men than women, reflecting the presence of twenty-eight predominantly male lodgers, only one flat could be described as a rooming house in miniature. Few of the women were in paid employment. Of the adult lodgers and household heads, most were tailors, pressers, cap makers and cloak makers. In other words, they were exactly the tenants for whom the building had been intended.

Following Wineberg's 'unloading' of the building around this time, it passed rapidly through a succession of owners, nearly all Jews living near The Ward.

The only non-Jewish and non-Torontonian owners were Mary and John Dooley and Walter E. Buckingham of Guelph, who acquired ownership in 1912. Buckingham was a lawyer and active in a variety of 'good works,' including the founding of the Guelph YMCA. But by 1915, the building was back in local Russian or Polish Jewish ownership.

Toward the end of the war, the composition of the Wineberg's occupants soon began to change. By 1918, more than half of the flats were occupied by unnamed 'Chinese.' The 1921 census reveals an extension of this trend. Fewer than 11 per cent of residents were women, and less than a quarter were children. The only nuclear families included two Jewish shopkeepers who still lived on the premises, a Welsh caretaker, a newly arrived Chinese Methodist minister and his family, and two mixed-race Chinese-English households: a Chinese Presbyterian and his English Anglican wife and kids, along with a B.C.-born Chinese husband with his French Catholic wife and family. The remainder were all single Chinese men. Most had migrated at least ten years earlier, implying previous addresses, presumably else-where in The Ward. Nearly all were employed in catering – mostly in restaurants, but also including a hospital cook and two 'private' or 'family' cooks – or in laundries. In total, 75 per cent of residents were now Chinese. Rents in 1921 ranged between $35 and $50, double Wineberg's expressed intentions, although not out of line with inflation in the intervening war years.

Despite *Construction*'s representation of the building as an almost philan-thropic improvement to The Ward, Wineberg's own interest did not last long. Following his short-lived career as a developer-cum-housing reformer, he bought the *Hebrew Journal*, moved to a lakefront home at Kew Beach and continued to pursue a political career, running again for mayor (in 1925) and, at least six times, always unsuccessfully, as an alderman for Ward 3, which included 'The Ward,' and Ward 4, Kensington Market.

In microcosm, the history of the Wineberg Apartments foreshadows the twentieth-century history of The Ward: promoted as a progressive form of private-sector housing reform that provided sanitary and economical accom-modations for blue-collar Jewish immigrant families, it quickly transformed into a Chinese lodging house. Unlike so many others in that part of Toronto, however, the building is a survivor. More than a century later, the Wineberg currently hosts renovated one- and two-bedroom apartments, convenience and discount stores, and Japanese, Korean and Taiwanese cafés.

Five Chinese children attending a picnic at the Toronto Exhibition, June 18, 1926.

BRIAN BANKS

AN UNTIMELY
DEATH

IT WAS LATE afternoon on October 2, 1907, when Delia Hazelton, a forty-two-year-old seamstress and charwoman, finished her day's work at a home on Roxborough Avenue in Rosedale. A widow for thirteen years who had originally immigrated to Canada from Ireland in her late teens, Delia lived with her children, Mary, twenty-one, and Robert, thirteen, in a boarding house on King Street near Yonge.

She headed home, walking south. When she got to Bloor and Yonge streets, Delia crossed Bloor first, then turned east across Yonge. The intersection was noisy with the clatter of horses, wagons, streetcars, pedestrians, traffic cops and the occasional automobile. Before she reached the far corner, a car coming north, driven by businessman Frank Mutton, hit her. Delia died instantly when, according to an account in the next day's *Toronto Telegram*, the front wheel of Mutton's 'very heavy' car 'passed over her neck.' This tragic ending not only left her two children alone, but it also immortalized her as one of Toronto's first auto-pedestrian fatalities.

Delia Hazelton was one of the many thousands of men and women of her era who lived in and around The Ward, each day leaving their crowded, rundown quarters for mean, low-paying jobs in all corners of the growing city. As it happens, Delia was also my great-grandmother, and her daughter, Mary, my mother's mom.

My brother Kerry unearthed the details of Delia's untimely death a few years ago. But it was only after some recent genealogical research that I came to realize how closely her life story, and that of two generations of my family on my mother's side,

is bound to the history of The Ward. In fact, after knowing The Ward only through archival photographs, I was surprised to learn that my brother and I – products of a middle-class, post-war, Scarborough upbringing – are only one generation removed from this dense, working-class slum.

Our mother, Elizabeth, was the eleventh of twelve children born to John and Mary Colestock (née Hazelton). Two of her four grandparents arrived in The Ward in the 1880s, and both sets of families, moving often, continued to live in the area as the second generation came of age post-1900. By the late 1910s and early 1920s, they were somewhat settled on Edward Street east and west of Terauley, parts of which were later cleared to make space for a bus station.

In that period, The Ward was a gateway for many immigrant groups. With my mother's family, both Delia and her husband, Benjamin, had emigrated separately from Ireland. Her other grandparents, Annie (Reel) Colestock and husband Robert, were from rural Ontario and England, respectively. Annie was born near Palgrave, in 1855, to Irish immigrant parents. Robert Colestock arrived in Canada in 1869 with the early flights of English 'home children'; he landed in Quebec City, age sixteen or seventeen, on the passenger steamship *Cleopatra*, along with nineteen other teen 'labourers.' Within a few years, he became a soldier, then a baker, the job he'd have all his life. He and Annie married in Toronto in 1876. Their eldest son, John, my mother's father, was born in 1877, when the couple was living in Corktown.

Toward the turn of the century, Delia and her two children drifted into The Ward after Benjamin died, living on Chestnut Street and Centre Avenue. The Colestocks, meanwhile, moved all over town with their five children, and even to Oshawa for a while, before returning to The Ward in 1903, stopping first on Hayter Street.

AUTO DRIVER IS EXONERATED

By Verdict of Coroner's Jury in the Case of Mrs. Delia Hazelton.

CONFUSED BY THE TRAFFIC

Story of the Policeman and Others Who Saw Accident, as Told at the Inquest.

"The deceased, Mrs. Delia Hazelton, came to her death on October 2, from injuries received from being struck by an automobile driven by Frank E. Mutton, and we exonerate Mr. Mutton from all blame."

The above verdict was returned by the jury which sat under Coroner R. J. Wilson in the Police Court last night. A rider was attached by which the jury recommended that all street traffic be placed in the hands of the police.

All the witnesses except one agreed that the car was going no faster than a walk when it struck Mrs. Hazelton. It was evident from the testimony given by Policeman Hobbs who was on duty at the corner of Yonge and Bloor streets, that the woman had been confused by the traffic.

Toronto Daily Star, *October 11, 1907*

It was sometime after this when my mother's parents met. Even though both their families relocated once or twice, they remained within The Ward, a few blocks from each other, making it easy to cross paths.

John was a teamster; Mary, a laundress. And that's the work they were doing in 1907, when Frank Mutton killed Delia with his car. A coroner's jury convened a week later, on October 10, and exonerated Mutton. It concluded Delia was confused by a police officer and a street railway road master both directing traffic, and that she had stepped in front of the car trying to avoid a streetcar. The jury recommended putting control of all traffic 'in the hands of the police.' (Mutton, for his part, later went on to become president of the Ontario Auto League.)

Curiously, records show that just two days after the inquest, Mary wed John Colestock. Had the marriage been planned earlier – a joyful event marred by Delia's death – or was it a hasty decision, born of Mary's suddenly difficult circumstances and intended to salve her grief? A few names and dates in the archives don't tell the whole story. What we do know is that Mary moved in with John's family. But we've yet to learn definitively what became of her younger brother, Robert.

By this point, John and Mary, and the rest of the Colestock family, were walking the same lanes and living the same sorts of lives as the figures in Arthur Goss's Ward photographs. Again, the archival record only hints at their struggle. In 1908, they lived on Chestnut Place, where expropriation for the new Toronto General Hospital began in 1909. In 1910, John's only sister died 'in confinement' (during/after childbirth). The following year, the census shows, three generations of Colestocks – the elder parents, four adults and Mary and John's first two infant children – were crammed into a shabby hovel at 9 Barnaby Place (previously known as Price's Lane). The records also reveal how The Ward's social and cultural life had evolved. Of the fifty names on the census page for Barnaby Place, thirty-eight were Jews of Russian or Austrian origin.

As John and Mary had more children, they moved out on their own. After the mid-1910s, they lived either on Edward or Terauley. John's three brothers were just doors away; two remained with their mother, each serving a stint in the Canadian Forces in 1917 and 1918.

John and Mary now moved less frequently and life appeared more stable economically, yet other records reveal a different sort of struggle. Of the seven

children Mary delivered between 1913 and 1921, six died, at ages ranging from a few weeks to six years. Their three youngest daughters, born in the more prosperous 1920s, all did fine.

The Colestocks gradually left The Ward as the area itself transformed, but upward mobility remained elusive throughout the Depression. During and after the Second World War, however, a recovering economy brought secure jobs in downtown warehouses and factories. By the mid-1940s, in fact, John and Mary, with my mother and her younger sisters, had moved to a brick semi-detached house on Niagara Street.

My grandparents lived their final years with my mother's next oldest sister, first there, and later in Scarborough, where several descendant Colestock families – our family – put down roots in the 1950s. The catalyst for that final move was the relocation of the Canada Foils factory, where my mother and father first met, from cramped quarters downtown to the modern spaciousness of the Golden Mile. After a century of migrant-family travails, shaped by the tides of global history, urban life and fate, it was my generation's turn to write the next chapter.

Credit for the initial inspiration and much of the archival research goes to my brother, Kerry Banks. At time of writing, our mother, Elizabeth Banks, lives in Scarborough. Her younger sister, Bernice, also lives in the GTA.

EVERY MORNING AT 6 a.m., brothers William and David Wolfish would leave their home at 142 Elizabeth Street, purchase newspapers and sell them to pedestrians on their way to work. The boys, aged fourteen and ten respectively in 1914, hawked papers before school to help support their family of eight. Their father, Samuel, ran a fledgling dry-goods store and rented space to two lodgers. But those income sources weren't sufficient, so his two eldest sons had to pitch in.

ELLEN SCHEINBERG

PAPER PUSHERS

Around the turn of the century, many working-class families required older children to take jobs to supplement the main breadwinner's meagre income. According to historian Michael Piva, a family with an adult male and older son who worked could earn approximately $1,600 a year and achieve 'a standard of living somewhere between abject poverty and health and decency.'

The school laws of Ontario, introduced in the early 1890s, required that children fourteen and under attend school full-time, but many poor families had to disregard the rules. According to the 1911 census, Ward children worked as cigar strippers, milliners, operators, storekeepers, errand boys, machinists, printers, messengers, labourers, apprentices, carpenters, servants and newsboys. Older Ward teens were commonly found working as factory operators, but many of the kids got their start in the street trades.

The streets afforded younger children an escape from overcrowded homes. 'The street was the ideal workplace,' notes American historian David Nasaw, author of *Children of the City*. 'It was outdoors, alive with activity, and away

Left: Sleeping newsboy, 1930s.

Wolfish family in front of their store on Elizabeth Street, 1913.

from the prying eyes of teachers and parents.' Many working-class boys, particularly the younger ones, had street jobs, such as polishing shoes, selling pencils or fruit, delivering messages or hawking newspapers – the most visible of all the street trades.

These boys, who had to be at least eight years old, were required to secure a city licence signed by a parent or guardian, and had to promise to attend school for at least two hours each day.

During the late 1910s, there were approximately 600 'newsies' in Toronto. They were from different backgrounds, and many of them, including the most influential newsies, were Jewish residents from The Ward. Sam Lichtman, known as the 'King of the Newsies,' arrived alone in Toronto in 1902 at the age of fourteen. Within several years, he built one of the city's largest newsstands, at the corner of King and Yonge. During his career as a newsie and agent, Lichtman mentored dozens of younger boys, became the first president of the Toronto Newsboys' Union and eventually launched the Lichtman's chain of newsstands. By 1913, at age twenty-five, he was worth $50,000 and retired from the business.

This was a booming trade for boys because Toronto, at the time, had six daily newspapers, with several publishing multiple editions each day. With no home delivery, consumers purchased their papers from street vendors working on street corners, railroad stations and the ferry dock. The older boys often sold morning and evening editions for several papers. In an interview for the Multicultural History Society of Ontario, Max Geller recalled selling the *World*, *Globe*, *Telegram*, *Mail and Empire* and *Toronto Star* on weekdays at Adelaide Street and University. On weekends, the thirteen-year-old would hawk the *Star Weekly* and *Toronto Sunday World*.

The youngest boys tended to sell only one newspaper – the evening and weekend *Telegram*. They would get out of school at 3:30, pick up their bundle of papers and sell them until around 7 p.m. The downtown at dinner hour, observed contemporary journalist C. S. Clark, was full of 'little shavers, yelling "six o'clock *Telegram*."' The newsies often worked weekends, toiling until midnight on Saturdays to sell the *Sunday World* – which couldn't be sold on Sundays due to the Lord's Day Act.

Sam Lichtman posing with some of his protégés, ca 1910.

The boys paid about one cent a paper and sold them for twice that amount, occasionally generating extra profits if the customer was wealthy, didn't have change or offered a tip. Since the boys couldn't return unsold papers, they had to calculate how many they were likely to sell before purchasing them.

These miniature entrepreneurs, however, didn't just sell papers. Before television and radio, newsies would shout out the day's top stories. In addition to informing the public about local and world events, this approach was one of the main sales tactics they employed to push their product. Because most

were independent agents who grappled with significant competition on the street, it was a job that required considerable business acumen, ingenuity and creativity. Some relied on other talents to bolster their income. For instance, two Ward boys, George White and Luigi Romanelli, would 'clog and buck-dance at the corner at his [White's] stand at King and Bay Streets' for tips. White later moved to New York City and performed in vaudeville productions while Romanelli grew up to become an internationally acclaimed conductor.

While the newsies mostly got on well with newspaper publishers, in April 1908 a move by the *Sunday World* to raise its wholesale prices and undercut the newsboys' profits prompted a protest. A newsie strike commenced when thirty to forty boys tried to block cars carrying bundles of papers for the *Sunday World*. Other local youngsters joined in. The boys overturned streetcars and wagons with bundles, scattering papers all over the street. Police were called in, and thirteen newsies were arrested. All but one were released to their parents. Soon after, the newsies formed a union, headed by Sam Lichtman, and built a clubhouse at 20 Pembroke Street.

Due to the number of children selling newspapers, the Elizabeth Street School set up a newsboy class under the supervision of teacher Mrs. J. M. Warburton. She helped them enhance their English and also taught them about business conduct and other useful skills, such as calculating correct change. The boys were extremely devoted to her, and she in turn found them extremely bright and industrious. They were, she said, 'as keen a group of boys in trade as can be found easily anywhere.' The main goal, however, was keeping the boys in school and off the streets. Central Neighbourhood House also provided the newsboys their own club space, as well as access to billiard tables.

The newsboys' union had a social component. In August 1914, president Harry Roher organized a picnic on the Toronto Island, an event that drew over 550 boys. A decade later, the union arranged a boxing competition, with bouts by local fighters and several newsies, some so small they qualified for the sixty-pound weight class.

Beyond the cost of their union dues and other small expenses, the news-boys were expected to hand over their earnings to their parents, although C. S. Clark pointed out that the older boys often spent the money on tobacco, drinking and theatres. Some reformers feared that newsies were exposed to physical and moral danger – one ten-year-old died after being struck by a

streetcar. Others, reformers said, imperilled their spiritual well-being by reading dime-store novels, smoking and going to the theatre. These activities inevitably led to 'idleness, theft and vicious habits.'

Indeed, the founder of Toronto's Children's Aid Society, J. J. Kelso, wanted to eliminate newspaper selling and keep children in school full-time. Kelso essentially dismissed the job as a 'pretense for idling on the streets, evading school and the learning of some useful trade or industry.'

Kelso and other reformers pushed legislation aimed at regulating child labour and keeping youngsters in school. Further, truancy officers were relied on to locate children, bring them to juvenile court, make house visits and keep tabs on offenders.

Authorities succeeded in targeting a number of newsies. Police brought nine-year-old Jacob Geller, Max's younger brother, to a CAS shelter after he was caught smoking and begging while selling newspapers. The police warned his parents they would be brought before the magistrate for neglected children if Jacob continued this behaviour. Others were hauled into juvenile court for truancy, theft and gambling. Civic authorities and reformers accused their parents of shirking their responsibilities. As a *Saturday Night* writer commented, '[P]arents will bring the child into the world, the police magistrate will do the rest.'

What reformers like Kelso failed to understand was that newsies had no choice but to help their parents make ends meet. They also derived benefits that served them well later on. For some, hawking papers was a short-term trade they later abandoned for a higher-paying factory or shop job. For others, the job provided entrepreneurial skills or the funds needed to return to school and pursue a career in business or as a professional. When they looked back, later in life, former newsies didn't feel as if they had been endangered or exploited. Conversely, many were very nostalgic about their experiences hawking papers, regarding those first forays into the world of work with a sense of purpose, pride and camaraderie.

142 Agnes Street, 1913.
Health Department
series on slum conditions.

I**N DECEMBER 1918,** just weeks after the armistice that ended the Great War, the Bureau of Municipal Research (BMR), a non-profit advocacy group, released a hard-hitting report on slumlike living conditions in The Ward. Entitled 'What Is "The Ward" Going to Do with Toronto?,' the seventy-four-page research document was both a warning and a call to action. Among the key findings:

**LAURIE
MONSEBRAATEN**

THE BMR'S WAKE-UP CALL

- Immigrant families were doubling up in crumbling rental housing because they couldn't afford to live anywhere else.
- Low-income children lacked safe places to play.
- Public schools should be open for community use after school hours.
- The lack of public transit in the city's outlying areas, where housing was more affordable but jobs were scarce, forced residents to live in The Ward's slum housing.
- Any new housing developments should include adequate municipal services and employment opportunities for residents.

The BMR was a progressive-era think-tank formed by civic-minded businessmen in 1914 to bring evidence-based policy-making and fiscal rigour to a rapidly expanding twentieth-century city. Under the directorship of Horace L. Brittain, the group released numerous studies and pamphlets on taxes, education and social conditions.

On the subject of The Ward, the BMR's analysts didn't mince words. In their letter of transferral, the authors warned that deplorable living conditions concentrated in the area were 'boiling over' and threatened to 'spring up sporadically' in other

parts of the city if municipal leaders didn't 'discover and eliminate or control the forces which produced it.'

After it was released, the report drew media attention for its call for more innovative use of the municipal property tax system to dampen land speculation in The Ward and encourage landlords to maintain their properties. But the authors also noted the report's recommendation to establish a planning commission to educate the public and advise local government on how to build more desirable living and working conditions in every part of the city.

At the turn of the century, The Ward was home to 10,527 people, mostly Italians, Jewish immigrants from Eastern Europe and 'a small sprinkling of Polish, Chinese, Negro and other foreign peoples, with a few English born,' the report noted.

There was no official data on household economic conditions, so the authors relied on 'family histories' written by social workers. These accounts revealed that a large number of area residents eked out a living 'by labour of the most unskilled variety or by peddling, rag-picking, second-hand and bottle dealing and other seasonal occupations.' Most adults had little formal education, and many children worked as messengers, hawked newspapers or toiled in factories to supplement their family's income.

Dr. Charles Hastings, Medical Officer of Health, in his office, January 13, 1925.

The perennial problem of inadequate settlement services for immigrants was highlighted even then: 'Insufficient care is taken with the immigrants on their arrival in this country to instruct them in the ways and methods of living here,' the report said. Of the Toronto Board of Education's ten adult night schools, average attendance at Hester How School, in The Ward, was almost four times higher than schools in other parts of the city, suggesting demand for these classes among

immigrants was high. In an observation that could be made today, the BMR warned, 'Each community suffers politically, socially and financially ... by neglecting its immigrants instead of making valuable assets of them.'

Just as the health of residents in low-income communities suffers today, the BMR study also concluded that there was 'a considerable amount of sickness' in The Ward in 1916. Even though the area made up just 2 per cent of the city's population, the overall cost of 'hospital orders' for Ward residents that year was $16,187.20, or 4 per cent of the city's total. And while The Ward's mortality rate was 10 per cent compared to the overall city rate of 12 per cent, the discrepancy was likely due to the area's high immigrant population, which tended to include fewer seniors and children, the report suggested. Among the 110 deaths in The Ward that year, twenty were from pneumonia, ten from paralysis and ten were children under two who died of enteritis. Of the various other causes of death, seven involved violence and six were from malnutrition.

Lastly, the BMR took aim at the area's crowded, degraded housing conditions. The Ward was a high-density neighbourhood with 60 per cent of the area occupied by buildings. By contrast, buildings in similar downtown residential neighbourhoods, such as the one bounded by Church, Sherbourne, Bloor and Carlton, took up just 40 per cent of available land.

About 60 per cent of the residential buildings were neglected and deemed 'combustible,' compared with just 22 per cent elsewhere. 'In many places windows are boarded up keeping out cold, wind and rain and also all light and air,' the authors note. In some houses, plaster was crumbling and there was no paint or whitewash on the walls. Partly collapsed fences, broken doorsteps, shutters sagging from their hinges and vermin infestation were rampant. Public health officials had recorded 'sanitary defects' in about half of The Ward's 1,656 buildings, mostly stemming from 'filthy conditions.'

Instead of lawns and gardens, the yards were 'cluttered with a confused collection of sheds and other framed buildings making a most depressing outlook for residents and depriving the children of any home playgrounds ... Unused personal and household effects lie about in front of stores and buildings. Boxes and furniture of all sorts are piled about without being placed on the street line.' Unpaved rear laneways and side streets were reportedly in 'disgraceful condition with children playing about in the dirt and disorder of the roadway.' To drive home the point, the report included many photos of cottages built behind houses.

With the expansion of institutional buildings, such as the Toronto General Hospital and the Hospital for Sick Children, as well as rampant real estate speculation that was driving up property values, landlords had little incentive to maintain their buildings.

The parallels to contemporary Toronto are striking. Just like today, many immigrant residents either didn't know they had a right to ask their landlord for repairs or didn't ask for fear of being evicted. And residential overcrowding remains common in the city's high-density inner suburbs, according to a 2014 University of Toronto report.

There are other echoes, such as the BMR's recommendation that school buildings be used as community centres 'for the socializing of all elements of the population.' Generations later, Toronto's SPACE Coalition has been advocating for more community use of schools since the Mike Harris government in the late 1990s changed the school funding formula. Another BMR recommendation – for 'suburban garden cities with rapid transportation' – is still relevant to the contemporary debate over the importance of connecting Toronto's suburbs with downtown employment areas. Interestingly, the report notes that 'a wage-earner should not spend more than one-fifth of his income on shelter.' Today the rent ceiling for residents in rent-geared-to-income housing is 30 per cent of their income.

But yesterday, as today, civic advocacy groups stopped short of recommending specific solutions. In 1918, the BMR authors insisted their purpose was to 'stimulate thought and inquiry as a basis for a community solution.' In 2011, the United Way Toronto released its 'Vertical Poverty' report, which documented the growth of low-income, immigrant communities living in crumbling highrise apartment towers; that report didn't prescribe solutions, either. In both cases, these advocacy organizations hoped that public awareness would propel municipal officials to craft new policies to tackle the problems.

In the case of The Ward, reform did come, eventually. In 1934, sixteen years after that alarming BMR study, Ontario's Lieutenant Governor Herbert Bruce led a Royal Commission that bluntly recommended the demolition of Toronto's worst slum districts. In the aftermath of the Second World War, city council finally took up his advice, bulldozing Cabbagetown to make way for Regent Park and demolishing much of The Ward, by then home to Toronto's original Chinatown, to make way for a civic square.

CHARLES J. HASTINGS

REAR HOUSES
AN EXCERPT FROM THE REPORT OF THE MEDICAL HEALTH OFFICER

SHORTLY AFTER HIS *appointment as Toronto's medical offi-cer of health, Dr. Charles J. Hastings went public with a report intended as a wake-up call. The language, as this excerpt shows, was inflammatory.*

This is a rear tenement under the morning shadow of the City Hall, occupied by six 'families.' There are six dark rooms in it. To the right is a 'Sanitary Convenience,' intended to be used by all the inhabitants of the row, except those in the third house. At the door of the third house may be seen the outside entrance to a closet in the cellar used not only by the people of that house, but by the workers in the 'factory' which occupies the top flat of all these four houses.

In the foreground is a muddy, dirty, unpaved yard and lane.

The tap with the pail under it is the sole water supply for all the houses, and the tenement house, and the workers in the factory – 40 persons in all. That tap is sometimes frozen in the winter.

These are rear-houses. They cannot be seen from the street.

The rent paid for these houses is high.

Finally, on the day the photograph was taken, the owner had for some unknown reason cut off the use of the sole

sanitary convenience for 30 people, by nailing it up as shown in the picture.

The bare branches of the tree shown to the extreme right mark the place where stands an outdoor privy of another type, the condemned and out-of-date privy-pit. That closet belongs to a house on the front street rented for $10 a month. One of the best-known real estate firms in Toronto collects the rent. The house is unfit for habitation. The outside privy has been for some time overflowing. Its disgraceful state may be seen from the open street across a vacant lot. Into that vacant lot the husband of the poor woman who still struggles to keep that house decent casts, under cover of night, the 'night soil.' The same thing is done from seven other dwellings of which we have reports.

In other words, what we have read of with disgust as having happened in the cities of Europe in the Middle Ages, happens in Toronto now before our very eyes.'

From Report of the Medical Health Officer Dealing with the Recent Investigation of Slum Conditions in Toronto, *Medical Health Officer, July 5, 1911.*

THELMA WHEATLEY

DR. CLARKE'S CLINIC

THE WARD CLINIC, Canada's first psychiatric outpatient facility, opened in 1909 on the corner of Chestnut and Christopher streets. It was an ideal setting for Dr. Charles Kirk Clarke to develop his idea of treating people with less severe mental illnesses in their own community instead of a large mental asylum. Clarke's humanitarian approach was ahead of its time, and he struggled to make his goals for the tiny facility understood.

As superintendent of the Toronto Insane Asylum, dean of the University of Toronto's Faculty of Medicine and a full professor of psychiatry, Clarke wanted to build a grand, world-renowned psychiatric hospital modelled on Dr. Emil Kraepelin's famous Munich Clinic. The Ontario government initially promised an endowment, but then reneged, leaving an incensed Clarke to press the Toronto General Hospital board to allow him to use a dilapidated house in The Ward for his new clinic. Clarke soon hired Dr. Ernest Jones, a renowned British psychiatrist who later wrote a biography of Sigmund Freud, to run the facility, for a salary of $600 a year. Jones was an authority on 'functional nervous troubles' as well as recent developments in psychology, and he had worked at the Munich Clinic.

One wonders what Jones, a seemingly sophisticated intellectual, thought of the broken-down house when he arrived from Munich. He was a proponent of the new psychoanalytic approach being developed by Freud. But the Canadian medical establishment, under Clarke's direction, adhered to a more traditional approach to psychiatry and viewed Freud with suspicion.

The new facility was open for a few hours each day. For the first year, Clarke himself was present for assessment of seventy-four of the clinic's 267 patients. But Jones, according to a 1911 report by Clarke, did the brunt of the work.

The building, noted Clarke, was adjacent to 'the foreign quarter of the city,' which accounted for the many immigrants who turned up. Notices promising free dispensary services were pinned askew to the outside of the house and written in several languages, including Yiddish and Italian. Another notice on the railing notified patients of similar services at the Toronto General starting at 9 a.m.

Of forty-seven male patients, eleven were born in Canada. The rest were from Russia (fourteen), England (ten), Austria (four) and two each from Scotland, China, Italy, Romania and Ireland. Twenty of these patients were Jewish. Similarly, eleven of fifty-four female patients were born in Canada. Thirty-six were Jewish. Jones surmised that the prevalence of Jewish patients was likely due to his familiarity with Yiddish.

Dr. Charles Clarke, 1907

Among the male patients, diagnoses included neurosis, hysteria, dementia praecox, catatonia and 'congenital idiocy.' The females presented with similar symptoms, with twenty-one suffering from anxiety neurosis and one from acroparesthesia.

The work was of the roughest description and the facilities 'exceedingly primitive,' Jones complained – there wasn't even a quiet room or an examination couch. Treatment was necessarily limited to advice regarding 'the regulation of their life.'

Clarke, a member of the National Council of Women of Canada, was well aware of the heightened public and professional concern about the so-called 'eugenic threat' apparently posed by immigrants. Poor, illiterate and often unemployed,

they were seen, particularly women, as bearers of sexually transmitted diseases, mental disabilities and mental illness. Some critics feared that such immigrants would outbreed intelligent, educated citizens – the hotly debated 'birth differential' – and overwhelm the upper classes.

The Council of Women had issued warnings in its 1895 annual report urging the sterilization of feeble-minded girls who were getting pregnant out of wedlock, and Clarke was certainly aware of that. In 1908, Clarke himself wrote an article entitled 'The Defective and Insane Immigrant' for the *University (Toronto) Monthly*. In it, he urged controls on immigration. His colleague, Dr. Helen MacMurchy, who served as 'inspector of the feeble-minded' for Ontario from 1905 to 1919, claimed that mental defectiveness and illegitimacy went hand in hand. A regular visitor to The Ward, where she often delivered babies, MacMurchy didn't mince words: 'The rich baby lives, the poor baby dies.'

The Ward Clinic, on Chestnut Street at Christopher, 1909.

Motivated in part by their experiences with patients in the Ward Clinic, both Clarke and MacMurchy supported the 1916 Canadian Conference of Charities and Public Corrections petition demanding the government reform immigration and establish humane – but segregated – farm colonies to curb 'the great menace of the feeble-minded to the moral and social life of our communities.' In 1919, the two doctors pushed for changes to the Immigration Act and the Marriage Act, calling for six-month jail terms for clergy who performed the marriage sacraments for 'feeble-minded' people.

Ironically, the Ward Clinic itself didn't survive. In 1913, the facility collapsed amid scandal after Jones was discovered to be living with his mistress on Brunswick Avenue, a revelation that shocked U of T's conservative administration. As well,

rumours, denied by Jones, had been circulating about his sexual conduct with students, for example, promoting masturbation. But even more serious were the accounts that had travelled across the Atlantic – of sexual assaults on several mentally disabled girls in a special school in London. In fact, Jones had been tried for sexual assault in 1906, three years before Clarke hired him. Incensed, U of T president Robert Falconer, a staunch Presbyterian, demanded Jones's removal. Jones returned to Europe, accusing Toronto of being too 'biblical' and 'Victorian' in its attitudes.

The demise of the Ward Clinic did not end Clarke's ambitions. At MacMurchy's insistence, he opened a second clinic, in April 1914, in the basement of the new Toronto General Hospital, on The Ward's northern boundary. Known as the Toronto General Psychiatric Clinic, it was soon dubbed by patients 'the Feeble-Minded Clinic,' to Clarke's annoyance. The Ward Clinic's files, and former patients who wished to continue receiving treatment, were transferred to the new centre.

Clarke's purpose was now well honed and focused – the identification, treatment and compilation of research data on the 'feeble-minded' for the Juvenile Court, especially the young delinquents and those suffering from the beginnings of mental illness. The TGH clinic proved to be a resounding success, with over 5,600 patients treated in its first five years.

His voluminous reports on the patients provide revealing insights into prevailing professional attitudes toward the 'feeble-minded,' particularly young girls and women – girls such as 'Maria P.,' an eighteen-year-old drifter undoubtedly living in The Ward whom he cites as 'immoral from an early age.' She ran away from home after incestuous relations with her father, and was now a 'menace to the community.' And then there was 'Betsy,' noted Clarke, 'a pretty little butterfly with an undeveloped brain.' She left school at thirteen and frequented dance halls – likely including the one on Elm Street founded by Central Neighbourhood House director Elizabeth Neufeld to keep an eye on the morals of young women – as well as nickelodeons and Shea's Hippodrome. Betsy had had numerous factory jobs where she claimed to have contracted 'chocolate poisoning' under her fingernails. As Clarke concluded, Betsy had no sense of morality, sex being simply an incident of no importance. He diagnosed her as a 'moral defective' and had her committed to Orillia's Asylum for Idiots and Feeble-Minded.

Young factory girls deemed to be 'night-hawks' who '[flitted] about the countryside at night' with questionable young men or frequented dance parlours on Yonge Street were pronounced by Clarke as 'morally defective' and sent to the reformatory, the Women's Jail Farm in Richmond Hill or the Orillia asylum.

Such girls, he said, came flouncing through the clinic, dressed in the latest wartime fashions, with bobbed hair and skirts above their knees, 'and not a brain in their heads.' As the case files show, Clarke considered the poor biologically and genetically 'unfit,' and in need of care and protection from themselves.

Before his death in March 1924, Clarke finally realized his dream: a full psychiatric hospital for Toronto, underwritten by a Rockefeller

Portrait of a 'feeble–minded' child, March 23, 1916.

Foundation grant, and located on Surrey Place, just north of the corner of College and Elizabeth Street. Clarke was a complex person who exhibited the prejudices and attitudes of his era. However, the Ward Clinic was an admirable step toward treating people with mental illness in a community setting, and as such he was seen as a pioneer. The obituary in the *Toronto Sunday World* noted: 'Canada Owes Immeasurable Debt to Dr. C. K. Clarke, Who Helped to Lift the Shadow of Misery and Hopelessness from Insane Asylums.' Meanwhile, the Ward Clinic became but a half-forgotten fragment in the annals of time in Toronto's medical history.

A CENTURY AGO, TWO Scots helped change the way Canadians viewed immigrant neighbourhoods. At the time, the prevailing response by governments and social welfare groups to urban over-crowding and poverty was to help families locally, either by improving people's physical living conditions or by founding settlement houses that eased the process of cultural adjustment. By the 1910s, both strategies were being pursued in The Ward, for example with the establishment of Central Neighbourhood House in 1911. Reformer Peter Bryce advocated an alternative approach. From 1906, he showed that, with a little help, newcomer families could make a better life for themselves in the suburbs. Then, based at a federal agency in Ottawa from 1914 to 1921, fellow Scot Thomas Adams worked to demonstrate how this goal might best be accomplished.

RICHARD HARRIS

SLUM-FREE
THE SUBURBAN
IDEAL

In the latter decades of the nineteenth century, progressives and social reformers in the U.S. and Britain sought to confront urban poverty and related ills, such as infectious disease outbreaks, overcrowding, noxious air and the lack of green space suitable for families. Ebenezer Howard, a British civil servant and inventor, developed his utopian vision, the garden city, which proposed new suburban towns surrounded by agricultural greenbelts. His 1902 book, *Garden Cities of To-morrow*, spurred the development of garden-city projects, like Letchworth, north of London.

Both Bryce and Adams were inspired by a new international movement of professionals who called themselves 'town planners.' Although commonly trained as engineers or

architects, these reformers believed that the growing industrial cities of the day faced a cluster of interrelated problems that required professional expertise and interventions. Important early initiatives, notably in the regulation of land use, had been taken in Germany. But by the early twentieth century, British advocates had moved to the forefront of the town-planning movement. In 1909, the British parliament made a symbolic gesture, passing the Housing, Town Planning &c. Act. Then, in 1914, a new professional association, the Town Planning Institute, was formed. Town planners believed that physical conditions lay at the root of most of the social and health problems facing urban areas. Their preferred solution was to open up 'slums' by widening roads and alleys and improving all types of transportation, thereby encouraging families to move to the suburbs.

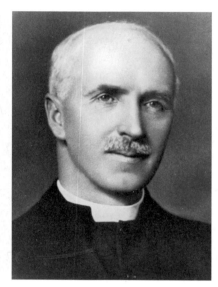

Planning reformer Peter Bryce, ca. 1935.

Bryce came to these sorts of ideas through experience. Born in Blantyre, Scotland, in 1878, he was deeply influenced by the writings and work of John Wesley, the father of Methodism. Bryce offered himself as a candidate for the Methodist ministry, travelling in 1903 as an evangelist to Newfoundland outports before moving to Toronto in 1906 to complete his training at Victoria College. He might have volunteered a few blocks away in The Ward, at the Methodist Mission established in 1904. Instead, he headed for the raw suburban district of Earlscourt, northwest of St. Clair and Dufferin, where he stayed and matured for fifteen years, making a local impact immediately. He organized and became the first president of the Neighbourhood Workers' Association in 1918, and was later elected moderator of the United Church of Canada in 1936.

Bryce's timing, and his choice of Earlscourt, was fortuitous. After the recession of 1890s, immigration to Canada had

resumed, and by 1910 it had reached a level unmatched to this day. The great majority of immigrants, especially those settling in Toronto, were British. Perhaps after a brief stay in one of the inner neighbourhoods, many acquired suburban plots of land and erected shacks that, in time, they improved. Land developers catered to their demand by marketing unserviced land. The real estate was inexpensive because, until the 1920s and the founding of the Toronto Transit Commission, such outlying districts lacked streetcar service. The Toronto Railway Company, the private firm that had long controlled the streetcar franchise, refused to extend service into the newly developing suburbs, believing that such lines would be unprofitable. Thousands of suburban residents, including Bryce, lobbied and fumed, but to no effect. For many years, these new suburbanites had to walk

View of Earlscourt,
October 14, 1916.

long distances to work, or at least to the end of the car line. Wary of risk, professional builders avoided these areas.

Earlscourt was the epicentre of the main concentration of this type of settlement, lying in the northwestern suburbs and straddling the municipal boundary with York Township. As an immigrant district, it soon became as famous as The Ward was infamous – the two areas were intriguing counterpoints. Reformers such as Mary Joplin Clarke, who had taken over from Elizabeth Neufeld as director of the Central Neighbourhood House, knew that the settlers in Earlscourt were just as poor and neglected as those in The Ward. But the suburbanites were British homeowners, and for contemporaries this made all the difference.

Suburban poverty was as grinding as anything found downtown in areas like The Ward. During the recession of 1907–1908, and during the First World War, when men were fighting in Europe, families almost starved or, in winter, froze. From the moment of his arrival in the area, Bryce dealt head-on with these and other pressing issues. As a student, and then from 1908 as an ordained minister, he directed the construction of Earlscourt Methodist Church, which opened in 1911. As neighbouring suburbs grew, he established six more churches. In effect, these undertook settlement work: they ran day cares, Sunday schools, libraries and a children's home; organized a cooperative club; lobbied for a recreation centre; advised families on how best to grow vegetables; and, in times of emergency, mounted city-wide campaigns to collect clothing and coal. He helped make suburban living possible.

Bryce, however, observed a substantive difference between downtown and suburban poverty. Referring to The Ward, in 1918, he compared Earlscourt residents to 'the foreigner, with his low standard of living' who has 'not been acquainted... with Canadian ideals of housing.' He was not alone in citing the contrast. Two years later, the author of a study of Earlscourt bluntly observed that 'poor as England's poor may be, they would appear to have reached a higher stage of social development than the Jews and Southern Europeans of which "The Ward" is made up.' Of course, Jews clustered downtown because that is where the garment industry was concentrated. Ignoring this economic logic, middle-class Anglo Toronto praised the British immigrants whose language and religion they shared, and who embraced the suburban solution – building homes in settings where, in a reporter's words, 'romping, sturdy children' thrived under

'a thrifty woman's care.' Bryce shared the cultural prejudices of the day, but believed there was hope for everyone. Pleading for 'a Canadian standard of living,' he argued for the establishment of a Municipal Town Planning and Housing Commission that would promote decentralization.

This proposal never came to pass, even though by 1918 Bryce's ideas were aligned closely with those of Thomas Adams and other self-styled planners of the day. Born in 1871 near Edinburgh, Scotland, Adams had trained as an architect and risen to prominence during the 1900s. He secured an early position as secretary to the Garden City Association, which advocated the planned decentralization of cities, played a vital role in the passage of the 1909 Planning Act and in 1914 was elected the first president of the Town Planning Institute. In a coup, Clifford Sifton, head of the recently formed federal Commission of Conservation, persuaded Adams to come to Canada to take up a position as the agency's 'Town Planning Advisor.' In this capacity, and until Ottawa abolished the commission in 1921, Adams crisscrossed the country, tirelessly promoting the ideology of planning. Inevitably, when the Town Planning Institute of Canada was established in 1920, he was elected its first president.

By virtue of his training, Adams was more interested than Bryce in the physical layout of the suburbs. When a short-lived federal housing program for veterans was launched in 1919, for example, Adams designed a model subdivision to fit it, while Bryce was more interested in ministering to people's needs once they had moved in. But both Scotsmen agreed that neighbourhoods like The Ward were a problem, and that suburbs were the solution.

Today, their conviction may make some people uncomfortable. We hear constantly about the problems of the low-density, auto-oriented suburbs that became the norm after 1945. But the views of Bryce and Adams made complete sense to contemporaries, including many of those who grew up in The Ward. From the 1920s until the 1940s, some of the children of Jewish and Eastern European immigrants moved north into Forest Hill and later North York, or west toward Roncesvalles, each seeking some version of the Canadian dream.

F RANCESCO GLIONNA WAS born in the province of Potenza in the Kingdom of Naples. Little is known of his European past, but he seems to have arrived in North America with his wife and children in the late 1860s or early 1870s. He and his brothers – Giovanni Battista, Donatantonio (Donato) and Rocco – were part of a growing migration from the south of Italy; they went first to Paris and later to New York, plying various trades. Laurenzana was one of a number of towns which sent harpists, violinists, and clarinetists, as well as boot makers, cordwainers and coppersmiths, throughout the world. On their journeys such tradesmen often brought children, the most conspicuous of whom were street musicians. They were especially evident in Paris, but after the expulsion of child street performers during the universal exposition there in 1867 and the start of the Franco-German War, they moved to such other European and American cities as Barcelona and New York.

JOHN E. ZUCCHI

THE GLIONNA CLAN AND TORONTO'S FIRST LITTLE ITALY

In the early 1870s, Francesco Glionna lived with some of his brothers in Crosby Street on the perimeter of New York's Little Italy, where the city directory listed him as a carpenter. By 1874 he was in Toronto, working as a cabinet-maker and carpenter; later in the decade and in the early 1880s he also worked as a musician and as a peanut vendor on Yonge Street. It is not totally clear why the Glionnas came to Ontario, but it seems that their move had something to do with New York's opposition to child street musicians, particularly in 1873. The Giovanni Glionna arrested in New Haven, Conn., in the

Left: Fiddler surrounded by children, ca. 1910.

| 239

summer of that year for keeping child street musicians was probably Francesco's brother, who appeared in Toronto a few months later. The Glionnas were followed by other immigrant families from Laurenzana who had been living in New York, among them the Laurias, the Brancieres, the Lobraicos and the Laraias. In 1877 Francesco and Anna Glionna became naturalized Canadian citizens.

At first the Glionnas rented homes on Chestnut Street, which had been settled a few years earlier by Genoese tradesmen and their families. In the late 1870s Francesco Glionna had invested in real estate and within a few years he owned eleven lots at Chestnut and Edward streets. On this corner, which became the heart of Toronto's first Little Italy, he constructed a number of houses and, in 1885, the Glionna Hotel, an immigrant saloon that was probably also a labour agency for Italian immigrants. In the 1870s Canadian contractors, following the lead of their American counterparts, were beginning to employ Italian immigrants on public projects, most notably the Welland Canal. They used Italian *padroni* (labour agents) to bring workers from Italy, and a number of the *padroni* in North America were from Laurenzana.

Francesco's prominence in Toronto's early Italian community came not only from his relative wealth – he also owned farmland in Scarborough Township – but also from his position as patriarch of the community's largest (over eighty members in 1908) and most influential family. The Glionnas were certainly visible as musicians. Francesco worked periodically as one before 1885. His brother Giovanni, a street performer in Paris in the 1860s, was a glazier and a *padrone* in New York but he went back to the music trade in Toronto. Each of the brothers had at least one son who was a musician. Francesco's son Donatantonio (Donato) Giuseppe, a sometime bartender at his father's hotel, was a musician, and another son, Egidio, also had his own orchestra, E. Glionna Sr Brothers and Company, which could be booked at the hotel. There was also Vincenzo Glionna, whose family connection is not certain; he had fifteen children, all of them musicians, and he directed his own orchestra, Glionna, Marsicano and Company. At a time when bands were few in the city, the Glionnas performed for entertainments, at tea parties for wealthy families, at department stores such as Eaton's, and in vaudeville theatres and churches. In 1895, for example, Vincenzo's orchestra performed a mass by Dvořák at Our Lady of Lourdes Church.

The second generation of Glionnas had an important place in the Italian community. Donato was the Liberal party's organizer there and he became involved in a number of high-profile projects and organizations. For instance, he founded the Umberto Primo Benevolent Society in 1888 and was its president until 1911. This society, of which Francesco was a member, and its colourful corps of *bersaglieri* (ceremonial guards) were present at all important Toronto Italian gatherings. At the turn of the century Donato tried to persuade the local Roman Catholic archdiocese to establish an Italian parish and offered to donate land for a church. As late as the 1920s he began a second friendly society, the Italian Aid and Protective Society. The first doctor and lawyer of Italian origin in Toronto were Glionnas – Francesco's grandson George and Joseph F. respectively – and two Glionnas served as Italian consular agents in the city between 1914 and the early 1920s.

Francesco Glionna had retired from his hotel business about 1903 but it was continued by the family until 1917, when it was closed and sold, probably because of the introduction of prohibition the previous year. A member of Our Lady of Mount Carmel Church, he died of pneumonia in 1918 and was survived by five children, forty-five grandchildren, and fifty great-grandchildren. His family's prestige in the Italian community continued into the interwar period, but the arrival of many more immigrants from various regions of Italy and the growth of fascist and antifascist movements in Italian Toronto marginalized the Glionna family and reduced its political power.

Adapted with permission from the Dictionary of Canadian Biography, Vol. xiv: http://www.biographi.ca/en/bio/glionna_francesco_14E.html.

MICHAEL POSNER

'THE HIPP'

IN THE ARGOT of the times, it was known simply as the Hip, or sometimes the Hipp. The entrepreneurial Shea brothers, 'Iron Mike' and his younger sibling Jerry – Canadian-born but U.S.-raised – already owned two flourishing vaudeville venues in Toronto, one on Yonge Street and another on Victoria, as well as a mini-empire of theatres in upstate New York.

But such was Toronto's dynamism at the turn of the century – its population would swell from just 96,000 in 1881 to more than half a million by 1920 – that the ambitious impresarios were convinced it could accommodate another. A small town compared to New York, Chicago, Philadelphia or Boston, Toronto nevertheless punched above its weight in the burgeoning world of mass entertainment.

Thus, on April 27, 1914, at a then-staggering cost of $250,000 (the equivalent of $5.8 million in 2014 terms), the brothers opened Shea's Hippodrome, designed by Rochester-based architects L. H. Lempert. It was Canada's grandest – and one of the world's largest – theatres, boasting 3,200 plush seats, twelve opera boxes, an orchestra pit, decorative plaster mouldings, a mezzanine smoker's lounge and a $50,000 Wurlitzer organ with 1,200 gold and ivory pipes. (A century later, you can still hear the organ's dulcet tones in concerts at Casa Loma.)

The theatre's location was entirely apposite. Just north of Queen Street, on Terauley, it lay due west of City Hall, towering symbol of civic propriety and Protestant rectitude. But it also stood on the eastern flank of The Ward. Nearby were other vaudeville houses, including the Colonial, on Queen Street just west of Bay, and the Gayety, a little further west.

A hip indeed, the Hippodrome thus mediated a tacit but very real social tension, brokering the city's Apollonian instinct for order with its Dionysian impulse for rule-breaking revelry. It hovered and thrived on the very cusp of the divide that separated Toronto the Good from the strange, polyglot Other –

everything that threatened the city's safe, perceived equilibrium. Among other groups, the Woman's Christian Temperance Union regularly raised alarms about the pernicious threats – disease, prostitution, alcoholism, family breakup – posed by the world to which the Hippodrome was seen as a gateway.

Inevitably, for the next four decades, until it was razed to make way for what became Nathan Phillips Square, the Hipp became the middle ground, a democratizing agora, Greek for 'gathering place.' This was true both literally and figuratively. White and black, Jew and Gentile – all were welcome here. While renowned organist Quentin Maclean performed his magic on the Wurlitzer, Ben Sherman, a young Jewish teenager from Kiev, played drums and clarinet in the pit orchestra (he would later open a hardware store on Queen Street West).

Previous: South side of Queen looking west from Bay, with two burlesque theatres, ca. 1960s.

Above: Ad for The Unholy Three *at the Hippodrome, 1925.*

At minimal expense – in 1926 and for years afterward, patrons could see five acts plus a feature film, newsreels, cartoons and serials, for twenty-five cents – the generation that successively experienced the First World War, the Roaring Twenties, the Great Depression and the Second World War could forget their troubles and be entertained.

Most of the greatest stars of the vaudeville era walked the boards of the Hippodrome, among them W. C. Fields and

George Jessel, Al Jolson and Fanny Brice, Maurice Chevalier and Ethel Barrymore, Eddie Cantor and Sophie Tucker, the Marx Brothers and Harry Lauder Jr., Red Skelton and Cab Calloway. Stan Laurel (before he teamed with Oliver Hardy) played here, as did, before his solo career in films, Buster Keaton and his parents, Myra and Joe. During their run at the Hipp, performers' names were emblazoned in lights on the building's impressive copper marquee.

Skelton, who often emceed the shows, became a Toronto favourite. 'I really got started in a big way when I went to Shea's in Toronto,' he once said. In one of his best-loved routines, he would demonstrate the many possible ways to eat a doughnut. In the process, twice a day, six days a week, Skelton would consume fourteen doughnuts, eventually earning the sobriquet 'Fatso with the Bottomless Belly.'

The Hippodrome's stage was a non-stop carnival, filled with knife throwers and lion tamers, comics and magicians. Ragtime singer Belle Baker sang through a megaphone, while proto-feminist Eva Tanguay, originally from Quebec and credited as the woman who created vaudeville itself, performed songs with – for the era – risqué titles ('It's All Been Done Before, But Not the Way I Do It' and 'I Want Someone to Go Wild With Me'). And Siegmund Breitbart, billed as the strongest man in the world, ripped metal chains in half with his bare hands and lay on a bed of nails while elephants and horses walked a wooden plank across his body.

Some homegrown Ontarians also graced the Hippodrome stage, among them May Irwin, née Georgina May Campbell; Maud Allan, née Beulah Maude Durrant; Margaret Anglin; and, hailing from what was then known as New Toronto, now Etobicoke, the O'Connor Sisters.

Always hip to the times, the Shea brothers early on began supplementing vaudeville acts with silent films and, after 1929, talkies. In 1938, they used the theatre's stage for the first public demonstration in Toronto of a revolutionary new medium, television – though it would be another fifteen years before it was commercially available. (Former heavyweight boxing champion Jack Dempsey was brought in for the event.) By the early 1940s, with vaudeville in eclipse, the Hippodrome had become a movies-only venue, managed by Famous Players.

A decade later, the city began to assemble land for a major urban redevelopment, ultimately spending $3 million acquiring neighbourhood properties,

Shea's Hippodrome, 1953.

including the Hippodrome site. By then, The Ward itself had begun to lose its cohesion, as the next generation of Jews and Italians literally moved upwards, geographically to the north and, metaphorically, within society. The Hipp's wrecking ball arrived in 1956. 'Times change,' the *Toronto Star* editorialized, in an accurate if not terribly eloquent send-off, 'and a new era requires new rules of comedy and entertainment.'

In due course, Finnish architect Viljo Revell's arresting new city hall was built in the very heart of the old Ward, on a site bounded by Bay, Queen and Chestnut streets, with Osgoode Hall on the west. Fronting it is Nathan Phillips Square, the vast public gathering place – a modern *agora*. The driving force behind the city hall project was Phillips himself – the city's first Jewish mayor and a sign of how much the times had indeed changed.

JOHN LORINC

BEFORE YORKVILLE

IN 1929, MARY John's Coffee Shop opened for business in a three-storey brick house at 79 Gerrard West. Near the bustling Elizabeth Street Playground and a three-storey Christian mission, the restaurant offered its patrons 'steak-chop' dinners and luncheons, tea and even the services of a tarot-card reader. Those Depression-era diners could scarcely have imagined that the modest eatery would become, some three decades later, the choicest hangout in the so-called Gerrard Street 'Village,' Toronto's first arts district.

Like Old Angelo's, the popular Italian restaurant/bar at the corner of Chestnut and Elm, just a few blocks away, Mary John's during the 1930s and 1940s gradually transformed into a destination for younger people, as well as writers, artists and photographers. The tumbledown dwellings on Gerrard west of Yonge, as well as LaPlante, Walton and Hayter, were gradually rented out to studios, antique dealers, framers and milliners. In the mid-1940s, the tenants at 20–22 Hayter, a block north, included Eaton's paint supplies shop, a costume maker and the Canadian Drama League.

The area soon attracted more tea houses, restaurants, boutiques, a bookstore and even a masseuse who called herself Madame Caya and cultivated flowers on the roof of her shop. Those who lived in the 'Gerrard-Hayter' district – once home to itinerant Italian labourers, and still ethnically diverse in the late 1940s and early 1950s – called themselves 'villagers.' They saw their gritty, laid-back neighbourhood as Toronto's Greenwich – a community that consciously opted out of the city's notoriously staid ethic. 'Just a year ago,' as a *Globe and*

Mail reporter dryly observed in late 1948, 'there was a party on Hayter St. that went on for six weeks.'

Ernest Hemingway was said to have wandered those streets during his brief and unhappy stint in Toronto in the early 1920s. Nicole Baute, a *Toronto Star* reporter, wrote that Pierre Berton described the Village in that era as 'our ghetto, our Bowery, our Chinatown, our East Side.' In the 1930s, 'our Soho, our Montparnasse.' By the 1950s and 1960s it was just 'the Village,' a bohemian enclave often compared to New York's Greenwich Village. Berton called it an 'intriguing island in the heart of downtown Toronto, whose doom has been predicted (wrongly) for so many years.'

By the late 1950s, the Village, with its colourfully painted storefronts and tree-lined sidewalks, had become home to a handful of popular coffee houses that offered a stage and a mic to the jazz combos, folksingers and rock musicians who also played gigs at venues like the Colonial Tavern, a bit further south, on Yonge Street. The Village, noted critic Rick McGinnis on blogTO in 2009, provided 'a respite from Toronto's famously Presbyterian character, but it was that character – and the city's draconian liquor regulations and famously strict blue laws – that [artist and actor Don Cullen, founder of the Bohemian Embassy on nearby St. Nicholas] has come to credit for the uniqueness of cultural life in the village.'

But the Village wasn't just about clubs and performances. On the block of Gerrard between Bay and Yonge, Martin Ahvenus opened the Village Bookstore, which attracted young, aspiring poets like Milton Acorn, Al Purdy, Michael Ondaatje and Gwendolyn MacEwen – some of whom scrawled poems on the walls. Avrom Isaacs, in 1955, opened a framing shop and art-supplies store that later became the Isaacs Gallery, representing artists like Michael Snow, William Kurelek and Joyce Wieland; another Village gallery sold paintings by Robert Bateman and Ken Danby. Marilyn and John Brooks, in turn, set up the Unicorn, a curio shop that launched their fashion lines and the North America–wide empire of Marilyn Brooks boutiques. General Idea, the conceptual art collective founded by Felix Partz, Jorge Zontal and AA Bronson, had its headquarters at 78 Gerrard in the late 1960s and early 1970s.

'In such a setting,' writes critic and filmmaker Stuart Henderson in *Making the Scene: Yorkville and Hip Toronto in the 1960s*, 'European owners and their clientele would mix with curious teens and twenty-somethings from around

the city – it was through this alchemy, a fruitful combination of Euro emigres, Beat youth, aspiring poets, musicians, artists and students, all breathing the air of difference, that the soon-to-be Yorkville scene found its genesis.'

In the midst of this Soho-like milieu, Mary John's, the vintage diner, continued to function as 'the social centre ... famous for its lacquered travel posters by Cassandre and 75¢ meals,' the Los Angeles musician Wolf Sullivan writes on his memoir blog, RochdaleCollegeBook.com. 'Sixty cents bought a lunch of soup and meat loaf, and a chicken pot pie cost a dollar.' A block north, on Hayter, Jack & Jill's, one of the first Hungarian restaurants in Toronto, operated out of a little cottage surrounded by a picket fence and an outdoor patio. Nurses and technicians from the Hospital for Sick Children would drift over for lunch and 'espresso,' as the yellow sign over the door proudly promoted.

In the late 1950s, Eva Lorinc, my mother, was one of those young hospital workers who liked to stroll over for soup on her break. She and my father, John, a physician, would meet at Jack & Jill's for coffee after their shifts ended. Later, in 1963, my mother wheeled me, as a newborn in a stroller, to the Village to visit with her friends at the coffee shops and to browse for books or pottery.

By that point, however, the Village's boutiques and tea houses had begun to decamp to Yorkville amid insistent rumours that the city was preparing to

demolish those quaint, century-old houses to make way for hospital expansions and modern high-rises. The Brooks moved their store to Cumberland. Albert Franck, who immortalized Toronto's working-class row houses and laneways in his paintings, relocated his gallery to Hazelton. Jack & Jill's leased space on the second floor of the newly built Colonnade shopping mall on Bloor Street.

'I remember when it was all torn down,' my mother, eighty-three, recalled one afternoon in late 2014. Most of the demolitions occurred in the mid-1960s, although a few of the storefronts on Gerrard hung on until the early 1970s, and the development of the Delta Chelsea Hotel.

Today, apart from a strip of original row houses on the northwest corner of Gerrard and Bay, there's absolutely nothing left to suggest that those few blocks – now dominated by featureless 1970s and 1980s office buildings, as well as one of Bay Street's few remaining parking lots – had once pulsed with the kind of youthful cosmopolitan energy so feared by 'Toronto the Good.' Nothing, not even a plaque, acknowledges that these blocks begat 1960s Yorkville and the ensuing cultural explosion in a city that had found its voice. The Village's thoughtless eradication, it seems to me, offers up some kind of lesson, although Toronto clearly has made versions of this mistake many times since.

My mother scrutinized the photo of Jack & Jill's languid patio that's posted on Wolf Sullivan's website. 'We were sad,' she told me, summoning up wistful memories that had been buried for over fifty years. 'It just sort of disappeared.'

Left: Colourful boutiques on Gerrard Street between Yonge and Elizabeth, 1960s.

Above: The terrace of the Jack & Jill Café, Hayter Street at Laplante, 1960s.

ELLEN SCHEINBERG

PUBLIC BATHS

SCHVITZING ON CENTRE AVENUE

HAVE FOND MEMORIES of my grandfather regaling me with stories about his regular visits to the schvitz, Yiddish for 'steam bath.' I had never seen this foreign place. But I knew that for him, it was a refuge from the daily grind, somewhere he could socialize with his male friends, spruce up and enjoy the health benefits associated with this pastime.

The Talmud mentions public baths, which have been a part of Jewish tradition for over 2,000 years. (The ancient Greeks and Romans also patronized baths, as do modern Nordic citizens.) As a result, many European immigrants who came to Toronto during the late nineteenth and early twentieth centuries had a connection to public baths and schvitzes.

In contrast to cities like New York and Boston, Toronto did not have many bathhouses or saunas at the turn of the century. In fact, before 1910, there were only seven in Toronto, and several didn't last. Typically situated far from the downtown core, they were intended for middle- and upper-class residents who could afford the entrance fees.

Immigrants in The Ward had no public baths nearby and most of the cramped housing in the area did not have room for a tub. Indeed, according to the 1911 'Report of the Medical Health Officer,' produced by Dr. Charles Hastings, only 160 out of the 1,653 Ward homes inspected by health officials had indoor plumbing. Most families relied on wells or outdoor spigots shared by as many as ten families. One resident interviewed by the *Globe* remarked that he had never been in a foreigner's home in The Ward that possessed a bath. Some could take advantage of public

beaches to bathe during the summer, but most had no way to clean themselves during the colder months of the year.

During this period, reformers like Hastings viewed Toronto slums like The Ward as breeding grounds for disease and sin that threatened the health and stability of the entire city. In *Washing 'The Great Unwashed,'* American public hygiene scholar Marilyn T. Williams notes that these health and hygiene advocates perceived dirt and poverty as linked to 'habits of laziness, weakness, degeneration, or thriftlessness.' By contrast, cleanliness, according to historian Andrea Renner, was a metaphor for the act of 'purging physical substances to eliminate vice and foreignness.' Bathing, in the mind of the reformer, could therefore have a transformative effect on slum

dwellers, rendering them physically and morally cleaner and ultimately more 'Canadian.'

Rather than exerting pressure on landlords to equip their buildings with indoor plumbing and baths, reformers blamed immigrants for their lack of hygiene and viewed the construction of public baths near these residents as the solution. The first local public bath was proposed by Alderman W. S. Harrison, who argued that 'a man with a clean and healthy body is more likely to have a clean and healthy mind, and one who respects himself is more likely to respect the rights of others.' Consequently, he perceived this civic project as a 'potent factor in the solution of social economic problems' afflicting The Ward. Dr. Charles K. Clarke, psychiatrist and head of the Toronto Asylum at the time, described public baths as 'one of the greatest moral levers in the community.'

Caricature of Dr. Charles Hastings attempting to scrub Toronto's 'slum element' in the bath, ca. 1912.

Relying on Buffalo's modest public bath as a model, city officials built a grand structure that generated a steamy controversy. The *Telegram* was particularly vexed by the exorbitant cost – $46,000 – as well as its ornate design, which the newspaper described as akin to 'the baths of the Shah of Persia.' The writer even went on to suggest that the new bath facility might be more suitable as a residence for the lieutenant governor.

The Harrison Baths opened on November 1, 1909, on 3 Stephanie Street, just off McCaul (it moved to 15 Stephanie during the First World War) and a few blocks west of The Ward. It included separate entrances and sections for men and women: each side was equipped with a change room, showers and a single tub. Harrison's also boasted a 26-by-60-foot pool, along with laundry facilities. Users were charged five cents to access the showers and the bath, and ten cents to swim in the dunk pool. The laundry was free. The swim tank was only open to the boys and men during the early years, swimsuits were mandatory and an

instructor was hired to provide swimming lessons to the kids.

The immediate response to the Harrison bathhouse was positive. During the first week, over 2,000 people visited the facility. Of that group, 795 used the baths and 1,527 the pool. Several months later, a *Globe* reporter noted that attendance continued to be extremely high, remarking, '[T]here is hardly a shower or tub left idle for any length of time.' Most of the patrons were boys and men using the pool. The reporter was also pleased to see many female foreigners such as Italians, 'who are dark-skinned and flashing eyed,' along with many 'Hebrews' who 'discovered with joy, and satisfaction the civic plant or ablutions.' Evidently, young girls and women of Finnish, Jewish, Italian, Polish and Ruthenian descent came in once a week, often with multiple children in their care, whom they

Swimming tank with male bathers, Harrison Baths, May 19, 1914.

bathed in the tub. According to the women's change-room supervisor, one 'foreign' mother scrubbed her four babies and then gave 'motherly help to the children who come [sic] alone to the baths.' During the 1920s, Harrison's provided free admission to children on Mondays and Wednesdays. Summer months were busiest: it wasn't uncommon to see hundreds of people lined up outside.

Besides such municipal facilities, private operators jumped

Ad for Riman's Russian Baths, 1925.

l 1910, Mendel Riman, a former peddler, opened a private Jewish bathhouse at 34 Centre Avenue, in The Ward. (The facility was behind the Goel Tzedec synagogue.) The ten-cent entrance fees would enable him to support his large family and honour the Jewish Sabbath. At first, he shared the business with a partner, operating out of a house equipped with a steam room, a shower and a mikveh (a ritual bath for Jewish women). It was open only on Friday afternoons and Saturday nights. Most of Riman's clients were Orthodox peddlers who came in to cleanse themselves before the Sabbath. The business was a family affair: Mendel dealt with the male clients and supplies, and his wife, Basha, assisted the women, preparing slivers of soap and towels for each paying customer.

As demand grew, Riman bought 36 Centre Avenue so he could expand the operation. According to his grandson, Nathan Bornstein, who wrote about the schvitz in an unpublished paper called 'Hot Rocks,' the renovated building had a brick-and-glass facade with a sign that read, 'Riman's Russian Turkish Steam Bath – Relieves the Pain of Rheumatism, Lumbago and Arthritis.'

The new facility no longer had a mikveh, but it was equipped with showers and a bath used by both genders at

different times. Bornstein says they attracted patrons from many backgrounds: Jews, Finns, Italians, blacks and others. The men would relax on one of the forty lounges after a schvitz, wrapped in white sheets, discussing religion, art, music, business, sex and politics. Their accents, he says, 'were so thick that a native Canadian could hardly make out what was being said, but they understood each other perfectly.' Although Riman sold only pop on the premises, customers would bring in food from Solomon's Deli on Dundas Street, as well as imported Scotch to wash it down. After finishing their repast, they would go back into the steam room to sweat it off.

Beyond the diverse clientele, Riman's also attracted men from many different trades. Bookies and gangsters liked to meet there, Bornstein says, because the naked bathers couldn't conceal weapons. Many athletes also used the schvitz: jockeys came in to lose weight before a race, and boxers used the facility to hit their weight class or have a post-bout massage. In fact, Canadian heavyweight champion Larry Gains was a regular before he went off to Europe to compete internationally during the 1930s.

Despite the presence of boxers and gangsters in Riman's, fights were rare. Indeed, the only major incident was a brawl between the internationally renowned cantor Bernard Wladowsky and another prominent local cantor. Both men were naked at the time. Other bathers, appalled by the melee, had to separate the scuffling cantors.

By the 1930s and 1940s, a handful of bathhouses opened in the Kensington Market area – including a Finnish Turkish bath. Riman's went bankrupt, as its clients now had many baths to choose from. Typically, they patronized the ones closest to where they lived. Also, most homes outside The Ward had indoor plumbing by this time, which meant the owners didn't need to visit bathhouses. Regardless, the older first-generation immigrant men continued to go for a schvitz with their friends. And from the 1950s to the 1980s, many of these bathhouses came to be patronized by gay men.

Today, there is little left of The Ward's original built form. The houses occupied by Riman's Russian Bath, at 34 and 36 Centre Avenue, were razed, and the land is now occupied by an office building fronting onto University Avenue. As for the Harrison bathhouse, it remains at 15 Stephanie Street, tucked between two apartment buildings just south of Grange Park. The city operates it as a public pool.

NDUSTRIALIZING CITIES LIKE Toronto were tough places to live, especially for women. Drawn to the seemingly abundant opportunities to buy freedom with a paycheque, they flocked to the city to escape dull or oppressive family and community environments. Many took up live-in domestic work, but long hours, overbearing employers and vulnerability to sexual harassment made work in the growing industrial and retail economies more appealing. Eaton's and Simpson's, two large department stores on The Ward's borders, were the largest such employers.

The trouble was that employers paid women half to two-thirds of what their male counterparts earned. For too many women, this meant living in poverty. To get by, they shared cramped rented rooms or lived in boarding houses. When wages didn't cover basic living expenses, or during periods of unemployment, women and men alike sometimes turned to the sex trade to keep food on their plates and a roof over their heads.

It is impossible to know all the ways women came to engage in sex work in the early twentieth century. The stigma surrounding the exchange of sex for money or goods meant that when women appeared in court or were interviewed by social workers, they were likely to tell a tale that would earn them the most sympathy. For a woman accused of prostitution, it made sense to portray herself as a victim of male lust or treachery, poverty or the need to support children and aged parents. A few asserted their right to do with their bodies what they

ELISE CHENIER
SEX WORK AND THE WARD'S BACHELOR SOCIETY

Left: The Rex Hotel, 193 Queen West. In the 1930s and 1940s, it was frequented by local men in search of alcohol and prostitutes. The Rex had two bars, one for men and another for women, as well as rooms on the second floor.

pleased. For some women, grossly disadvantaged in the job market, sex work became an acceptable and legitimate way of earning a living. For others, it was the last and most desperate option.

The popular image of the sex worker as a 'fallen woman,' pitiful and morally corrupt, does not represent the reality of how the sexual economy functioned. While it was once thought that poverty produced immorality, we now know that poverty forces people to make choices that others never have to face. Another common association with sex work is street prostitution, usually visible in the most depressed neighbourhoods. By the 1920s, however, an active sex trade extended into the heart of The Ward, where small and large hotels such as the Continental on Dundas, the Ford on Bay and the Rex on Queen Street West rented rooms by the hour. In doing so, the hotel owners disregarded municipal bylaws – aimed at quashing immorality, including prostitution – that prohibited them from renting rooms to unmarried couples.

The expansion of The Ward's sex trade had a great deal to do with the rapid growth in the number of male immigrants from China. Since the 1860s, labourers were recruited from China's Guangdong province to work in mines and on railway construction projects. Once the railway was completed in 1885, many sought out new opportunities in cities across Canada. By the 1910s, Chinese-owned shops, laundries and restaurants opened among The Ward's Jewish- and Italian-owned butchers and bakeries. At that time, most Asian men planned to stay overseas just long enough to earn enough money to buy land and build a home in their natal village, but some, preferring the life they had cobbled together in Toronto, stayed on. Others found their plans to return to their country of origin disrupted by the war with the Japanese and the establishment of the People's Republic of China.

Until men were permitted to sponsor their Chinese spouses in 1946, the majority lived alone or with other men. By the 1930s, about a third were married to or living common-law with white women, but many never had the opportunity to learn English and earned even less than white women. For them, marriage or even dating was simply out of the question.

These conditions created a strong demand for sex workers, which was filled by underemployed and unemployed working-class women, some born and raised in Ontario, others from the U.S., Ireland and Quebec. (Men also sought out other men for sexual relations, but my research has so far uncovered only female sex

workers.) Most of these women were white, some were of mixed ancestry, some of Aboriginal or African heritage. Like other professions, even the sex trade was racially segregated. Black women who worked outdoors, for example, occupied a single back alley. Only a minority worked on the streets, however. Much of the trade was organized in and through restaurants and small hotels owned by men (and sometimes women, as was the case with the Rex) of Chinese heritage.

Lorraine, a local sex worker who resided in a boarding house owned by the Rosenthal family in Chinatown, posing in front of Eaton's factory, ca. 1940.

White women were warned against having any contact with men of Asian heritage. Toronto's tabloid headlines screamed warnings about Chinese men as sexual predators who enslaved white victims by introducing them to opium.

Non-Asian working women desperate for a cheap meal ignored such warnings and sought out not only food, but jobs.

Social prejudice against whites 'race-mixing,' especially with people of Chinese heritage, along with the belief that women's sexuality should be regulated by the state, meant that any association with people of Chinese heritage involved considerable social risk for white women. Women who were deemed to be misbehaving – typically this meant engaging in sexual relations – could be charged under the Female Refuges Act and sentenced to a reformatory. Women found in Chinese restaurants at night and women known to 'fraternize' with men of Chinese heritage were harassed and picked up by police officers who charged them under vagrancy and similar laws aimed at punishing women for having sexual relations outside of marriage. Velma Demerson, who in 1939 was charged by her father with the crime of incorrigibility, was sent to prison as punishment for her ongoing relationship with Harry Yip. As her autobiography, *Incorrigible*, attests, many women ignored the threat to their personal lives and developed intimate relationships with men of Asian heritage based on a shared desire for intimacy and affection. Others sought only to maintain their freedom and autonomy by exchanging sex and intimacy for cash and other material goods.

Hotels were important spaces where such exchanges could occur, but once again the stereotype hides the lived reality. Many, if not most, 'dates' took place in the boarding rooms where the men resided, saving on the additional expense of renting a room, which was usually double the cost of sex. Some dates were relatively anonymous, such as those arranged through local tongs (community halls whose members belong to the same clan), but many such liaisons lasted months and even years. Some women found Chinese men to be more respectful of them than were white men. They would often cook meals for their female companions, purchase them gifts and generally allow them greater autonomy. It was, for many women, a much better arrangement than what they could expect from men of white European heritage.

Those who lived in The Ward understood the reality of life on the sexual, social and economic margins. When asked about attitudes toward sex workers, many former residents interviewed for this research responded with a story about Tom Lock, the owner and operator of a pharmacy on Dundas Street West. Lock, the first Chinese pharmacist in Toronto, was known to stand

outside his shop on slow afternoons and keep time as couples entered and exited the boarding house across the street, often quipping, 'That was quick!' The Lock family later adopted the mixed white-Asian child of a local sex worker. When one white wife protested the comings and goings of sex workers in the boarding house she and her husband ran, her husband explained that if they did not accept them, they would go out of business. Over the years, some of the sex-worker regulars became close friends of the family, earning the honorific 'Auntie.'

By the 1920s and well into the 1950s, sex workers were as much a part of the neighbourhood as the butcher, the grocer and the restaurant cook, their comings and goings observed with equal parts humour and concern. The history of The Ward shows how two socially and economically marginalized groups formed a unique community defined by very human needs: food, shelter and intimacy. Interestingly, the image of Chinese men as dirty, deceitful enslavers of innocent young women has withered away, yet early-twentieth-century stereotypes about sex workers as morally corrupt victims of male lust persist into the present day, reminding us that historical change is always an uneven process.

JOHN LORINC

THE HEALTH ADVOCATES

McKEOWN ON HASTINGS

I N AN OTHERWISE unprepossessing office in Toronto Public Health's Victoria Street headquarters, Dr. David McKeown, the city's medical officer of health, makes a point of working under the stern, watchful gaze of an important mentor. He shares the space not with a colleague but rather with an arresting portrait of Dr. Charles Hastings, who served as the city's MOH from 1911 to 1929.

From the moment he took office, the snowy-haired obstetrician focused intensively on eradicating slum conditions in The Ward and other poor areas. Hastings promoted dramatic changes to water, milk and meat quality standards, infectious disease control, vaccination and housing. By the time he retired, in 1929, Toronto had attained a global reputation for its public health practices. Almost ninety years later, Hastings' outspoken brand of advocacy – and a track record of reform that begins in The Ward – continues to characterize the TPH's approach to contemporary urban public health issues such as air quality and obesity.

Was The Ward really Toronto's first 'priority neighbourhood'?
McKeown: I like the idea of the first priority neighbourhood, because what we talk about today in Toronto is 'place-based' risk and 'place-based' services. In the early twentieth century, Hastings' approach was basically a place-based approach. He talked about the importance of housing, income, sanitation and services at the household level – [filtered] water instead of privies and wells. It was a relationship between people's living circumstances and their health outcomes.

Was 'outcomes' a concept in public health at the time?
Hastings' period was very much a transitional period, when we're moving from a less science-based approach into measuring health outcomes. The infrastructure that Hastings put in place, in terms of staffing and qualifications and data, was the beginning of the modern approach to public health. They measured things. That's how they knew that some areas of the city were less healthy than other areas of the city. They were looking at where the public health staff were going and what they were finding. They were knocking on doors and finding out how many people were living in this place. Do you have a well, ventilation, running water, a privy? Those kinds of data-driven assessments helped identify the size of the problem.

What else did he discover about this community?
He was an early proponent of a 'social determinants of health' approach. He didn't use that language, but he was looking at things other than health services that made a big difference in people's health: income, housing, community safety, access to non-health services like clean water. These were critical elements in determining how healthy people are. He also recognized patterns of immigration as being a factor. People in overcrowded, substandard housing were new to the city.

Hastings played quite a large role in creating a network of public health nurses.
Hastings was instrumental in bringing public health nursing as a profession into the delivery of public health services. When it was started twenty or thirty years earlier, it was very regulatory- and inspection-based. Public health employees acted more like police officers. But nurses, he felt, brought a very different set of skills, particularly around maternal and child health. The idea of sending nurses out into the community to connect with people in their own homes, whether it was for the purposes of TB, communicable diseases control or teaching new mums how to adapt to their babies, was an innovation in public health.

How important was it that he'd been an obstetrician who had a practice on Wellesley Street, delivering babies in both Cabbagetown and Rosedale?
He was not initially a public health expert. But he brought that experience as a physician for people living in very poor circumstances, and he brought a reforming missionary's zeal to his work because of the experiences he'd had.

Can you talk about Hastings and Toronto's milk supply?

Hastings lost a child to unpasteurized milk. So he was very much a pro-pasteurization advocate before he became MOH, and he managed to achieve pasteurization reforms at the municipal level during his tenure. Interestingly, that kind of measure, although it may have benefited people living in places like The Ward, was a classic example of a population-wide public health intervention. Everyone would have benefited.

What other major changes was he responsible for?

He's best known for his innovative approach to advocacy. He had seen with own eyes the conditions in which people live. The decision-makers may or may not have. He would have wanted to bring that information to decision-makers, so he hired Arthur Goss to document conditions in slum housing. He did use the photos in his 1911 report on housing conditions, and in his advocacy about people living in very poor circumstances. He built up the political will to make the changes that were necessary in the neighbourhood later on.

Why did he become such an effective public health advocate?

He started with a great deal of good will. When he was hired, there was a widespread view in the medical field that he was the guy for the job. He [also] used data to support his advocacy in ways that hadn't been done [before]. He wasn't shy about making his views known, either. He published a health bulletin, which was widely circulated and served as a soapbox.

Did he have political opponents?

As today, there are always people who will oppose health and progressive moves forward. He struggled, as did all public health people in that era, with anti-vaccination sentiment. There was backlash on the pasteurization issue as well.

Did conditions change in The Ward as a result of Hastings' efforts?

They brought in measures to improve the physical conditions – the regulations on privies and the water system. It was after his tenure when [Ontario lieutenant governor Herbert Bruce] did the big housing report in 1934. That highlighted The Ward in terms of housing quality. So [Hastings] certainly didn't solve all

the problems. The big physical changes in the neighbourhood came afterward.

What does Hastings' career tell Toronto in the twenty-first century?

It says that leaders can make a difference. If they'd had a different medical officer of health, we might not have got the progress we did get. Also, public servants sometimes have to be advocates and not stick to their knitting – really get outside their narrow job description and advocate for what's best for the city.

Female resident of The Ward breastfeeding in the kitchen with her family, October 27, 1913.

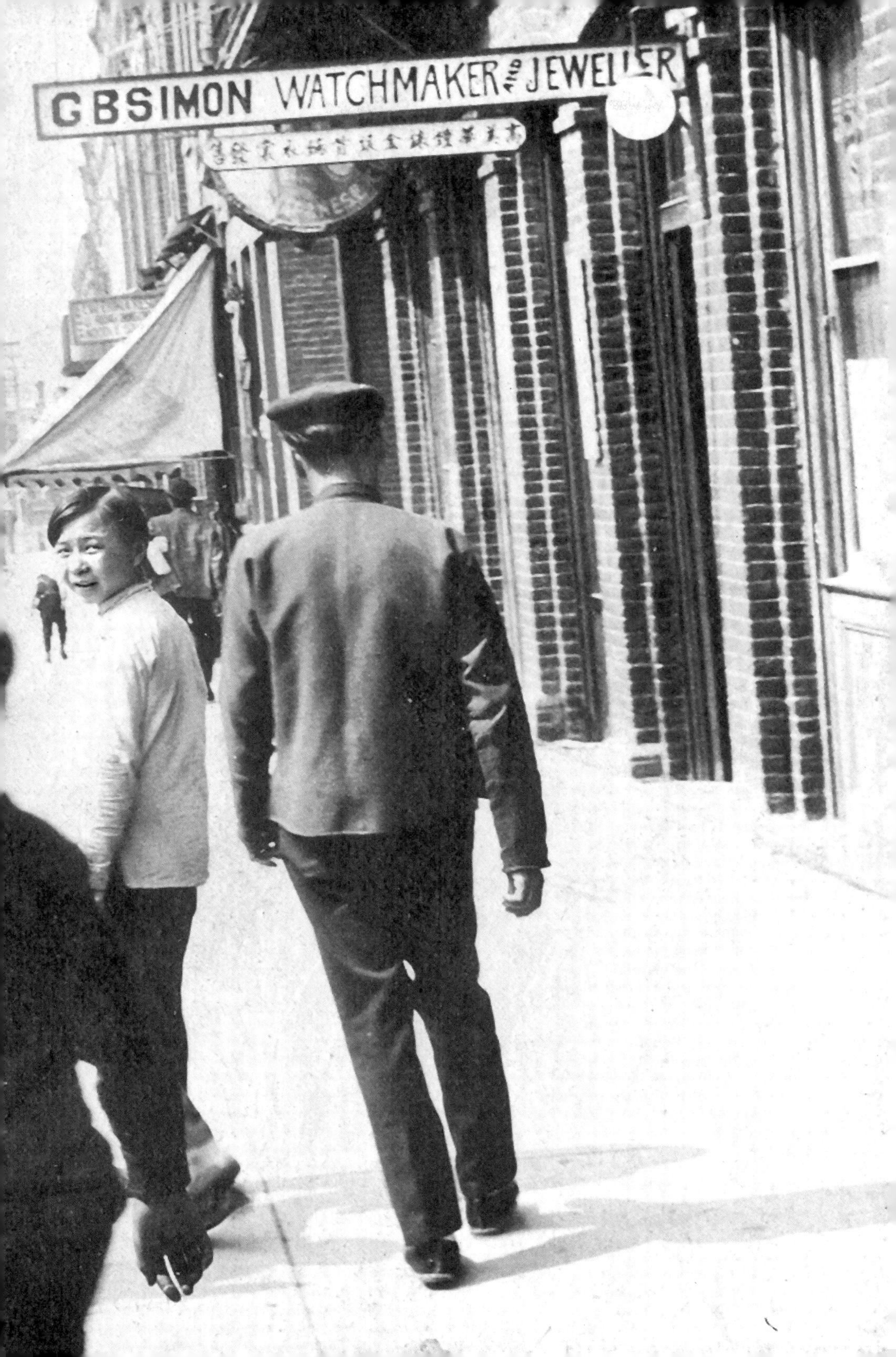
G B SIMON WATCHMAKER AND JEWELLER

MY CITY HALL office faces north onto Elizabeth Street – a non-descript stretch of grey sidewalks, concrete walls, family-run restaurants and a condo aptly named One City Hall. But when I look out the window, I also see a streetscape haunted by the spirit of Chinese settlers, long gone and mostly forgotten.

In my mind's eye, Elizabeth Street is lined by sunlit batten-board storefronts, with Chinese script painted on lead glass windows. My imagined Elizabeth Street is influenced by archival photographs, their details etched into my subconscious through ancestral connections I cannot readily explain.

KRISTYN WONG-TAM

REMEMBERING TORONTO'S FIRST CHINATOWN

I sense here the indomitable spirit of the Chinese settlers from places like Guangdong and my native Hong Kong – poor migrants who fled poverty and civic unrest beginning in the late 1880s. They toiled on the railways and then had to fight racist laws for the right to remain. These pioneering men and women clustered together and supported one another by building homes and businesses on streets that would become some of the most valuable commercial real estate in Toronto: the 'first' Chinatown.

The Chinese-owned groceries, laundries, restaurants, theatres, benevolent societies and apartments that once dominated the lower Ward are old history now. Very few Torontonians, including those of Chinese descent, know why the city tore down the original Chinatown and displaced its inhabitants.

I confronted this history in 2006, when I was president of the Toronto chapter of the Chinese Canadian National Council. Heritage Toronto officials told me the plaque commemorating

Previous: Street scene in Chinatown, ca. 1913.

Left: View of Elizabeth Street looking north toward College, 1955.

Toronto's first Chinatown would have to be relocated due to renovations at Nathan Phillips Square. The agency's historian, Gary Miedema, wanted to know whether we were interested in replacing the old bronze plaque with a new enamel one designed to accommodate archival photographs.

Heritage Toronto asked me to raise $4,750 to cast and install the new plaques. Using my own funds, I donated prizes and sold raffle tickets at our annual banquet. We collected the money easily. The hard part was confronting the little-known history of the sanctioned demolition of the original Chinatown.

Chinatown grew up in the middle of The Ward, home to waves of non-English speaking 'Orientals,' Italians and Jewish refugees fleeing persecution in Europe. These newcomers were told to stay out of other neighbourhoods. Few business owners would serve them, let alone rent them properties. The Ward became home to everyone who wasn't white, Anglo-Saxon and Protestant.

Chinese opera singers in local production, March 1946.

In 1945, Toronto council decided to build a new civic square capped with an architectural shrine to symbolize a budding metropolis. Eager to shed its colonial past and move out of 'old' City Hall, the elected officials ordered up an ambitious plan to assemble land in The Ward. Chinatown, where Chinese-Canadians owned 55 per cent of the property, stood directly in the path of council's grand vision. Two-thirds of the area would be expropriated in the late 1940s and early 1950s.

Few Toronto residents today know this story better than Doug Hum. A learned man with a kind face and strong brow, Hum was born in 1940 and lived in Chinatown. His old home was a semi-detached building with moon-shaped windows at 111 Elizabeth. In the 1930s, there were two stores on the ground floor: a Chinese laundry and a Jewish bakery. The structure was demolished to make way for this new civic project. But in the

end, the new City Hall precinct did not extend north of Hagerman Street. The entrance to a luxury condo is now where Hum's home once was. His family also operated Cathay Gardens, a Chinese restaurant located on the southern end of Elizabeth, just north of Queen Street, about where the west end of the Nathan Phillips Square fountain now stands.

109 and 111 Elizabeth Street, March 30, 1937. Doug Hum lived at 111. The site is now a condominium.

    Hum's Chinese-born father and uncle arrived in Canada in 1912 through the Vancouver port, on an ocean ship known as *Empress of Japan*, and paid the $500 head tax, which represented at that time two years' worth of wages. They prayed that China's instability would pass and the new country could offer them an opportunity to make enough money to return to the brides and wives they'd left behind. Sadly, Hum's father's young wife, who had remained in China, died shortly after his departure. He eventually remarried a Cantonese opera singer, who arrived in 1936. The small, tight-knit Chinese community, Hum recalls, was capable of supporting the fundraising efforts of three local Cantonese opera houses in The Ward. In the 1930s, he tells me, Chinese expats from across the region

Celebration on Elizabeth Street at Hagerman, 1974.

would flood into Chinatown and fill these venues to raise funds to support China and its refugees in a 'life-and-death struggle' with Japan. He describes the community's preoccupation with the 1931 invasion of Manchuria, the subsequent fall of Peking (now Beijing) and the Japanese army's incursions down the coastal regions. In fact, some Chinatown residents were refugees fleeing the war and could recount in horrific detail the Nanking (now Nanjing) massacre.

After the Second World War and the defeat of Imperial Japan, Chinese immigrants in Canada realized they could return home. Yet many had established roots in cities like Toronto, Montreal and Vancouver. Many continued to send home money, but returning to China was no longer their primary objective. Families ripped apart by oceans and wars had grown estranged.

With the city's post-war plans for a civic square, Toronto's Chinese community was again forced to defend itself against

mass displacement. Merchants and property owners banded together with community leader Jean Bessie Lumb, who would receive the Order of Canada for her resistance efforts through the Save Chinatown Committee.

Its members marched, lobbied and launched a lawsuit to fend off the expropriation of their homes, businesses and buildings, covering about two-thirds of Chinatown. In the end, Lumb and her followers lost a long battle. After a decade of uncertainty, the buildings deteriorated, as the owners didn't want to invest in properties destined to be torn down. The city expropriated the properties at 'market value,' but Hum says the building owners never received payments reflecting the true value of the property taken from the Chinese community.

Though some Chinese businesses hang on, many owners left Chinatown, broken and defeated. Few merchants were able to relocate to the Chinatown on Spadina. And most, including Hum's father, didn't own the buildings where they had their businesses, and were forced to close their doors for good, without compensation.

The perfunctory text on the 1983 plaque commemorating Toronto's first Chinatown made no mention of mass displacement and expropriation. But after raising the funds for a new one, I advocated for the inclusion of language that better reflected the story of the destruction of the first Chinatown. I wanted to reveal the injustice imposed on the Chinese-Canadian community. I felt it would be wrong to once again erase a community that had been scrubbed from The Ward many years earlier.

Heritage Toronto agreed. In 2007, two new Chinatown plaques were installed in Nathan Phillips Square next to the new children's playground, and then removed and stored for years while the square underwent extensive renovations. In 2014, the plaques finally settled into their permanent location, northwest of the square, next to the Winston Churchill statue near the corridor in which Elizabeth Street had once thrived. The new plaques now tell a fuller story of Toronto's first Chinatown.

VILJO REVELL, THE Finnish architect of the Functionalist school, died too young, in 1964. He was not yet fifty-five, and his design for Toronto City Hall would not be completed until the following year, rising from this razed square of The Ward. From that moment, the curving asymmetric twin towers and flying-saucer central council chamber of the design would prove iconic. Functionalism is not always so optimistic in execution as here, but the basic commitment to the classical ideals of firmness, commodity and delight are everywhere evident in this exemplary civic structure. 'Two curved white towers gave onto a great square,' Dennis Lee wrote in his complicated song of citizenship, *Civil Elegies* (1968; revised 1972); 'at the time, such a dramatic public space was new in Toronto.'

MARK KINGWELL

TABULA RASA

Lee's poem offers an extended reflection on the Canada of the mid-1960s – the clearing away of old neighbourhoods to make way for new ambition. This is the Canada of the Montreal Expo 67 world's fair, Pearsonian global citizenship, economic and cultural confidence. But as the poem's narrator sits in the square and watches his fellow citizens make their way across it, in the smooth urban dance of many people on their way to different places, he considers those who are absent, not part of what G. K. Chesterton called 'the small and arrogant oligarchy of those who merely happen to be walking about.'

Previous: Site of City Hall, from Conditions of Competition, City Hall and Square, 1957

> *Often I sit in the sun and brooding over the city, always*
> *in airborne shapes among the pollution I hear them, returning;*
> *pouring across the square*
> *in fetid descent they darken the towers*

Left: Engineer surveying construction of new City Hall, 1964.

and the wind-swept place of meeting, and whenever
the thick air clogs my breathing it teems with their presence.

The new confidence of 'Canada's century' delivers a booby-trapped gift, the narrator will go on to suggest, one compromised by what we would later call neo-liberalism.

The narrator ponders how everything new is bracketed by what has been scraped away, and haunted by what is yet to come:

I sat one morning by the Moore, off to the west
ten yards and saw though diffident my city nailed against the sky
in ordinary glory.
It is not much to ask. A place, a making,
two towers, a teeming, a genesis, a city.

The dream is, as ever, ambiguous in significance: Is it merely a fantasy? An alternative history? Perhaps a premonition? A better past, we are told, but in what way? Henry Moore's *Three-Way Piece No. 2 (The Archer)*, unveiled on the plaza in 1966, is a mute prompt for these thoughts. The city's dead, the narrator says, 'dawdle about in our lives and form a destiny, still / incomplete, still dead weight, still / demanding whether Canada will be.'

Even with all the uncertainties of this moment, the city is still capable of glory – the ordinary kind, as befits our modesty about ambition, but glory all the same. And such glory is, as Machiavelli argued in *The Prince*, the end or purpose that all civic energy must serve. Toronto is not wicked in this pursuit, nor as eager to obliterate and rebuild as some cities. Whole blocks of New York or Shanghai may disappear in a matter of days, built over by new towers that first obscure and then eliminate any memory of what was there before.

This image of the planned site of Toronto City Hall and Nathan Phillips Square demonstrates that sometimes our civic leaders rouse themselves to similar exertions of creative destruction. The plan was deliberately bold, a gesture meant to send the message of thrusting modernist certainty. It was also, to be sure, convenient that what was being swept away was a most troublesome sector of the shifting downtown core.

The image itself is dreamy, almost childish: the god's-eye view of the city, the grid-square footprint, the clean blankness of a tabula rasa where anything is possible. It reminds me of an illustration from some kind of building set, perhaps like the SuperCity construction kits that allowed the children of the 1960s, myself among them, to build the future metropolis on the smooth floor of a basement playroom. It has the abstract quality of the architectural imagination, like those scale models where all the buildings are present, but the people – and the noise, the smells, the pollution – are left out. Abstraction that enables concrete rendering, the results of which we must then contend with.

Nathan Phillips Square has not quite lived up to Revell's promise of public-space glory: its bare expanse is notably inhospitable even for the many lunching office workers who, perforce, take their midday break there. Nevertheless, it occupies the centre of Toronto's sudden material maturation in the late 1960s and early 1970s – a prelude to Mies van der Rohe's Toronto Dominion Centre and then First Canadian Place, the Bank of Montreal's flagship tower, designed by Bregman + Hamann, which made its singular claim to dominance in 1975. The CN Tower, still the clearest visual metonym of Toronto, opened a year later.

City Hall's towers, meanwhile, have entered the larger cultural imagination. Among other things, they have been obliterated by CGI neutron-bomb explosion in *Resident Evil: Apocalypse*, provided the backdrop for a hostage scene in a political thriller and appeared as a time-travel destination on an episode of *Star Trek: The Next Generation*. Now half a century old, Revell's design still feels futuristic, though tinged inevitably by the same City of Tomorrow nostalgia that pervades the Futurist designs of Oscar Niemeyer, who built Brasilia, or even the confident mid-century Modernism of Philip Johnson. The future of those utopian desires never really arrived. Or, as science-fiction writer William Gibson once put it, the future is already here; it's just unevenly distributed.

The business of politics is being conducted even now in the disk-like council chamber, resonating with scandals and accusations that the generation that built this place likely never imagined possible. Revell and his kind are gone, or going. As for the even older ghosts of the blocks wiped clean to make way for the square, they take their place in the long roster of the city's departed, their thousand individual stories of love, longing, toil and heartbreak forgotten by time and then wiped clean by civic ambition.

Let us remember them this way: they were Torontonians.

J. DAVID HULCHANSKI

UNREALIZED
RENEWAL

IN THE PERIOD after the Second World War, The Ward quickly lost any remaining significant remnants of its past diversity. It evolved into an almost totally new physical and social landscape.

With the pressure to expand existing downtown institutional uses for a growing metropolitan population, The Ward's central location meant dramatic change was inevitable. There had been very little new development during 1930s and during the war. After 1945, however, 'renewal' planning became a priority.

During the 1950s, The Ward was part of Toronto's first designated urban renewal study area. Civic officials feared that Toronto's downtown would further deteriorate, as was happening in large cities in the United States. During the heyday of the automobile, millions of young families flocked to the suburbs. Suburban shopping malls, with their large free parking lots, took business away from the downtown retailers, in Toronto and elsewhere. The question facing civic leaders and planners was, what should be done with the old central area?

We need to recall that in 1950, Toronto remained a sleepy outpost in North America. With a metropolitan population of about 1 million, the Toronto area ranked sixteenth in North America, well behind twelfth-ranked Montréal, with 1.3 million people, and Detroit, ranked sixth with 2.8 million people.

Urban renewal was seen as the answer to The Ward's blighted streets – it meant clearing away much of what existed and starting over. Existing government buildings, like the Land Registry Office, were replaced with a new city hall and

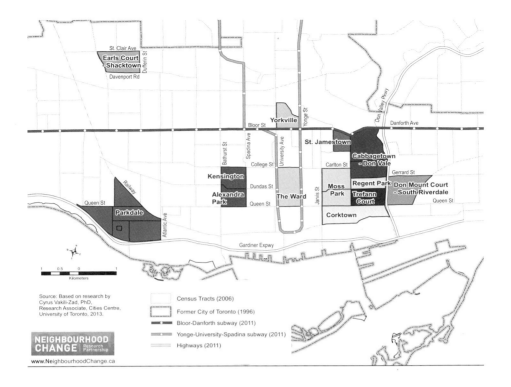

Source: Based on research by
Cyrus Vakili-Zad, PhD,
Research Associate, Cities Centre,
University of Toronto, 2013.

NEIGHBOURHOOD
CHANGE | Research
Partnership
www.NeighbourhoodChange.ca

Census Tracts (2006)
Former City of Toronto (1996)
Bloor-Danforth subway (2011)
Yonge-University-Spadina subway (2011)
Highways (2011)

a new courthouse. The city also expropriated and then demolished The Ward's residential areas. East and west of the core,
so-called slum districts were levelled and replaced with large
public housing communities.

*Areas considered to be
'slums' in early-20th-
century Toronto.*

In 1964, the city designated the north section of The Ward
as a 'housing improvement area,' even though there was very
little housing left by then. Five years later, the Official Plan
decreed that parts of The Ward would become a 'designated
improvement study area.' But by 1974, when the city was looking for federal funds for a neighbourhood improvement
program geared toward inner-city neighbourhoods, it left The
Ward off the list. The reason? The area was no longer residential and was undergoing 'renewal' due to the construction of
new government, hospital and office buildings.

Over time, these city and regional institutions – the new
city hall and Nathan Philips Square, additions to the provincial

courthouse, and regional hospitals and associated medical services – expanded to occupy more of The Ward. Today the northern part of The Ward is branded Toronto's biotechnology

'Discovery District,' while the southern section is dominated by municipal government and justice services.

The radical shift in land use obviously impacted the residential cross-section. In the early years of the twentieth century, The Ward's population density rivalled that of contemporary Paris, with thousands of inhabitants packed into a crowded enclave. By the 1950s, the population had fallen to 3,000, and to just 900 by the early 1980s. Post-war, children under fifteen accounted for about 10 per cent of The Ward's inhabitants, a number that fell to just thirty, or 3 per cent, by 1981.

And then the population

Redevelopment in The Ward, 1971. Mary John's Café, at Elizabeth and Gerrard, occupied the small building in the foreground from the late 1920s. pendulum started to swing back as the city's 1970s policy of bringing residential back to the downtown took root. Reformers like David Crombie and John Sewell openly opposed the bulldozer approach to renewal, and recognized that the central business area would likely continue to decline unless it became more like a neighbourhood, with round-the-clock and weekend users. The reformers proposed mixed-use development throughout the city, but especially in the central area.

Though private developers initially resisted building housing downtown – they worried that no tenants would materialize – the city leveraged a new federal non-profit social housing program to build neighbourhoods such as St. Lawrence.

The 1980s saw new residential mixed-use development, mostly condos, in The Ward, and the population has grown steadily ever since, from 900 in the early 1980s to 7,300 today.

This community bears virtually no resemblance to the one that existed in the area during the early twentieth century. From the 1980s until the mid-2000s, the average income in The Ward was much higher than the city average. In 2004, however, the University of Toronto bought the former Holiday Inn adjacent to City Hall and transformed it into a residence for about a thousand students. This development lowered the area's average income and introduced a different population mix from that of the more affluent condominium residents.

Yet, unlike some of the newly developed downtown residential areas, The Ward today is not a place for families with children. The share of families, about one-third, is currently at its lowest level in the post-war period. The population comprises two dominant groups: working-age professionals (twenty-five to forty-nine) with good incomes, and university students (under twenty-four). Only 7 per cent of the population in 2011 was under fifteen years old, and 15 per cent were over fifty.

Is there a sense of community among the people who now live in The Ward? Not likely. Condominiums have security systems, internal management and social structure, and underground parking. Also, a large number of The Ward's residents are transitory – students in the University of Toronto's Chestnut Street residence. The area's public spaces serve the general public, not just the local population. It's safe to assume that most of the current residents know very little about the dense, immigrant community that once existed there.

JOHN LORINC

A SHORT HISTORY OF THE 'CIVIC SQUARE' EXPROPRIATION

WITH THE SECOND World War raging, Toronto politicians in 1943 advanced an ambitious master plan that called for the creation of open space, as well as a new city hall in the area north of Queen between Bay and University: Chinatown.

Over the next three years, the 'Civic Square' vision took shape, for example, with a proposal to build a four-storey garage beneath the square to generate revenue and help solve the mounting problem of car theft in downtown lots.

But in 1946, city officials became anxious about cost. The assessed value of the property and buildings – including the Land Registry Office and Shea's Hippodrome – totalled about $2 million. Mayor Robert Hood Saunders reckoned the city could acquire the land for $3 million, assuring voters that new development would recoup the outlay. Nevertheless, council approved a more modest scheme that called only for a new police headquarters, court building and civic square.

Media reports claimed that Chinese merchants in the area had accepted the plan. 'Chinatown Is Getting Ready to Move,' blared a *Toronto Star* headline on March 30, 1946. 'The biggest part will be wiped out by the proposed civic memorial square and the police building but the unobtrusive Oriental is taking it in his stride. "We're a pretty flexible lot," said Yick Wong, publisher of the *China Daily Times*. "We Chinese residents of Toronto have expected this for a long time… "' Contrary to such reports, many of Chinatown's residents deeply resented the plan and later fought further attempts to expropriate their community.

On January 1, 1947, Toronto electors eligible to vote on money bylaws – i.e., property owners, lease holders and corporations – were asked to approve the unfunded plan, which enjoyed the endorsement of the Toronto Board of Trade. Herewith, a partial chronology of what followed:

January 2, 1947

• In a New Year's Day plebiscite, voters approve plans for an affordable housing project in Regent Park and a civic square. As Saunders told the *Toronto Star*, 'I supported the Civic Square project because I think that one of the misfortunes of this city is that we have no open spaces in our downtown district.' Regarding Regent Park, he added, 'We must remove housing conditions which contribute to juvenile delinquency. In that respect, we have a moral duty to our fellow man...'

MUNICIPAL ELECTIONS

CIVIC SQUARE

VOTING ON THE QUESTION IN RELATION TO THE ACQUISITION OF CERTAIN LANDS AND BUILDINGS FOR A CIVIC SQUARE

Notice is hereby given that the votes of the Electors

ENTITLED TO VOTE ON MONEY BY-LAWS

will be taken at the Municipal Elections to be held on

WEDNESDAY, THE FIRST DAY OF JANUARY, 1947

on the following question (which is correctly stated) viz:

"Are you in favour of the City acquiring, for the purposes of a Civic Square, certain lands and buildings within the area bounded by Bay Street, Queen Street, Chestnut Street and a line approximately 460 feet north of Albert Street, and having an assessed value of approximately $2,000,000.00?"

EACH ELECTOR IS ENTITLED TO VOTE ON SAID QUESTION IN EACH WARD IN WHICH HE OR SHE HAS THE RIGHT TO VOTE ON MONEY BY-LAWS

A tenant, who has a lease which extends for a period of at least twenty-one years and who has, by such lease, covenanted to pay all municipal taxes in respect of the property leased (other than local improvement rates), shall, if he or she makes and FILES WITH THE CLERK OF THE MUNICIPALITY NOT LATER THAN THE 21st DAY OF DECEMBER, 1946, being a date not later than the tenth day before the day appointed for taking the vote, a declaration under "The Canada Evidence Act," so stating, be entitled to have his or her name entered on the list of Electors to vote on the said question.

A CORPORATION assessed on the last revised assessment roll as owner or as lessee, having a lease for a period of at least twenty-one years, shall be entitled to appoint a nominee to vote on its behalf on this question. All such appointments must be in writing and filed with the Clerk of the Municipality not later THAN THE 21st DAY OF DECEMBER, 1946, being a date not later than the tenth day before the day appointed for taking the vote. When a Corporation is a lessee, a declaration in accordance with the preceding paragraph must also be filed. (Blank forms for the above may be had upon application at this office.)

Notice is further given that the thirtieth day of December, 1946, at 11.00 o'clock in the forenoon at the Mayor's Office in the City Hall, is the time and place which has been fixed for the appointment of persons to attend at the various polling places and at the final summing-up of the votes by the Municipal Clerk, on behalf of the persons interested in voting in the affirmative or negative on this question.

City Clerk's Office.
Toronto, December 5, 1946.

J. W. SOMERS,
City Clerk.

January 8, 1947

• Council's Board of Control instructs the city solicitor to apply to the Ontario Municipal Board 'for an order from that Board approving of the undertaking of the work and dispensing with the assent of the electors.'

Notification of plebiscite on Civic Square. Toronto Daily Star, *December 19, 1946.*

February 12, 1947

• Ontario Municipal Board issues order No. 5777, approving the authorization of the use of powers and 'the provision of moneys' to proceed with a civic square.

February 17, 1947

• Council unanimously passes Bylaw 16834: 'The establishment of a Civic Square within the area of the City bounded

by Bay Street, Queen Street, Chestnut Street, and a line approximately 460 feet north of Albert Street.'
- Bylaw 16835, passed the same day, authorizes the city to expropriate 'certain lands' within that area. Council authorizes city officials to issue bonds up to $2 million to fund the property acquisitions.

April 1, 1947
- Council passes Bylaw 16548: 'To restrict to use for parks, playgrounds, government buildings and certain other purposes lands and buildings' with the area designated for the civic square.
- The Board of Control retains 'real estate expert' W. H. Bosley to negotiate the acquisition of the properties in the area and directs the 'Head of Civic Departments to cooperate with Mr. Bosley in every possible manner...'

November 10, 1947
- Council passes Bylaw 17087, authorizing the city to borrow another $1 million for purchasing property within the civic square site.

November 24, 1947
- 'There has been some criticism of the prices at which a real estate agent, acting for the city, has purchased properties which Toronto requires for the new civic square,' a *Toronto Star* editorial noted. 'The complaint is that these prices are greatly in excess of the assessed value. It is a fact, however, that municipalities very seldom get properties at or near the assessed value. Certainly Toronto has not done so in the past... An owner is naturally entitled to more when his property is taken away from him than when he voluntarily sells it.'

January 12, 1948
- Alderman Harold Fishleigh (Ward 3, which included the area) 'gives notice that he will on tomorrow move that the City acquire and demolish as many small buildings as possible immediately on the Civic Square site and make same available immediately for parking purposes.'

July 14, 1948
- Recommendation to Board of Control from Mr. W. H. Bosley, OBE, regarding

the acquisition of 19 and 19½ Elizabeth Street. 'The lands required for the establishment of the Civic Square were expropriated by By-law No. 16835, passed by Council February 17th, 1947. Included in the expropriation is No. 19 and 19½ Elizabeth Street having a frontage of 22 feet by a depth of 80 feet. The building is 2 storeys in front and 1 storey at rear, ground floor divided into two portions, the front part... is a grocery store, rear apparently a commission merchant's. No. 19½ has corridor leading back to two rooms, which have concrete floors and metallic ceilings, second floor belongs to No. 19. No cellar or heating; plumbing fair, but no bath; flat or deck roof covered with ready [roofing]; small roof in front over store window felt and gravel.' Bosley negotiated the $13,500 purchase with agents for Mr. Lee Sam and Mr. Yung Ing Lee. The property was assessed for the sum of $7,850.

January 10, 1949
- According to the council minutes, 'Alderman Fishleigh gives notice that he will move... that the Committee on Works be given copies of the attached report of the Union Square Garage, "the largest underground garage of its type in the world," in San Francisco, and that said Committee study the same and submit a report in respect to applying a similar plan to our own Civic Square.'

January 20, 1949
- Council passes Bylaw 17567. With the expropriation budget exceeding initial projections, council votes '[t]o authorize the issue of debentures to the amount of $1,000,000 on account of the cost of the new Civic Square.'

It took another six years before Toronto council approved an $18 million plan to erect a new city hall and square on that land. Mayor Nathan Phillips famously rejected a dull Beaux-Arts proposal and persuaded council to support an international design competition. The jury, led by architect Eric Arthur, selected the Finnish designer Viljo Revell in 1958. Construction crews broke ground in 1961 and finished the $31 million structure, which came to be called the 'eye of the government,' in 1965 – fully a generation after that initial wartime proposal. Journalist and critic Robert Fulford dubbed the instantly iconic structure a 'break with the past.'

TATUM TAYLOR

STORYTELLING IS PART OF THE STORY

I N 1964, AS the new City Hall became a concrete reality, a *Toronto Star* journalist wrote an obituary for the neighbourhood it had replaced. The headline waxed lyrical: 'The Ward of 1900 was a harsh ghetto, but to thousands it symbolized freedom.' At the turn of the twentieth century, however, Toronto's newspapers had portrayed the immigrant precinct of St. John's Ward in a far drearier light. An article in 1905 warned of an 'Invasion of Foreigners ... which presents grave problems of a sociological and religious character.' Now that few physical traces of the neighbourhood remain, The Ward exists for us in stories. But how can we reconcile these disparate accounts to reconstruct a singular, truthful depiction of The Ward? Should we even try?

Traditional history has often cast shadows on marginalized communities such as The Ward's inhabitants. As popular history has shuffled fragments of experience into a dominant narrative, these groups have been largely neglected or forgotten for any number of reasons: political oppression, poverty, illiteracy, secrecy, controversy, inattention. Social historians in recent years have sought to document the stories of neglected communities. To further understand the underdocumented past, we must look critically at what impressions remain. Because media both affects and reflects public perception, it provides insight into the evolution of The Ward within Toronto's collective memory. The Ward was not an area that many non-residents frequented, so published descriptions had heightened potential to shape public opinions. Newspapers help us to chart the arc of how The Ward was narrated over time – how it was perceived, remembered and

CLASSIFIED WANT AD SERVICE
TELEPHONE EMPIRE 8-3611
8.30 a.m.-5 p.m. (Mon. to Fri. only)

TORONTO DAILY STAR

MORE CLASSIFIED WANT
ADS THAN ANY OTHER
NEWSPAPER IN TORONTO

FEBRUARY PAID CIRCULATION **402,244** COPIES PER DAY   FRIDAY, APRIL 1, 1955   SECOND SECTION

Drew 'Arrogant', Now Frost 'Smiles Us To Death'--Labor

QUAINT CHINESE SHOPS AND RESTAURANTS HANG "CLOSED" SIGNS ON THEIR DOORS, AS COUNCIL CLEARS AREA FOR A CIVIC SQUARE

almost forgotten. But as language, politics, race relations and city demographics evolved, so did the tone of the media portrayals. Just as we might trace the neighbourhood's history through atlases and photographs, we can find vestiges of The Ward by considering diction and details in the news. For this community, storytelling is very much a part of the story.

The end of Chinatown is front page news. Toronto Daily Star, *April 1, 1955.*

Early characterizations struck an alarmist tone: journalists warned of the 'evils of overcrowding' (1897) and 'undesirable immigrants' (1907). In 1909, the *Globe and Mail* published an exposé so 'that *Globe* readers might know what a Toronto slum looks like.' A journalist posed as a missionary and knocked on every door along an unnamed street in The Ward. He documented the crowded conditions he discovered and the immigrant interactions he witnessed. The reporter concluded by pointing out the relative scarcity of Canadian and British inhabitants, and expressed sympathy for those living among so many non-Anglophones: 'Truth to tell, these English

speakers, a number of them industrious, respectable people, did not look upon their new fellow-citizens with much favor. The aversion of the latter to soap and water in their houses and persons was certainly obvious.' These descriptions exemplify one of two approaches toward the Ward that seem to have prevailed at the time. They use broad observations and negative generalizations to convince readers of a dichotomy: there are clean, respectable, hardworking Torontonians – and then there are those other people in The Ward.

Some journalists in the early twentieth century achieved similar ends with a second rhetorical approach. Several articles emphasized the otherness of Ward inhabitants by romanticizing their homes and lifestyles. 'There is one part of the city that the people seldom boast about,' noted one reporter, 'although it is picturesque and interesting' (1923). Rather than decrying the perils of poverty, such writers gleefully recorded peculiar details of life in The Ward. One reporter marvelled, 'The Italians amuse themselves by singing in their rich, sweet voices the songs of their far-away homeland or dancing their native dances to the music of a mandolin or guitar in the open roadway beneath the stars' (1910). Another observed, 'How many Orientals crowd into the room-houses, from which the weird tinkle of Celestial stringed instruments floats over the street, cannot be told' (1922).

It is clear in retrospect that The Ward wasn't all starlit dances and floating music. While this second group of writers should be credited with acknowledging the neighbourhood's character, they also exaggerated its foreignness. Their version of The Ward depicted an enclave of exotic yet quaint customs that had no other place in the city. It was a way of explaining the clannishness that caused a certain disquiet among Anglo-Torontonians: 'The people from a dozen different countries have come together. They love their religion and their traditions and they want friendship, so they huddle in together where they can enjoy to the fullest possible extent the only kind of life that they know how to live' (1923).

By mid-century, with plans underway for the city's expropriation and redevelopment of the area, media accounts of The Ward echoed that earlier romanticized tone. However, the post-war coverage increasingly treated the neighbourhood not as a threatening curiosity but as a nostalgic landscape. These depictions mingled historic biases about The Ward with the modernizing spirit of the 1950s. With The Ward slated for demolition and 'renewal,'

Torontonians could view it more comfortably; it was no longer a menace but a transitory spectacle.

Some journalists commemorated the doomed Chinatown as a place 'where you can take your pick of two mayors and five kinds of chop suey and buy a package of "dragon's teeth" for whatever ails you' (1955). When city council discussed expropriating the northern portion of Chinatown in 1955, it was reported that 'this final action very nearly has some of the Chinatown people reverting to the custom of rubbing the stomachs of P'o Tai images. (P'o Tai is an oriental god of good fortune and you win his help by rubbing his stomach).' These disparaging descriptions suggest that The Ward's destruction might even be a shame – but still acceptable: 'Despite the expropriation troubles, the pedestrians on Elizabeth St. continue along at the same unhurried pace. Business is just as leisurely. After all, who wants to rush into paying $19 a pound for the wherewithal to make bird nest soup? (The material, in fact, does come from bird nests on Chinese islands)' (1955).

Even after the Second World War, Chinese-Canadians could expect condescending coverage.

The racist language of this period's coverage was less overtly anxious than in the past, and perhaps less self-conscious. Whereas journalists in the 1920s referred to Jews, Italians, Russians and Black inhabitants as 'human derelicts,' the Asians of the 1950s were called 'Chinatown's characters.' Pre-war accounts warned of 'moral leprosy' and inventoried the distasteful sights and smells of an Italian/Jewish neighbourhood: the 'squalor and hubbub,' 'the odors of decayed fruits and vegetables and of hundreds of unwashed men,' 'the swarthy, smudgy-faced children' (1923). In contrast, post-war journalists noted curiosities, such as a Chinese cook smoking a bamboo water pipe ('They're not for opium, despite the suspicions of sightseers'), and ran photographs of beaming Chinese women displaying silk slippers and paper lanterns.

Chinatown Rubs P'o Tai Hopes Good Luck Image Saves One-third of Area

By TED HONDERICH

The neon lights are going out in the town where nobody hurries, where you can take your pick of two mayors and five kinds of chop suey and buy a package of "dragon's teeth" for whatever ails you.

Toronto's Chinatown, or at least most of it, is on the way out. The city of Toronto, with plans

In 1947. No action to possess the land had been taken until several months ago when tenants on three blocks received notices. The blocks, two of them largely parking lots, are those bounded by: Bay St., Elizabeth St., Queen St., Albert St.; Elizabeth St., Chestnut St., Queen St., Albert St.; and Bay St., Elizabeth St., Louisa St., Albert St.

Most of the Chinese tenants

While the explicit taunts of an earlier era were mostly absent from post-war media accounts, the condescension was unmistakable: 'Bowing to the inevitable with typical Oriental calm,' observed one writer, 'most members of Toronto's Chinese community have accepted the absorption of the greater part of Chinatown in the name of progress' (1957). Mainstream newspapers claimed to speak on behalf of all Chinese citizens of The Ward, declaring that expropriation of their charming homes and businesses was perfectly agreeable. In their patronizing generalizations, these writings are hardly less bigoted than those of prior decades. Instead, the prose seems less self-aware; while earlier writers made no pretenses about their revulsion toward Jews and Italians, post-war journalists cloaked their racism in a dubious sort of admiration for a dying Chinatown.

Soon, it was all gone. In 1956, the painter Reginald Capel recalled a time, thirty years prior, when artists like Lawren Harris roamed The Ward's streets to sketch its unusual scenery and inhabitants. Capel wrote in the *Globe and Mail*, 'Many of us will remember the quaint old dwellings that housed them – many of patched stucco, shuttered and painted gaily in an attempt to keep up an air of respectability ... With the contemplated civic square, these places have practically disappeared. So interesting were these houses that from the artist's point of view they were a must for many a study.' Capel reminisced that, in the 1920s, a pile of Ward paintings seemed worthless. But years later, he visited the home of a wealthy acquaintance and discovered, by coincidence, a number of his own images of The Ward hanging on the wall. Time's passage can burnish our perspectives and reframe our values; what once was blight might later be deemed beautiful.

As a *Toronto Star* reporter wrote in 1964, The Ward was

a huge, threadbare ghetto in which Jews cheerfully shared a raw-knuckle hardship with immigrant Irish and Italian Catholics ... They fled to Canada in the stinking holds of big ships but they were too joyously preoccupied with being alive, safe and free – or well-fed – to be unduly bothered by the sweaty smell of the steerage decks ... Jews from Hungary and Italians from Palermo moved into the tiny cottage houses of Chestnut St. where, on summer weekend afternoons, they affably greeted one another in mutually unintelligible tongues. Now and again, they shyly exchanged gifts – a bottle of dark red wine for a steaming hot loaf of chala [*sic*].

Whether the writer meant to mourn The Ward as a symbol of immigrant freedom or silo it in a former era, he provided a poignant image that shaped readers' ideas about a place that no longer existed, and also resonated in an Anglo city now teaming with European newcomers. Society's perceptions of The Ward had gained the buffer of two decades following the Second World War, during which mass resettlement had become more commonplace. Perhaps the general public was ready to view The Ward with more empathy.

The most recent articles have offered a more pragmatic outlook. The city's memory of The Ward has dwindled over the second half of the twentieth century, and rare references in the media have offered a more objective portrayal of a little-known history. Unlike earlier accounts, they are based on historic reports and photographs rather than eyewitness experience. Adjectives are straightforward and observations are factual: 'Theirs was a milieu of congested streets, noisy markets, cramped workplaces; of ragpickers and junk dealers; of pushcarts and peddlers' (1992).

Contemporary coverage also draws parallels to our age, indicating that 'Toronto continues to face many of the same issues that troubled civic leaders at the turn of the 20th century' (2002). An article in 2011 exemplifies our current challenge of negotiating disparate assessments of The Ward's conditions: 'Life played out in rooming houses and tiny cottages and along alleyways. Some said the conditions were deplorable, but they were a far cry from the ghettos of other North American urban centres. Still, it was tough.'

This vacillating statement demonstrates the difficulty of describing places such as The Ward. We are reluctant to bluntly assess poor social conditions for fear of echoing bygone bigotry, and we turn instead to euphemism. Equivalent areas in contemporary Toronto are branded 'priority neighbourhoods'; inhabited by 'low-income families.' Like the generations before us, we have developed our own hesitant rhetoric of poverty. Toronto, it seems, has all but forgotten what happened in and to The Ward. But unless we read into the stories of past social injustices, how can we directly confront the poverty and racism in our city today?

Toronto archivist and photographer Patrick Cummins has been documenting the city's storefronts and the changes that wash over retail strips as neighbourhoods change. His work includes photos of row-houses on Dundas between Elizabeth and University, and Gerrard Street west of Yonge – both areas where The Ward's early housing stock somehow survived to the present.

PATRICK CUMMINS

HOW WE THINK ABOUT WHAT (LITTLE) SURVIVES

ORIGINALLY THOUGHT THE building at 149–151 Dundas was an example of Second Empire style, albeit a rather plain one. I didn't know if it was a fragment of a former row or if it was always a stand-alone structure. But I photographed it as an example of an architecture that predates the rest of the surviving commercial buildings in the area. As I researched the building, however, I discovered it was built much later than I had thought – not in the Second Empire period (1865–1880), but sometime in the early 1900s, in the Edwardian period (1901–1914), the same as the rest of what survives.

There was a time when I thought this might have been built as a hotel or a rooming house. Yet right from the beginning, it was commercial at ground level, with basic services – grocers, butchers, druggists, etc. – and apartments above. As for why it survives, that's an interesting question, and it caused me to look at other older buildings along that stretch of Dundas. What survives from the late nineteenth and early twentieth centuries? These buildings, built during the heyday of The Ward, which had already been around for some time as a gathering place for immigrants, are all that we have left of The Ward.

Looking at other survivors along that stretch, what becomes clear is that these were really very basic examples of late Victorian or early Edwardian architecture. In some cases, the survivors were clearly built as residential and converted to commercial. This is easily verified using old city directories, fire insurance plans and assessment rolls.

The block of Dundas toward University, at 181–187, was built as a row of houses in the late 1880s. Not very ornate at all – nothing like you'd see in Cabbagetown or Parkdale in the late nineteenth century. Why they survive, I don't know. The north side of Dundas was developed in this area, but not the south side. With the south side, the buildings appear to survive due to an endless turnover of mostly dining establishments.

When you look at the city directories, initially there's a shift from residential to commercial, with a range of shops you would need in a neighbourhood. But as time goes by, in the 1970s and 1980s, this stretch becomes a mini–food court, servicing City Hall and the other office buildings in the area. In my earliest photographs, from the 1980s, you still see things like luggage shops. You might see specialty shops, but they're servicing offices more than they would be servicing the residential area, which was eradicated. It will be interesting to see what happens to these with the arrival of the Ryerson University residences and the other condo developments in the area.

Up on Gerrard, at 68–74, another nineteenth-century row survives, one that is far more substantial than those on Dundas. These are three storeys, with bays and gables, and were built between 1880 and 1884. The area itself was more removed from the lower part of The Ward. It also took a lot longer for those buildings to transition to commercial.

This row doesn't become fully commercial until well into the 1970s. It stayed residential for much longer, and at one point would have been an extension of the Village, an artist's enclave that once existed on Gerrard between Elizabeth and Bay streets, which was largely eradicated in the 1960s, with some occupants moving to nearby Yorkville. But again, I don't know what's going to become of this stretch with the incredible number of condominiums going up.

So why did these pockets of late-nineteenth-century and early-twentieth-century architecture survive? Really, it's just happenstance – economics, location, etc. In both cases, with Dundas and Gerrard, they always found tenants who would service the needs of the area. But now what do you do? Do you

declare them historical because they're the last vestiges of an area and an era that's extremely important to the city's history?

They don't have much going for them architecturally. In neither case are they stunning examples of their era's styles. So what happens to these structures that we've inherited from another era, and that are not what you would choose if you were selecting representative architectural examples? Still, an argument

can be made that they're worth preserving because they're all *Left: 149-151 Dundas*
we've got from that time period. *St W, August 11, 1997.*

    They're like those lone gravestones poking up through the
grass of a long-neglected, largely abandoned cemetery. You *Right: 149-151 Dundas*
know there are hundreds of bodies buried there, but there are *St W, April 30, 2004.*
only one or two gravestones left to draw you visually.

T HE PHOTOGRAPHS OF The Ward taken by city photographer Arthur S. Goss are perhaps the best-known images in the City of Toronto Archives. They reveal, in astonishing detail, the living conditions faced by the wave of immigrants arriving in the neighbourhood known as The Ward in Toronto at the beginning of the twentieth century. Not surprisingly, these photos have long been the subject of books, articles, reports, websites, exhibitions and theses. Simply, Goss's body of work is an important historical document, and Goss himself is now recognized as a significant contributor to our understanding of the history of the city.

**SCOTT JAMES &
VICTOR RUSSELL**

INSTITUTIONAL MEMORY

However, the survival of these images is as much a story of good luck as good management. Since its incorporation in 1834, the City of Toronto had been creating records. But until 1960, no city official was formally responsible for the care and management of a rapidly growing trove of documents. In fact, there were no municipal archives in all of English-speaking Canada. In 1960, however, the city, acting on a recommendation of a 1957 Woods Gordon management report, appointed a librarian trained in England, A. R. N. (Bob) Woadden, as city archivist and director of records.

The timing of Woadden's appointment was fortuitous. New City Hall was under construction and it is a matter for speculation how many of the old records would have survived the transfer to the new quarters in 1965 without the oversight of the archivist.

Woadden immediately recognized the significance of a huge collection of some 26,000 images created by Goss during his

Left: Mrs. Ansky and her child, 37 Agnes Street, March 23, 1916.

time as city photographer. Discarded and neglected in the attic of Old City Hall, the glass plates of Goss's photos were being used to channel water from roof leaks. Unprotected and of little apparent value, the images had been free for the taking prior to Woadden's appointment, which is precisely what happened. In one instance, a wealthy collector of transportation memorabilia, Andrew Merrilees, carted away many of the glass-plate negatives for his collection. In another, a city employee in the mid-1950s, Michel Lambeth, later a well-known photojournalist, removed a small but significant number of Health Department prints, which later appeared in a booklet entitled *Made in Canada*. Lambeth attributed the images to 'an unknown photographer.' In the end, the good news is that all these Goss photos in private collections survived to be later donated to Library and Archives Canada.

Goss worked as the city photographer for nearly thirty years, until his death in 1940. His job, created by Streets and Properties Commissioner Roland C. Harris in 1911, had been primarily to document the construction and maintenance of the city's public works (roads, bridges, sewers, etc.). As well, Goss regularly worked on assignment for other municipal divisions, such as the Department of Public Health. He documented a wide range of civic activity through the first half of the twentieth century.

In 1967, Woadden hired a new archives assistant, Scott James, who spent a portion of his workday for two years cleaning, rehousing and organizing this invaluable collection. The subsequent development of the city archives and the resulting improved access to historical resources coincided with a new interest, among scholars and the general public, in the research and writing of local history. Historians Robert Harney and Harold Troper made extensive use of the Goss photographs in their book *Immigrants: A Portrait of the Urban Experience, 1890–1930*. Published in 1975, their study was the first major example in Canada of the use of photographs as historical evidence, rather than simply as illustrative material, subject to the same sorts of critical analysis as the written record.

Slowly, awareness of Goss's work and significance spread. Without an exhibition facility of its own, the city archives partnered in 1978 with the Baldwin Street Gallery of Photography to present the first public curated exhibition of his work relating to The Ward. Then, in 1979, the city archives opened the Market Gallery in the St. Lawrence Market as a showcase for its collections and

a year later mounted a major one-man Goss exhibition. Numerous exhibits of Goss's work have followed, most recently one entitled *Arthur S. Goss: Work and Days*, held at the Ryerson Image Centre. Curators Dr. Blake Fitzpatrick and John Bentley Mays acknowledged that Goss 'has long been best known for his eloquent pictures of slums, destitute immigrants, and other dark elements.' However, the curators chose to examine and mount an exhibit 'featuring and deliberately highlighting Goss's quotidian, prosaic output in contrast to his more humanistic imagery of unfortunate city dwellers.'

Today, much of Goss's acclaim is certainly the result of his technical skill as a photographer. Along with his day job working in a purely documentary mode, Goss, in his private life, was an early and ardent advocate of photography as an art form. As a pioneer participant in the Toronto Camera Club, he created and regularly exhibited his pictorialist images. He was also a long-time and active member of the Toronto Arts and Letters Club, which led to his friendships with the members of the Group of Seven. Goss was especially close to A. J. Casson, and the two men shared sketching and camping trips into the north. All of this activity sustained his involvement in the arts, and there is little doubt these interests affected his sense of composition and his treatment of subject material.

The City of Toronto Archives is now the repository of hundreds of thousands of historic photographs. Since 1960, many valuable archival collections have been added, including the William James Collection, the *Globe and Mail* Collection, the Canada Pictures Collection (Strathy Smith's subway series) and the priceless photos of the city taken by Armstrong, Beere and Hime in 1856. Yet it could be argued that Goss's 26,000 photos form the core of the collections. Certain sub-series, like those concerning The Ward, are heartbreaking and haunting, and offer a poignant reminder of a long-lost time and place. Rescued by the civic administration through the creation of the City of Toronto Archives, the Goss images have survived to provide future generations with a rich visual record of the complex history of Toronto in the early twentieth century.

WHY DOES THE WARD matter to me? My family didn't live in The Ward – they were poor elsewhere. They emigrated, mostly from England, and became farmers in Muskoka, as if anyone could imagine farming there among all those rocks. I moved here as a teenager, and Toronto is now my home, the way this city has become the home to so many people from so many places. What interests me is how we understand the history of our city, and specifically whether that understood history accurately reflects the remarkable diversity that is the hallmark of Toronto.

MICHAEL McCLELLAND

ALTERNATIVE HISTORIES

History is a verb. The passage of time is a constant. But what we seek to preserve from our past and what we choose to cast away has always been a selective process often informed by unexamined motives and biases. Each generation sees its history differently. Each generation assigns heritage value differently.

In Toronto, probably the first effort to preserve some physical evidence of the post-contact past was the relocation of Scadding Cabin in 1879. John Scadding had been a clerk for Lieutenant-Governor John Graves Simcoe. His modest log cabin, built on the east bank of the Don River in the 1790s, was dutifully dismantled and reassembled on its new site in the Exhibition grounds.

The civic act of saving a log cabin was one way to strengthen the ties between a community and its pioneer genesis. The connection to Simcoe underscored Toronto's British roots. This recognition of a significant historical artifact was one way to provide legitimacy, authority and a legacy to those in power.

Left: Furniture warehouse, ca. 1910.

Most official histories, in fact, tend to solidify our understanding of the past and give subsequent generations the sense that the story is complete and nothing could have been otherwise. But official histories can ignore and marginalize the many alternative histories that represent the complexity and the richness of a living city.

Since Scadding Cabin, Toronto city council has formally amassed an 'Inventory of Heritage Properties' that now includes more than 7,000 structures. We continue to add very old buildings to the list, and even some that are quite recent, like New City Hall. But there is more to an understanding of the city's history than creating a list. While the inventory of heritage buildings is a symbol of our official history, the story doesn't end there.

In Europe, the abundance of things historical, and the ever-increasing interest in what might have heritage value, has led to some radical rethinking of how to understand history in the context of cities. There are two distinct ways this paradigm shift in heritage preservation could help us to see Toronto's past – and its present – with greater clarity.

First, heritage is to be understood as a value that could be shared as opposed to a selective expression of events that would favour one cultural group over another. In 2005, the Council of Europe adopted the Faro Convention on the Value of Cultural Heritage for Society. Disturbed by the purposeful destruction of cultural sites in sectarian war zones, especially Bosnia, the delegate nations agreed that cultural heritage was a resource to be held in common. The convention further recognized the need to put people and human values at the centre of an enlarged and cross-disciplinary concept of cultural heritage. Similar to human rights charters, the Faro Convention states, "[E]very person has a right to engage with the cultural heritage of their choice, while respecting the rights and freedoms of others." Toronto, with its great diversity, needs to more clearly articulate the principles embedded in the convention. As an immigrant city, Toronto's heritage is not simply about who came first or who has greater wealth, but rather how we all embrace the places we live.

Second, history is pervasive. In Europe, the expanding definition of what has heritage value has created something of a crisis in cities. Not only old buildings, but buildings from the 1960s and 1970s, broadly defined cultural landscapes and even traditional patterns of activity – like how a particular community makes wine or cheese – are now all understood to relate to heritage.

It is clear that almost everything in our built environment has value to some-one, even buildings or communities deemed to be problems, like The Ward, with its cramped housing and dense mix of uses. In describing this paradigm shift in understanding the value of history, Graham Fairclough, an official from English Heritage, observes:

> New heritage suggests that instead of finding the best, calling it heritage and fighting to keep it, we should look with open eyes at all that exists, accept that at some level it is all heritage and then decide how best to use it for social and future values.

History, in other words, is everywhere and it exists in all communities, even while the communities themselves may be constantly changing.

Because the development of Nathan Phillips Square demanded the creation of a completely clean slate, we can say that the history of The Ward was largely excluded and undervalued for many years. Indeed, there's scant physical evidence that the immigrant communities that forged their futures in the teeming streets and laneways between College and Queen, University and Yonge, ever existed. The eradication of The Ward has been a loss for the City of Toronto. When proposing or supporting change elsewhere in the city, we should now try to understand our motives and biases more clearly. We need to open our eyes. We need to appreciate the larger and broader histories that exist around us, and imagine our way into undocumented and unrecognized lives. We need to rebuild these forgotten, alternative histories so we can better understand our present, as well as our future. We owe this to our many ethnic communities, to our aboriginal communities and to our future as a city.

TORONTO'S GHOST MAP

A   Little Italy

B   Chinatown

C   Gerrard Street Village

D   St. John's Shtetl

1   Osgoode Hall

2   The Armouries

3   Goel Tzedec Synagogue

4   British Methodist Episcopal Church,

5   Land Registry Office

6   House of Industry/stone yard

7   Presbyterian Mission

8   Elizabeth Street Playground

9   Hester How Public School

10 Toronto General Hospital

11 Victoria Hospital for Sick Children

12 Bishop Strachan School

13 Central Neighbourhood House

14 Eaton's factories

15 Agnes Street Methodist Church (Yiddish-language Lyric Theatre after 1909)

16 Ford Hotel

17 Italian consulate

18 Wineberg Apartment

19 Church of the Holy Trinity

20 City Hall

21 Lung Kong Brotherhood

22 Nanking Restaurant

23 Angelo's Hotel/Glionna's

24 The Ward Clinic

25 Shea's Hippodrome

26 Globe Theatre

27 Casino Theatre

28 Arts and Letters Club

29 Riman's Russian Baths

30 Toronto Soda Company

31 Peerless Bicycle Company

32 Mary John's Café

33 Jack and Jill's Cafe

34 Shumacher family home

35 Merle Foster's studio

36 Wilson Ruffin Abbott's tobacco shop

37 Site of Elsie Mokryzcka's murder

38 Mary Pickford's family cottage

39 Slumans' family home

40 Colestocks' family home

41 Hum family home

COLLEGE ST.

⑪   ⑫

BUCHANAN ST.

⑩

㉝

HAYTER ST.

[C]

⑬

GERRARD ST. W.

㉜㉚   ㉟

WALTON ST.

㉔   ⑧

⑨

㊲   ⑦   ㉘

ELM ST.

PRICE'S LANE

[A]   ⑥

ELM PL.

㉓

㉞

EDWARD ST.

㉛   ⑱   ⑮ ⑯

AGNES (DUNDAS) ST.

⑰

CENTRE AVE.

CHESTNUT ST.

ELIZABETH ST.

TERAULEY (BAY) ST.

ALICE ST.

③   [D]   FOSTER PL.

⑲   TRINITY SQ.

㉙   ④   ㉒   ⑭

⑭

HAGERMAN

ARMOURY ST.

LOUISA ST.

②   ⑤   ⑭   ⑭

OSGOODE ST.

[B]

ALBERT ST.

①   ㉑   ㉕   ㊱

JAMES ST.

⑳

UNIVERSITY AVE.

YONGE ST.

QUEEN ST.

------- STREETS ELIMINATED SINCE WWII
     NEW CITY HALL   ㉗   ㉖

THE CONTRIBUTORS

ANDREA ADDARIO lives with her partner and their two sons in Toronto, where she works in the labour movement.

HOWARD AKLER is the author of *The City Man*. His new book, *Men of Action*, will be published by Coach House Books in Fall 2015.

DENISE BALKISSOON s a freelance journalist and editor-in-chief of the Ethnic Aisle, a blog about race and ethnicity in the Greater Toronto Area.

DEREK BALLANTYNE divides his time between managing social impact investment funds, two of which deliver affordable housing, and his consulting practice in affordable housing development.

BRIAN BANKS is an editor and writer in Toronto with a special interest in landscapes, conservation and the environment.

RANJIT BHASKAR is a journalist who has worked with leading international news organizations, including Al Jazeera English. On immigrating to Canada, he joined the Maytree Foundation as Content Manager in 2013.

STEPHEN BULGER has been interested in photography since he was a child, and since 1995 has owned a gallery that is devoted to celebrating the medium.

JIM BURANT has a Master's in Canadian Studies from Carleton University, and worked at Library and Archives Canada from 1976 until April 2011. He has published and lectured widely on art, photography and archives, and has an international reputation in the fields of art history and archives.

ARLENE CHAN is a third-generation Chinese Canadian raised in Toronto's Chinatown. She has penned seven books about the history, culture, and traditions of the Chinese in Canada. When she is not researching, writing or leading tours of Chinatown, she can be found paddling around Lake Ontario on a dragon boat.

ALINA CHATTERJEE has over fifteen years of experience working in the Toronto non-profit and community-based sector in various capacities, both as an employee and as a volunteer. Most recently she worked as Executive Assistant to Toronto City Councillor Kristyn Wong-Tam before joining United Way Toronto.

ELISE CHENIER is professor of history at Simon Fraser University where she teaches courses on the history of sexuality, oral history and modern Canadian history. She is also the creator of the online archives and learning tool www.interracialintimacies.org

CATHY CROWE is a long-time street nurse who works on homelessness and advocates for the solution, a national housing program. She is currently a Distinguished Visiting Practitioner in the Department of Politics and Public Administration at Ryerson University.

PATRICK CUMMINS has worked in archives in Toronto since 1986, curating several archival exhibitions. Photographer of Toronto's vernacular architecture since the late 1970s. Work is represented in holdings of Canadian

Museum of Contemporary Photography, Ottawa, and published in *Full Frontal T.O.* (Coach House, 2012), shortlisted for the Toronto Book Award and winner of the Heritage Toronto Award of Excellence.

RICHARD DENNIS is Emeritus Professor of Geography at University College London, U.K. He has written numerous articles about apartment housing and the social geography of Toronto, which also features prominently in his book, *Cities in Modernity: Representations and Productions of Metropolitan Space, 1840–1930* (Cambridge University Press, 2008).

RUTH A. FRAGER teaches Canadian history at McMaster University. She is the author of *Sweatshop Strife: Class, Ethnicity, and Gender in the Jewish Labour Movement of Toronto, 1900–1939* and co-author of *Discounted Labour: Women Workers in Canada, 1870–1939*.

KAROLYN SMARDZ FROST is an archaeologist, historian and award-winning author who specializes in African Canadian/American transnationalism. She has a particular fascination for Toronto's special role as an urban terminus of the Underground Railroad. Karolyn is the Senior Research Fellow for African Canadian History at the Harriet Tubman Institute, York University, and a Visiting Professor at Acadia University in Wolfville, Nova Scotia.

RICHARD HARRIS teaches urban geography at McMaster University, Hamilton. He writes about the history of housing, neighbourhoods and suburban development in Canada and the United States.

DR. CHARLES HASTINGS (1858–1931) was an obstetrician who served as Toronto's medical officer of health from 1910 to 1929.

GAETAN HEROUX is a member of the Ontario Coalition Against Poverty who has worked in East Downtown Toronto since 1988.

J. DAVID HULCHANSKI is a professor of housing and community development in the Factor-Inwentash Faculty of Social Work, University of Toronto.

SCOTT JAMES joined the City of Toronto Archives in 1967, and served as city archivist from 1975 to 1984. From 1984 to 1996 he was managing director of the Toronto Historical Board. He was the archives assistant responsible for the original cleaning and organizing of the Goss Collection. In retirement, Scott remains active as archivist for the Toronto Arts and Letters Club.

EDWARD KEENAN is a city columnist for the *Toronto Star* and hosts a weekly radio show on Newstalk 1010. He is the author of *Some Great Idea: Good Neighbourhoods, Crazy Politics and the Invention of Toronto*, published in 2013 by Coach House Books.

BRUCE KIDD is Vice President and Principal of the University of Toronto Scarborough, a Professor of Kinesiology and Physical Education at U of T and a lifelong participant in Toronto sport and recreation.

MARK KINGWELL is a Professor of Philosophy at the University of Toronto and the author of many articles and books on political theory and urbanism. His most recent book is the essay collection *Unruly Voices* (2012); a new collection of his essays, *Measure Yourself Against the Earth*, will be published in Fall 2015.

JACK LIPINSKY holds a doctorate in Canadian History and has published a number of scholarly books and articles about the Toronto Jewish community. He is an educator

and curriculum writer for both Facing History and the Associated Hebrew Schools of Toronto.

CYNTHIA MACDOUGALL is a Toronto municipal lawyer who loves the City of Toronto and is proud of her Italian heritage.

DR. DAVID MCKEOWN is the Medical Officer of Health for the City of Toronto. He is a community medicine specialist who has worked in the public health field for over twenty years.

SHAWN MICALLEF is a *Toronto Star* columnist, co-owner and an editor of *Spacing* magazine, co-founder of the mobile phone public space documentary project [murmur], and instructor at the University of Toronto. He is the author of *Stroll: Psychogeographic Walking Tours of Toronto, Full Frontal TO, The Trouble with Brunch: Work, Class and the Pursuit of Leisure*, and was the Toronto Public Library's non-fiction writer in residence in 2013.

LAURIE MONSEBRAATEN has been a reporter at the *Toronto Star* for more than thirty years specializing in municipal affairs and social policy. Her work has received four National Newspaper Award nominations and three nominations for the Michener Award for Public Service Journalism. She currently covers the *Star*'s Social Justice beat.

HOWARD MOSCOE's grandparents settled in the ward around 1911 when they immigrated to Canada from Ivansk in Poland. Howard served for thirty-two years on North York, Metro and Toronto councils as the Councillor representing the largest Jewish community in Canada. His careers included President of the North York Elementary Teacher's Federation, a nine-year stint as chair of the Toronto Transit Commission (TTC) and the Chairmanship of Toronto Licensing and Standards.

TERRY MURRAY has written extensively about architectural sculpture. She is the author of *Faces on Places: A Grotesque Tour of Toronto* (Anansi, 2006) and the forthcoming *Come to Dust: The Long Life, Short Art and Shorter Afterlife of Merle Foster*.

DEENA NATHANSON is a public relations and communications consultant living in Toronto. She has written about Jewish peddlers in Toronto and the history of some of the Canada's formative Jewish institutions.

RATNA OMIDVAR is the founding Executive Director of the Global Diversity Exchange at the Ted Rogers School of Management, Ryerson University. Previously, she was the President of Maytree.

STEPHEN OTTO has been an administrator and scholar in the heritage field for forty years. He was the first head of Ontario's heritage conservation programs in the mid-1970s and a founder of The Friends of Fort York in 1994.

VINCENZO PIETROPAOLO is an award-winning social documentary photographer who has distinguished himself as a photographic bookmaker, exploring Canada's immigrant communities, working-class culture and social justice issues. His most recent book is *Invisible No More: A Photographic Chronicle of People with Intellectual Disabilities*, in which he combined photographs and his own original writing.

MICHAEL POSNER is an award-winning author, journalist and playwright, and a former senior writer for the *Globe and Mail*.

MICHAEL REDHILL is a novelist, playwright and poet. His novel about Toronto, *Consolation*,

won the Toronto Book Award and was long-listed for the Man Booker Prize.

PATTE ROSEBANK was born. She's a writer, voice-artist, comedy historian, burlesque performer, and several other things, because she can't decide which one she likes best. www.patterosebank.com.

VICTOR RUSSELL worked at the University of Toronto Press before joining the City of Toronto Archives in 1973, becoming the City's Manager of Archives and Heritage until 1993. Victor went on to teach Urban Studies at Seneca College until his recent retirement. He is the author of numerous books and articles on the history of the City.

SANDRA SHAUL is passionate about Toronto's history. She is the project lead for Toronto's Great War Attic, an initiative of the City's Museums and Heritage Services department, led the City's Bicentennial Commemoration of the War of 1812 and was one of the principal creators of the Toronto in Time website and app.

MYER SIEMIATYCKI is Professor in the Department of Politics and Public Administration at Ryerson University, and past, founding director of its MA Program in Immigration and Settlement Studies.

KIM STOREY AND JAMES BROWN are partners in the architectural and urban design firms of Brown and Storey Architects Inc. and Office for Responsive Environments. Their research and design work over the past thirty years of practice includes a broad spectrum of civic infrastructure, public spaces and built form.

MICHAEL VALPY is a journalist and continuing senior fellow at Massey College. He teaches in the University of Toronto's book and media studies program.

MARIANA VALVERDE researches urban law and governance, both historically and in the present. Among other things she is the author of the 2012 prize-winning book *Everyday Law on the Street: City Governance in an Age of Diversity* (University of Chicago Press).

THELMA WHEATLEY is the granddaughter of a Welsh coal-miner and the author of *And Neither Have I Wings To Fly: Labelled and Locked Up in Canada's Oldest Institution,)* Inanna Publications, 2013). It was shortlisted for the 2014 Wales Book of the Year Award, winner of the Bronze Medal for Non-Fiction Independent Publishers Awards 2014 and winner of the Media Medal of the Protective Services of Ontario, 2014.

KRISTYN WONG-TAM is a Toronto City Councillor and human rights activist. When she's not advocating for sustaintable urbanism, economic justice, Kristyn can be found reading books under a big maple tree at her favourite park.

PAUL YEE has published fiction and non-fiction about Chinese immigration to Canada since 1983.

JOHN E. ZUCCHI is a professor of history and classical studies at McGill University, as well as the author of *Italians in Toronto: Development of a National Identity, 1875-1935.* (McGill Queen's University Press, 1988).

THE EDITORS

JOHN LORINC is a Toronto journalist who writes about urban affairs, politics, business, the environment and education. He has reported for the *Globe and Mail*, the *Toronto Star*, *Walrus* magazine, *Canadian Business*, *Reader's Digest*, *CPA* magazine and the *New York Times*, and has won numerous awards for his journalism. He also writes a weekly politics column for *Spacing* magazine, where he is a senior editor. Lorinc is the author of three books, including *The New City* (Penguin, 2006), and was a contributor to every volume of Coach House's UTOPIA series. He is married to Victoria Foote and they have two sons, Jacob and Samuel.

MICHAEL MCCLELLAND, OAA, FRAIC, is a registered architect with over twenty years of experience. He is actively involved in the promotion of Canada's architectural heritage and is a founding member of the Canadian Association of Professional Heritage Consultants (CAPHC). Prior to establishing ERA Architects with Edwin Rowse in 1990, McClelland worked for the Toronto Historical Board. He is the recipient of a certificate of recognition from the Ontario Association of Architects and the Toronto Society of Architects for his outstanding contributions to architecture and a Fellow of the Royal Architectural Institute of Canada.

DR. ELLEN SCHEINBERG is the President of Heritage Professionals, a heritage consulting company in Toronto that delivers archival, museum and information management services. She holds a Ph.D. in history from the University of Ottawa and has worked as a heritage specialist and manager for the past twenty-five years. Ellen has published many articles in the areas of archival studies, women's history, labour history, Canadian Jewish studies and immigration history. She was the recipient of the Ontario Historical Society's Scadding Award of Excellence and the Alexander Fraser Award, which recognizes individuals who have significantly contributed to the advancement of the Ontario archival community throughout their careers. She is currently in the process of completing an illustrated history of Toronto's Jewish community.

TATUM TAYLOR is a writer, heritage specialist and Texan transplant, currently at ERA Architects in Toronto. She holds a master's degree in historic preservation from Columbia University, where she wrote her thesis on interpreting the heritage of marginalized communities. She is actively involved with the boards of several heritage organizations and previously worked on the editorial team for the *Future Anterior Journal*. Further to her interest in inclusivity within heritage practice, she has published work on graffiti sites as cultural landscapes. She also writes fiction and poetry based on her experience as a preservationist.

ACKNOWLEDGEMENTS

IT TOOK ALMOST two years for the editors to transform our vision into this book. During that time, we received support from many individuals. First and foremost was Alana Wilcox, editorial director at Coach House Books, who believed in this project from the beginning and dedicated an enormous amount of time and energy to ensuring its successful completion. Stuart Ross and Ingrid Paulson were instrumental in producing a wonderful product that surpassed our expectations, and Sarah Smith-Eivemark did an excellent job getting the word out. Thanks to Amy Norris, Clint Langevin, Will MacIvor and the rest of the team at ERA Architects for their assistance and encouragement.

This book is a compilation of many unique, diverse and compelling stories. We would like to express our gratitude to the authors who penned these brilliant contributions, as well as their patience during the editorial process. We would also like to pay homage to the men, women and children who resided in The Ward and whose lives are captured in these photographs and articles.

We spent considerable time delving into the archival holdings of a number of different repositories, and received generous assistance from several heritage professionals: Jill Delaney, Joanne Guillemette and Andrew Rodger (retired) (Library and Archives Canada); Cathy Leekam and Pasang Thackchhoe (Multicultural Historical Society of Ontario); Ann MacDonald (Doris McCarthy Gallery); Donna Bernardo-Ceriz and Melissa Caza (Ontario Jewish Archives); the reference staff, Lawrence Lee and Gillian Reddyhoff (City of Toronto Archives); Nichole Vonk and Lea de la Paz (United Church Archives); and Julia Holland and Anna St. Onge (York University Archives). We would also like to thank other individuals who have contributed: *Toronto Star* editor Dan Smith, John Court from the CAMH Archives, historians Craig Heron and Harold Troper, Jane's Walk and filmmaker Hadley Obodiac.

Finally, we would like to thank our families, partners and friends for their enthusiasm, commitment and support throughout the course of the project. We wouldn't have been able to carve out the necessary time and energy required to tackle such an ambitious initiative without their support.

IMAGE CREDITS

p. 2. *Goad's Atlas of the City of Toronto*, 1910, Volume 1, Plate 9. Toronto Public Library, M912.7135 G57 BR.

p. 7. Photographer: William James. City of Toronto Archives, Fonds 1224, Series 2119, Item 39.29.

pp. 8–9. Photographer: John Boyd. Library and Archives Canada, PA-069966.

p.10. Toronto Public Library, T1842/4Mlrg C1, Winearls, MUC no. 2077.

p. 14. City of Toronto Archives, Fonds 1231, Item 1843.

p. 24–25. City of Toronto Archives, Fonds 200, Series 372, Sub-Series 32, Item 29.

p. 26. Photographer: Shawn Micallef.

p. 28. Photographer: Patrick Cummins.

p. 31. City of Toronto Archives, Fonds 200, Series 372, Sub-Series 33, Item 694.

p. 32. *Top*: Toronto Public Library, E-5-60b; *Bottom*: City of Toronto Archives, Fonds 200, Series 372, Sub-Series 3, Item 281.

p. 35. Boulton map: Images from this set are courtesy of the Toronto Public Library, 912.71354B5941858. Winearls, MUC no. 2133.

p. 37. *Top*: City of Toronto Archives, Fonds 200, Series 372, Sub-Series 3, Item 732. *Bottom*: Image courtesy of Beverley Ballett.

p. 38. City of Toronto Archives, Series 1317, Item 379.

p. 41. Archives of Ontario, Fonds 4436, F4436-000112.

p. 42. City of Toronto Archives, Fonds 200, Series 372, Sub-Series 55, Item 43.

pp. 44–45. City of Toronto Archives, Fonds 1257, Series 1057, Item 229.

p. 47. Image courtesy of Terry Murray.

p. 49. *Chatelaine*, December 1928, page 28.

p. 50. City of Toronto Archives, Fonds 1244, Item 2348.

pp. 52–53. United Church Archives, Toronto, 90.115P/686.

p. 54. Bill Gladstone/Speisman Collection.

p. 57. Photographer: William James Topley. Library and Archives Canada, PA-025990.

p. 60. Toronto Public Library, S 1-2315.

pp. 64–65. City of Toronto Archives, Fonds 200, Series 372, Sub-Series 58, Item 2450.

p. 69. City of Toronto Archives, Fonds 1244, Item 2373.

p. 73. Toronto Public Library, Baldwin Collection, 1911.SundayLaws.s.

p. 74. City of Toronto Archives, Fonds 1244, Item 722.

p. 77. *The Toronto Daily Star*, March 31, 1927, page 1. Courtesy of Torstar Syndication Services, a Division of Toronto Star Newspapers Limited.

p. 81. *The Toronto Daily Star*, March 31, 1927, page 1. Courtesy of Torstar Syndication Services, a Division of Toronto Star Newspapers Limited.

p. 85. Archives of Ontario, F 1075-16-0-0-200.

p. 86. Courtesy of the Art Gallery of Hamilton. Used with the permission of Stew Sheppard.

p. 87. Courtesy of the National Gallery of Canada. Used with the permission of Stew Sheppard.

pp. 88–89. City of Toronto Archives, Fonds 200, Series 372, Sub-Series 32, Item 35.

p. 90. City of Toronto Archives, Fonds 200, Series 372, Sub-Series 32, Item 251.

p. 93. City of Toronto Archives, Fonds 200, Series 372, Sub-Series 32, Item 40.

p. 94. Photographer: John Boyd. Library and Archives Canada, PA-069995.

p. 98. Photographer: E. D'Angelo. Library and Archives Canada, PA-091114.

p. 101. Courtesy of Andrea Addario.

pp. 104–105. City of Toronto Archives, Fonds 200, Series 372, Sub-Series 11, Item 96.

p. 108–109. City of Toronto Archives, Fonds 1231, Item 2182.

p. 110. City of Toronto Archives, Fonds 200, Series 372, Sub-Series 41, Item 597.

p. 112–113. City of Toronto Archives, Fonds 200, Series 372, Sub-Series 32, Item 150.

p. 116. Toronto Public Library, s1a-3239a.

pp. 118–119. City of Toronto Archives, Fonds 1035, Series 810, File 2.

p. 122. City of Toronto Archives, Fonds 1244, Item 3509.

pp. 124–125. City of Toronto Archives, Fonds 1244, Item 8029.

pp. 126–127 City of Toronto Archives, Fonds 1244, Item 291.

p. 128. Toronto Reference Library, Plate 1, 'Report of the Civic Improvement Committee for the City of Toronto,' 1911. 917.1354T59033.

pp. 132–133. City of Toronto Archives, Fonds 1244, Item 598.

p. 134. City of Toronto Archives, Fonds 1244, Item 7034a.

p. 137. City of Toronto Archives, Fonds 200, Series 372, Sub-Series 32, Item 547.

p. 139. City of Toronto Archives, Fonds 200, Series 372, Sub-Series 1, Item 278.

p. 140. City of Toronto Archives, Fonds 200, Series 372, Sub-Series 32, Item 404.

p. 143. City of Toronto Archives, Fonds 1005, Series 8, File 6.

p. 146. Courtesy of Marc Wanamaker/Bison Archives.

p. 147. City of Toronto Archives, Fonds 1266, Item 2249.

p. 148. City of Toronto Archives, Fonds 200, Series 372, Sub-Series 33, Item 250.

p. 150. City of Toronto Archives, City of Toronto Directory, 1922, page 1717.

pp. 152–153. Photographer: Dick Loek. York University Libraries, Clara Thomas Archives & Special Collections, *Toronto Telegram* fonds, ASC02735.

p. 155. Archives of Ontario, F 229-308-0-372.

p. 157. *Top*: Kheel Centre, Cornell University, ILGWU Collection, 5780P, Image 1600. *Bottom*: City of Toronto Archives, Fonds 1251.

p. 161. Toronto Public Library, 910.7135 T59 – 406707.

pp. 162–163. Image courtesy of the MacDougall family.

p. 165. City of Toronto Archives, Fonds 200, Series 372, Sub-Series 32, Item 226.

p. 167. Photograph courtesy of Scott Weir.

pp. 168–169. City of Toronto Archives, Fonds 1244, Item 7346.

p. 170. Ontario Jewish Archives, Item 471.

pp. 172–173. Ontario Jewish Archives, Fonds 22, Item 61.

p. 174. Ontario Jewish Archives, Item 4346.

p. 178. *Goad's Atlas of the City of Toronto*, 1910, Volume 1, Plate 9. Toronto Public Library, M912.7135 G57 BR.

p. 180. ©iStockphoto.com/Mastamak.

pp. 182–183. City of Toronto Archives, Fonds 200, Series 372, Sub-Series 52, Item 70.

p. 185. City of Toronto archives, Fonds 200, Series 372, Sub-Series 52, Item 67.

p. 187. City of Toronto Archives, Fonds 200, Series 372, Sub-Series 52, Item 688.

p. 188. Photographer: E. D'Angelo. Library and Archives Canada, PA-091101.

p. 191. City of Toronto Archives, Fonds 1005, Series 8, File 10.

p. 192. Ontario Jewish Archives, Item 3306.

pp. 194–195. University of Toronto, Thomas Fisher Rare Books Library, 'Report to the Civic Transportation Committee on Radial Railway Entrances and Rapid Transit for the City of Toronto,' Volume II, E-10.06108.

p. 196. United Church Archives, Toronto, 93.049P/3515.

pp. 198–199. Courtesy of the Estate of William Kurelek, Wynick/Tuck Gallery, Toronto.

pp. 202–203. City of Toronto Art Collection, Museum and Heritage, EDC.

p. 205. *Construction*, Vol. 1, No. 2, November 1907, page 51.

pp. 208–209. City of Toronto Archives, *Globe and Mail* fonds 1266, Item 8020.

p. 211. *The Toronto Daily Star*, October 11, 1907, page 6.

p. 214. City of Toronto Archives, Fonds 1257, Series 1057, Item 1950.

p. 216. Ontario Jewish Archives, Item 1312.

p. 217. Ontario Jewish Archives, Fonds 43, Item 5.

pp. 220–221. City of Toronto Archives, Fonds 200, Series 372, Sub-Series 32, Item 259.

p. 223. City of Toronto Archives, Fonds 200, Series 372, Sub-Series 32, Item 749.

p. 229. Centre for Addiction and Mental Health (CAMH) Archives, Griffin-Greenland Fonds (F-12), Photographic Series V-14.

p. 230. Centre for Addiction and Mental Health (CAMH) Archives, Griffin-Greenland Fonds (F-12), Photographic Series VI-I.

p. 232. City of Toronto Archives, Fonds 200, Series 372, Sub-Series 32, Item 447.

p. 234. United Church Archives, Toronto, 76.001P/703N.

pp. 234–235. Library and Archives Canada, PA-69932.

p. 238. City of Toronto Archives, Fonds 1244, Item 132.

pp. 242–243. City of Toronto Archives, Fonds 124, File 15, Item 17.

p. 245. Image courtesy of Silent Toronto (www.silenttoronto.com). Used with the permission of Eric Veillette.

p. 247. Toronto Public Library, S 1-2569.

p. 250. City of Toronto Archives, Fonds 124 File 1, Item 146.

p. 251. City of Toronto Archives, Fonds 124, File 1, Item 114.

p. 253. Archives of Ontario, C 301-0-0-0-171.

p. 254. City of Toronto Archives, Fonds 1244, Series 2119, Sub-Series 25, Item 7.

p. 256. Toronto Jewish Directory, 1925, Ontario Jewish Archives.

p. 258. Ontario Jewish Archives, Accession 2010-3/1.

p. 261. Courtesy of J. Rosenthal.

p. 267. City of Toronto Archives, Fonds 200, Series 372, Sub-Series 32, Item 243.

pp. 268–269. United Church Archives, Toronto, 93.049P/3503N.

p. 270. Toronto Public Library, S 1-2576.

p. 272. Archives of Ontario, C 3-1-0-0-80.

p. 273. City of Toronto Archives, Fonds 200, Series 372, Sub-Series 33, Item 161.

pp. 274–275. York University, Clara Thomas Archives & Special Collections, *Toronto Telegram* fonds, ASC02797.

pp. 276–277. City of Toronto Archives, Series 60, Item 661.

p. 278. City of Toronto Archives, Fonds 1257, Series 1057, Item 6478.

p. 283. Courtesy of David Hulchanski and Richard Maaranen.

p. 284. City of Toronto Archives, Fonds 1526, File 10, Item 5.

p. 287. *The Toronto Daily Star*, December 19, 1946, page 19.

p. 291. *The Toronto Daily Star*, April 1, 1955, page 33. Courtesy of Torstar Syndication Services, a Division of Toronto Star Newspapers Limited.

p. 293. *The Toronto Daily Star*, April 1, 1955, page 33. Courtesy of Torstar Syndication Services, a Division of Toronto Star Newspapers Limited.

p. 298. Photographer: Patrick Cummins.

p. 299. Photographer: Patrick Cummins.

p. 300. City of Toronto Archives, Fonds 200, Series 372, Sub-Series 32, Item 441.

p. 304. Photographer: William James. City of Toronto Archives, Fonds 1224, Series 2119, Item 39.31.

For further information, including notes on sources, visit www.twitter.com/TheWardTO.

Typeset in Celeste, Gotham, Caslon and Knockout

Edited by John Lorinc, Michael McClelland, Ellen Scheinberg and Tatum Taylor
Designed by Ingrid Paulson
Cover by Ingrid Paulson

Coach House Books
80 bpNichol Lane
Toronto ON M5S 3J4
Canada

416 979 2217
800 367 6360

mail@chbooks.com
www.chbooks.com